Microorganisms, biotechnology and disease

Student's book

Dedication

To our husbands, Derrick and Richard, for their support and encouragement, and our children, Mark, David, Emily, Sarah and Christopher.

Microorganisms, Biotechnology & Disease

Student's book

PAULINE LOWRIE B.A., C.Biol., M.I.Biol.
Sir John Deane's College, Northwich, Cheshire

SUSAN WELLS B.Sc., C.Biol., M.I.Biol.
Frodsham High School, Cheshire

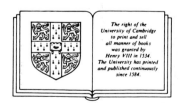

The right of the
University of Cambridge
to print and sell
all manner of books
was granted by
Henry VIII in 1534.
The University has printed
and published continuously
since 1584.

Cambridge University Press
Cambridge
New York Port Chester
Melbourne Sydney

Published by the Press Syndicate of the University of Cambridge
The Pitt Building, Trumpington Street, Cambridge CB2 1RP
40 West 20th Street, New York, NY 10011, USA
10 Stamford Road, Oakleigh, Melbourne 3166, Australia

First published 1991

Typeset by VAP Publishing Services, Kidlington, Oxon

Printed in Great Britain
by Scotprint Limited, Musselborough, Scotland

Lowrie, Pauline
    Microorganisms, biotechnology and disease,
    Students' guide.
    1. Industrial microbiology
    I. Title   II. Wells, Susan
    660.62

ISBN 0 521 38746 9

Contents

Preface

Microorganisms, biotechnology and disease is a supplementary Advanced level biology text written by two experienced 'A' level teachers and examiners. It is designed to meet the needs of the many changing Advanced and Advanced Supplementary level syllabuses of the 1990s, as well as first-year undergraduate courses. Many new syllabuses at this level include modules or special sections based on recent advances in biology, particularly in the field of biotechnology. At the same time, more flexible approaches to learning are being introduced into schools and colleges, so the book is designed for use in a variety of contexts. The comprehensive glossary and the questions inserted into the text will be particularly useful to students learning through supported self-study, and the authors have tried to reflect the philosophy of GCSE and balanced science in the style of many of the questions.

The authors have followed the latest Institute of Biology recommendations on biological nomenclature, units and symbols, and the Association for Science Education's recommendations on chemical nomenclature, symbols and terminology for use in school science.

A companion to this volume, entitled *Microorganisms, biotechnology and disease – Teachers' guide* contains 21 practical exercises with a teacher's and technician's guide and suggested assessments for Advanced level.

Acknowledgements

The authors would like to thank Jackie Grieves and Dr Stuart Chant for reading the text and making helpful suggestions; Edith Garrett for locating books, references and information; and John Houghton and Phill Evans for their encouragement. However, the authors accept full responsibility for the final content of this book.

The authors and publishers would like to thank the following for giving permission to reproduce photographs and diagrams in this book:

Fig 1.2 – photographs of *Staphylococcus aureus* and *Escherichia coli*, Dr Tony Brain/Science Photo Library; Fig 1.2 – photograph of *Vibrio cholerae*, London School of Hygiene and Tropical Medicine/Science Photo Library; Fig 1.32 – photographs of *Penicillium chrysogenum* and *Aspergillus oryzae*, Glaxochem Ltd; Fig 1.32 – photograph of cultivated mushrooms (*Agaricus* sp.), Mushroom Growers' Association;

Fig 1.32 – photograph of brewer's yeast, The Brewing Research Foundation, Nutfield, Redhill, Surrey, RH1 4HY; Fig 1.34 – photograph of tobacco mosaic virus, Omikron/Science Photo Library; Fig 1.34 – photograph of adenoviruses (common cold), Science Source/ Science Photo Library; Fig 1.34 – photograph of bacteriophages, B. Heggeler/Biozentrum/University of Basel/Science Photo Library; Fig 3.5 Cellmark Diagnostics, Blacklands Way, Abingdon Business Park, Abingdon, Oxfordshire, OX14 1DY; Fig 5.2 Marlow Foods; 5.6 National Dairy Council; Fig 6.3 Energy Efficiency Office of the UK Department of Energy; Fig 7.2 SmithKline and Beecham Pharmaceuticals; Fig 7.12 Imperial Chemical Industries PLC; Fig 9.2 John Walsh/Science Photo Library; Fig 10.4 Moredun Animal Health Ltd/Science Photo Library; Fig 10.10 St Mary' Hospital Medical School/Science Photo Library; Fig 12.1 ICI Agrochemicals; Fig 12.11 Geoff Schell; Fig 13.1 a Shell photograph.

The following questions have been reproduced with the permission of the Joint Matriculation Board: summary essay question at the end of chapter 7; chapter 9, question 6; chapter 11, questions 7–11; chapter 12, question 6; chapter 13, question 1.

1 Microorganisms

1.1 Introduction

Microorganisms (microbes) are so small that they can only be seen individually with the aid of a microscope. Microbiology is the study of microorganisms and is divided into several specialist branches, such as bacteriology, the study of bacteria, mycology, the study of fungi, and virology, the study of viruses. Not all groups of microorganisms receive equal attention and this text will concentrate only on some of those which affect the activities of humans, either beneficially or detrimentally.

Viruses are dependent on other cells for their reproduction and are not fitted into a classification of living organisms. All the prokaryotic organisms are grouped into the **kingdom Monera**. The cells of prokaryotes lack a true nucleus and do not have membrane-bound organelles or the typical 9 + 2 arrangement of microtubules found in the eukaryotes (fig 1.1). Eukaryotic cells have a true membrane-bound nucleus and organelles. Eukaryotic microorganisms are found in the kingdom Fungi, and in the kingdom Protoctista. Some further differences between prokaryotes and eukaryotes are shown in table 1.1.

Table 1.1
The differences between eukaryotes and prokaryotes

Feature	Eukaryote	Prokaryote
volume	large (up to 10^5 μm^3)	small (1–10 μm^3)
form	multicellular, unicellular or filamentous	unicellular or filamentous
cell wall	rigid, contains polysaccharides: plants – cellulose, fungi – chitin, animals – no cell wall	rigid, polysaccharides with amino acids – peptidoglycan (murein)
genetic material	DNA in linear form packaged with histone to form chromosomes in the nucleus; nucleolus present	naked circular DNA in cytoplasm; no nucleolus
cell surface membrane (plasmalemma)	contains phospholipids, sterols and proteins; phagocytic or pinocytic, microvilli may be present (animals only)	phospholipids and proteins only; no phagocytosis or pinocytosis
organelles	double membrane-bound include nucleus, chloroplasts and mitochondria; single membrane-bound include Golgi body, vacuoles, lysosomes, endoplasmic reticulum (ER)	none found; cell surface membrane may infold to trap photosynthetic pigments, mesosomes
ribosomes	80S (larger) in cytoplasm or attached to ER	70S (smaller) in cytoplasm
flagella or cilia	9 + 2 arrangement of microtubules; powered by ATP	single microtubule, made of flagellin; powered by H^+ pumps
storage compounds	glycogen or fats in animals, starch in plants	various, e.g. polymerised fatty acids, glycogen, rarely starch, phosphate granules (volutin); sulphur in purple sulphur bacteria

Fig 1.1
(*a*) **Diagram of a generalised eukaryotic cell.**
(*b*) **Diagram of a generalised prokaryotic cell**

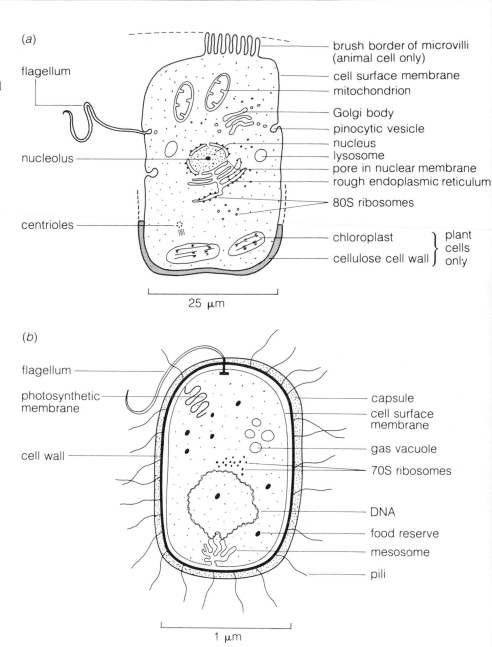

(*a*)

flagellum

nucleolus

centrioles

brush border of microvilli
(animal cell only)

cell surface membrane

mitochondrion

Golgi body

pinocytic vesicle

nucleus

lysosome

pore in nuclear membrane

rough endoplasmic reticulum

80S ribosomes

chloroplast ⎫ plant
cellulose cell wall ⎬ cells
 ⎭ only

25 μm

(*b*)

flagellum

photosynthetic membrane

cell wall

capsule

cell surface membrane

gas vacuole

70S ribosomes

DNA

food reserve

mesosome

pili

1 μm

1.2 Kingdom Monera

1.2.1 Class Bacteria

Examples: *Escherichia coli, Salmonella typhimurium, Streptococcus lactis*

Bacteria are very versatile and are found in a wide range of habitats; in the soil, the air, water, as well as in or on the surface of animals and plants. They range in size from 0.1–10 μm in length and are usually found in enormous numbers. One gram of soil may contain 100 million

Fig 1.2
Some examples of bacteria.
(*a*) Scanning electron
micrograph (SEM) of the
rod-shaped Gram negative
bacterium *Escherichia coli*
(× 14500). (*b*) SEM of the
comma-shaped bacterium
Vibrio cholerae, the cause
of cholera. The bacterium
moves by means of a single
terminal flagellum, as seen
in the picture (× 9000).
(*c*) Transmission EM of
Staphylococcus aureus
showing two organisms.
The cell on the right is in
the process of cell division
with the new wall half-way
to completion across the
centre of the organism
(× 62000).

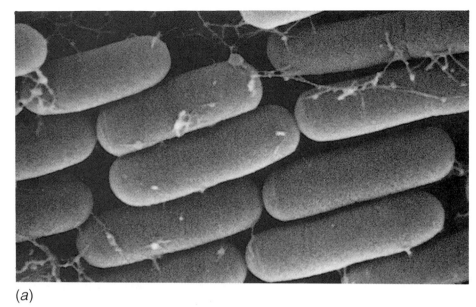

(*a*)

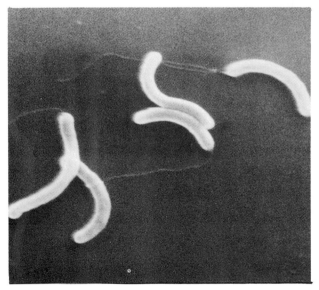

(*b*)

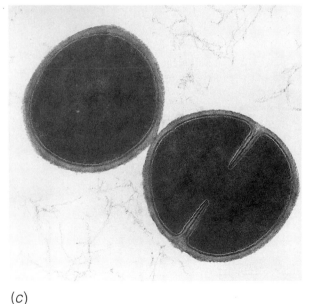

(*c*)

bacteria. Some thermophilic bacteria can withstand extremes of
temperature and may live in hot volcanic springs at around 70° C.
Others, called psychrophiles, can withstand long periods of freezing.
Bacteria are important because they help to decay and recycle organic
waste. Some do cause disease, but most are harmless and many are of
increasing economic importance in biotechnology.

1.2.2 *Structure of bacteria*

Fig 1.3 shows the structure of a generalised rod-shaped bacterial cell
and table 1.2 presents a summary of the structure of bacteria.

Fig 1.3
A generalised rod-shaped
bacterial cell

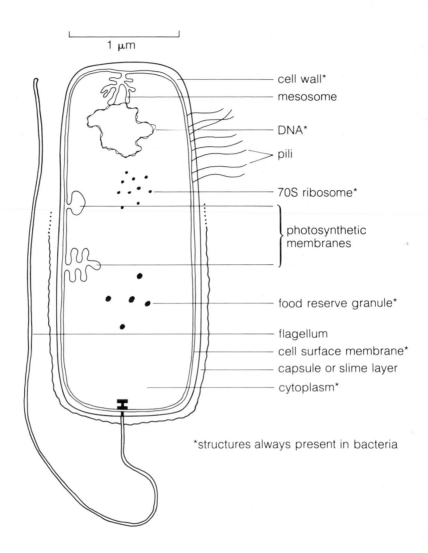

1 μm

cell wall*
mesosome
DNA*
pili
70S ribosome*
photosynthetic membranes
food reserve granule*
flagellum
cell surface membrane*
capsule or slime layer
cytoplasm*

*structures always present in bacteria

1.2.3 *The bacterial cell wall and the Gram staining technique*

In 1884, Christian Gram developed a way of staining bacteria which seemed to divide them into two groups. These were called Gram positive and Gram negative. It is now known that bacteria have two basic types of cell wall which react differently to the stain. The staining technique developed by Gram is still commonly used today.

The technique involves heat-fixing a smear of bacteria to a clean microscope slide and then flooding it with crystal violet. All bacteria take up this stain. The smear is then washed with Gram's iodine to fix the stain and then decolourised with alcohol or propanone. Gram positive bacteria retain the crystal violet/iodine complex, but Gram negative do not. Finally the smear is counterstained with a red stain, such as safranin or carbol fuschin. Gram negative bacteria take up this stain and become red. Gram positive stay purple.

Table 1.2
Summary: the structure of bacteria

Structure	Features	Examples of bacteria
Always present		
Cell wall	10–100 nm thick, often multilayered, main component is murein which forms a rigid framework. The murein molecule consists of parallel polysaccharide chains, cross-linked by short peptides forming a net-like structure. Two distinct types are distinguished by the Gram's stain:	
	Gram positive: murein network is filled with proteins and polysaccharides forming a rigid box	*Lactobacillus*
	Gram negative: thinner but more complex, murein coated with smooth layer of lipids. Thus protected from lysozyme, an anti-bacterial agent, and more resistant to penicillin.	*Escherichia coli*
Cell surface membrane (plasmalemma)	This does not contain sterols, except in mycoplasmas and has a high proportion of protein to phospholipids. These proteins are mainly enzymes used in DNA synthesis, electron transport, respiration and photosynthesis.	
Ribosomes	The site of protein synthesis. Bacterial ribosomes are of the smaller 70S type.	
Cytoplasm	Since bacteria are so small, they do not need to be divided into compartments. The cytoplasm is uniform and has few organelles. It contains storage granules, ribosomes and plasmids. A nucleoid (nuclear region) is usually found.	
Sometimes present		
Flagella	Found in many motile bacteria. Resemble one microtubule of eukaryotic flagella. A hollow cylinder of the protein flagellin; it is rigid and the base rotates so the cell is propelled along.	*Rhizobium* and *Azotobacter*
Capsule or slime layer	An outer protective layer found in some slime layer bacteria which shows up by negative (background) staining. It helps bacteria to join together into colonies. Many soil bacteria help to bind soil particles to give a good 'crumb' structure. Functions of capsule include: protection against chemicals, such as drugs, and desiccation, storage of waste products, as a food reserve and as a resistance to attack by other organisms, e.g. by phagocytes.	*Azotobacter*
Photosynthetic membranes	Some bacteria have tubular or sac-like infoldings of the cell surface membrane in which is found bacteriochlorophyll and other photosynthetic pigments.	*Chromatium*
Mesosomes	Thought to be the site of respiration, these are very tightly folded invaginations of the cell surface membrane. Mesosomes may also be involved in cell division and DNA uptake.	*Bacillus subtilis*
Pili or fimbriae	Like flagella, these project out of the cell surface membrane through the cell wall but are much more numerous and found all over some bacterial cells. Made of a protein called pilin, they are antigenic. Fine pili may bind cells together. In a few types they are used in conjugation, an exchange of genetic material.	*Escherichia coli* and *Salmonella*

Table 1.2 *(Cont.)*

Structure	Features	Examples of bacteria
Endospores	Some bacteria form very resistant endospores which ensure survival in severe conditions such as drought, toxic chemicals and extremes of temperature. Anthrax spores are known to be viable after 50 years.	*Bacillus anthracis*

The different reaction to the stain is due to the structure of the two basic types of cell wall. Gram positive bacteria have a cell surface membrane surrounded by a rigid cell wall about 20–80 nm thick (fig 1.4). This rigid layer is made of a peptidoglycan called **murein**, which has a complex three-dimensional structure. Gram negative bacteria also have a rigid layer outside the cell surface membrane but it is much thinner, only 2–3 nm thick (fig 1.4). On the outside of this is an outer membrane which contains lipopolysaccharides instead of phospholipids. This forms an extra physical barrier to substances, such as antibiotics and enzymes, like lysozyme, which normally destroy or inhibit bacteria. This means that infections due to Gram negative bacteria are more difficult to treat.

It is thought that the crystal violet/iodine complex is a large molecule that becomes trapped in the cell wall. It is more easily washed out of the thinner Gram negative cell wall.

1.2.4 Form of bacteria

When viewed with a microscope, several distinct shapes are obvious and these may be used to help in identification (fig 1.5).

Fig 1.4
The structure of bacterial cell walls (based on electron micrographs of the cell walls of *Bacillus* (Gram +ve) and *E. coli* (Gram −ve))

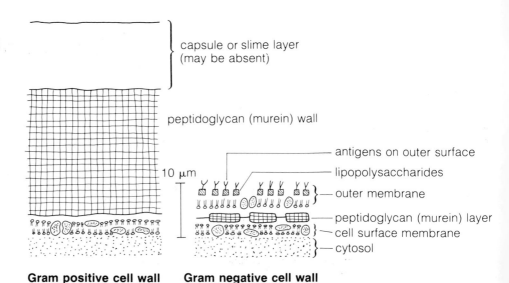

capsule or slime layer (may be absent)

peptidoglycan (murein) wall

10 μm

antigens on outer surface
lipopolysaccharides
outer membrane
peptidoglycan (murein) layer
cell surface membrane
cytosol

Gram positive cell wall   **Gram negative cell wall**

Fig 1.5
The form (shape) of bacteria

1(a) Cocci

coccus

(b) Staphylocci

e.g. *Staphylococcus aureus* causes boils and food poisoning

(c) Diplococci

e.g. *Diplococcus pneumoniae* causes pneumonia

capsule

(d) Streptococci

e.g. *Streptococcus pyogenes* causes sore throats

S. thermophilus used in yogurt making

2(a) Rods (bacilli)

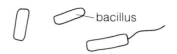
bacillus

e.g. *Salmonella typhimurium* causes severe food poisoning

Escherichia coli common symbiont of gut

(b) Chains of rods

e.g. *Azotobacter* a free-living soil nitrogen-fixing bacterium

endospore

e.g. *Bacillus anthracis* causes anthrax

3 Spirilla

spirillum

e.g. *Spirillum rubrum* saprophyte of fresh water

Treponema pallidum causes the venereal disease syphilis

4 Vibrio

e.g. *Vibrio cholerae* causes cholera

1.2.5 Reproduction

Bacteria grow very quickly in favourable conditions. The generation time may be as little as 20 minutes, though for many species it is 15–20 hours. Reproduction is asexual by **binary fission** (fig 1.6).

(1) The circular bacterial chromosome divides but there is no mitotic spindle. The chromosome attaches itself to the cell membrane, or in some cases to the mesosome.

(2) A septum starts to be synthesised to divide the cell. This often starts growing where there are mesosomes.

(3) The septum grows right across the cell, dividing it into two daughter cells.

Fig 1.6
Binary fission in bacteria

circular DNA

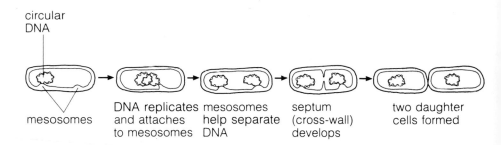

mesosomes

DNA replicates and attaches to mesosomes

mesosomes help separate DNA

septum (cross-wall) develops

two daughter cells formed

1.2.6 Conjugation, transformation and transduction

Some bacteria have 'mating' cells which come together and are joined by their pili. Some genetic material, either a copy of the chromosome or a plasmid is passed between them. The donor cell passes genetic material, usually deoxyribonucleic acid (DNA), to the recipient. In this way, the recipient acquires new characteristics. For example, it is known that resistance to antibiotics is passed on by **conjugation**.

Griffith first observed the phenomenon of **transformation** in 1928. One bacterium releases DNA into the medium and this is absorbed by a second bacterium. This cell therefore acquires new characteristics.

Transduction is where new genes are inserted into a bacterium by a bacteriophage virus (see section 1.7.3).

Conjugation, transformation and transduction are not sexual reproduction since this implies an exchange of genetic material. In each of the above cases, DNA has been transferred from a donor to a recipient.

1.2.7 Plasmids

The cytoplasm of certain bacteria may contain small circles of DNA called plasmids which are able to replicate independently of the main circular chromosome. Plasmids are known to carry genes which may aid the survival of the bacterium in adverse conditions (table 1.3). In several ways, plasmids have been found to resemble viruses. Plasmids can be transferred to another bacterium by conjugation.

1.2.8 The economic importance of bacteria

Tables 1.4 and 1.5 describe some examples of bacteria which are useful or harmful to humans. Some of these bacteria and their effects will be described in more detail in later chapters.

**Table 1.3
Plasmids**

The effect of plasmids on their host
R-factors cause resistance to antibiotics, virus infection and UV radiation (sections 10.6 and 11.10)
F-factors increase fertility
Help in the production of enzymes, antigens, antibiotics and toxins
Ti plasmids induce tumours in plants (sections 3.4 and 12.4.8)
Are involved in the metabolism of hydrocarbons and sugars

Similarities between plasmids and viruses
They reversibly integrate into the bacterial chromosome
They are specific to a few bacteria
They confer characteristics on the bacterial host
They code for their own transfer
They may pick up and transfer genes from the bacterial chromosome
They replicate independently of the bacterial chromosome

**Table 1.4
Some useful bacteria**

Name	Gram stain	Form (shape)	Use
Lactobacillus bulgaricus	+ve	rods	yogurt
Streptococcus thermophilus	+ve	filamentous	yogurt
Streptococcus lactis	+ve	cocci	cheese
Streptococcus cremoris	+ve	cocci	cheese
Methylophilus methylotropus	variable	cocci	methane, methanol
Clostridium autobutylicum	+ve	rods	propanone (acetone) and butanol
Leuconostoc mesenteroides	+ve	cocci	dextran
Bacillus subtilis*	+ve	rods	enzymes
Streptomyces spp.	+ve	filaments	antibiotics
Escherichia coli*	−ve	rods	insulin, growth hormone, interferon
Pseudomonas denitrificans	−ve	rods	vitamin B_{12}

* Using genetic engineering.

**Table 1.5
Some harmful bacteria**

Name	Gram stain	Form (shape)	Disease
Staphylococcus aureus	+ve	cocci	boils
Salmonella typhimurium	−ve	rods	food poisoning
Salmonella typhi	−ve	rods	typhoid fever
Mycobacterium tuberculosis	variable (acid-fast)	fine rods	tuberculosis
Bordetella pertussis	−ve	very short rods	whooping cough
Neisseria gonorrhoea	−ve	cocci	gonorrhoea
Treponema pallidum	variable	long spirals	syphilis
Vibrio cholerae	−ve	curved rods	cholera
Clostridium tetani	+ve	rods	tetanus
Clostridium botulinum	+ve	rods	botulism
Corynebacterium diptheriae	+ve	short rods	diphtheria
Listeria sp.	+ve	round-ended rods	listeriosis
Shigella sonnei	−ve	rods	dysentery
Pasteurella pestis	−ve	small rods	plague

1.2.9   Archaebacteria

Some bacteria are quite different from other prokaryotes in that they have different sequences in their ribosomal RNA (ribonucleic acid) and do not have murein in their cell walls. These bacteria are chemoautotrophic and methanogenic (methane-producing). They are strict anaerobes and produce methane from carbon dioxide and hydrogen, and obtain their energy in the process. They are so fundamentally different that it is thought they may have originated more than 3 billion years ago when the atmosphere of the Earth was anaerobic and rich in carbon dioxide and hydrogen. Some scientists even classify them in a separate kingdom – the Archaebacteria.

1.2.10   Class Cyanobacteria (blue-greens)

Examples: *Anabaena cylindrica*, *Nostoc muscorum*, *Spirulina platensis*

Cyanobacteria are prokaryotic microorganisms similar to bacteria. They are photosynthetic but not true algae and are considered to be very primitive life forms. They have been found in fossil remains from over 2 billion years ago and are considered by some to be one of the first living organisms to colonise the Earth. They are found in the surface layer of fresh and sea water. On land, they will grow wherever there is both light and moisture and are found as slime on the surface of mud, rocks, wood, and on some living organisms. They are so-called because of their photosynthetic pigments which give them a distinct dark greenish-blue colour.

1.2.11   Structure of Cyanobacteria

Blue-greens have a typical prokaryotic cell structure since they have no true nucleus and a naked coil of DNA (fig 1.7). The cell wall is similar in structure and composition to that of Gram negative bacteria. Protein synthesis takes place on 70S ribosomes in the cytoplasm. Blue-greens are photosynthetic. The pigments are incorporated into the many membranes which form layers called **lamellae**, which are simple infoldings of the cell surface membrane. The pigments are chlorophyll and others such as **phycocyanin** and **phycoerythrin**, which give the cells their distinct colouration. The cells may be single or in colonies, but members of a colony remain independent.

1.2.12   Nitrogen fixation

Only a very few organisms are capable of fixing atmospheric nitrogen by reducing it to ammonia and combining it with organic acids to produce amino acids and proteins (fig 1.8). This is one of the most important biological processes and is essential for maintaining a supply

Fig 1.7
Diagram of a typical blue-green cell (based on electron micrographs)

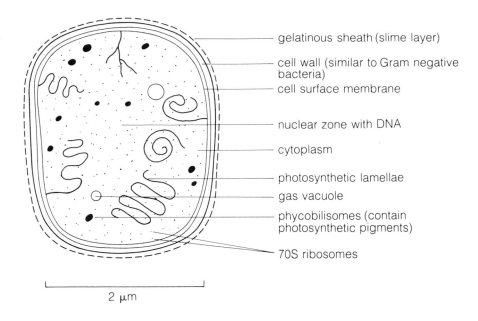

gelatinous sheath (slime layer)

cell wall (similar to Gram negative bacteria)

cell surface membrane

nuclear zone with DNA

cytoplasm

photosynthetic lamellae

gas vacuole

phycobilisomes (contain photosynthetic pigments)

70S ribosomes

2 μm

Fig 1.8
Nitrogen fixation

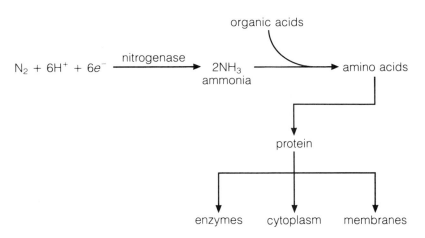

organic acids

$$N_2 + 6H^+ + 6e^- \xrightarrow{\text{nitrogenase}} \underset{\text{ammonia}}{2NH_3} \longrightarrow \text{amino acids}$$

protein

enzymes   cytoplasm   membranes

of organic nitrogen compounds for the whole biosphere. Nitrogen-fixing bacteria can do this and so can some blue-greens. Cells able to fix nitrogen contain the enzyme **nitrogenase**. This enzyme is inactivated by oxygen and so conditions inside the nitrogen-fixing cell have to be anaerobic. Some blue-greens have special thick-walled cells called **heterocysts**. *Anabaena* is a blue-green which has filaments made up of many normal photosynthetic cells. These cells produce sugars and oxygen. Scattered along the filaments are a few distinct **heterocyst** cells that generate combined nitrogen (fig 1.9). Whenever the external medium is rich in nitrates or organic nitrogen, the heterocysts disappear from the filament. If the surrounding medium is low in nitrates or organic nitrogen, then the number of heterocysts has been found to increase.

Fig 1.9
A filament of *Anabaena*

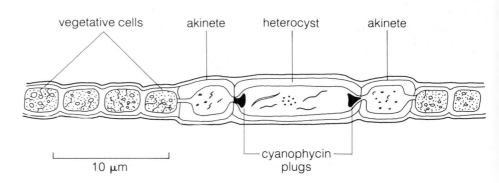

Within the heterocyst, **anaerobic** conditions exist. The thick wall, with a coating of mucilage, helps to prevent diffusion of oxygen from the external medium. A plug of **cyanophycin** prevents communication with adjacent photosynthetic cells. Within the heterocyst, most photosynthetic membranes break down. Some do remain but contain only the pigments and enzymes necessary for photosystem 1 to function (fig 1.10). This process will enable the cell to make adenosine triphosphate (ATP) but does not result in carbon dioxide fixation and the manufacture of glucose. Anaerobic respiration takes place within heterocysts. This means that the heterocyst is able to produce the ATP required to fix nitrogen.

Many filamentous blue-greens are also able to produce **akinetes**, or spores, which are able to survive adverse conditions such as during a period of overpopulation known as an algal 'bloom' (fig 1.9). They seem to develop from a vegetative cell near to a heterocyst. The cell increases in size and accumulates large food reserves. Photosynthesis within the akinete is reduced and gas vacuoles disappear (fig 1.11). This means that the akinete slowly sinks to the bottom. It may survive for several years, but will germinate as soon as conditions become favourable.

1.2.13 *The economic importance of blue-greens*

Spirulina platensis is a filamentous blue-green found naturally in shallow alkaline lakes in parts of Africa and South America. It has been collected and dried by the local people and used as a food for thousands of years. It is also used as a cattle food. In agriculture, nitrogen-fixing blue-greens may be used as an organic fertiliser. They are grown on a large scale in China, India and the Philippines, particularly where rice is cultivated in paddy fields. The water may be seeded with a starter culture of blue-greens at the start of the growing season. This method has been shown to increase the yield of rice by 15–20%.

Nostoc is another blue-green which is used as a food in Peru and in the Far East.

Fig 1.10
The structure and function of a heterocyst

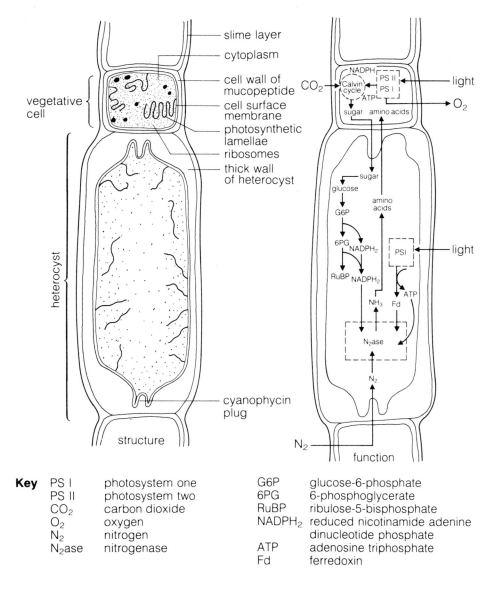

Key

PS I	photosystem one	G6P	glucose-6-phosphate
PS II	photosystem two	6PG	6-phosphoglycerate
CO_2	carbon dioxide	RuBP	ribulose-5-bisphosphate
O_2	oxygen	$NADPH_2$	reduced nicotinamide adenine dinucleotide phosphate
N_2	nitrogen		
N_2ase	nitrogenase	ATP	adenosine triphosphate
		Fd	ferredoxin

Research is taking place into the use of blue-greens in a solar energy conversion system. *Anabaena cylindrica* has heterocysts and is able to give off oxygen by photosynthesis in the vegetative cells and at the same time (in the absence of nitrogen) gives off hydrogen by nitrogenase-catalysed electron transfer to H^+ ions in the heterocysts. Both products are in demand industrially. Genetic engineering of blue-greens may enable new strains to be produced which can fix nitrogen, give off hydrogen or release ammonia with even greater efficiency.

Questions

1 Why are blue-greens considered to be prokaryotes?

2 By means of a table, compare and contrast the characteristics of bacteria and blue-greens.

13

Fig 1.11
An akinete

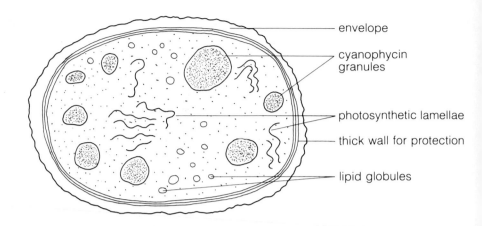

- envelope
- cyanophycin granules
- photosynthetic lamellae
- thick wall for protection
- lipid globules

3   Blue-greens are very important ecologically. Why is this? Give as many reasons as you can.

4   It is thought that blue-greens were the first photosynthetic organisms on the Earth and that they represent a very early stage in the evolution of life. Give as many reasons as you can why this might be so.

1.3   Kingdom Protoctista

This kingdom contains all eukaryotic organisms which are neither animals, plants, fungi nor prokaryotes. Members of this kingdom have been long claimed and disputed by both botanists and zoologists. So this new kingdom has been created to contain a number of different groups which are not really related though they all have some similarities. It includes all protozoa, all nucleated algae and the slime moulds.

1.3.1   Phylum Protozoa

Protozoa are found wherever moisture is present, in sea water, fresh water and soil. There are commensal, symbiotic and parasitic species in addition to many free-living types.

1.3.2   Structure of Protozoa

Protozoa are eukaryotic. The cell is surrounded by a single unit membrane beneath which is a layer of gelatinous **ectoplasm**. Below this there is a more fluid internal cytoplasm called **endoplasm**. Ectoplasm and endoplasm are two different colloidal states of protoplasm and are reversible. Some species have non-living external coverings to protect the cell. These may be either cellulose or gelatinous envelopes, or distinct shells of inorganic material cemented together. The nucleus is typical of eukaryotes, with a nuclear membrane, nucleoplasm, chromatin granules and one or more nucleoli. Movement is by means of a variety of locomotory organelles such as flagella, cilia or pseudopodia. Freshwater protozoans have contractile vacuoles to act as pumps to remove excess water from the cytoplasm. Water tends to enter by osmosis since the cytoplasm is usually hypertonic to the aqueous environment. However, contractile vacuoles may also be found in some marine protozoans. All types of nutrition are found in protozoans; some are autotrophic, others are saprotrophic, and many are heterotrophic. Digestion of food takes place intracellularly, within food vacuoles. Exchange of gases is by diffusion across the cell membrane. Waste products from cell metabolism diffuse out of the cell; the main nitrogenous waste is ammonia.

1.3.3 Class Rhizopoda

Example: *Amoeba proteus*
Fig 1.12 shows the structure of *Amoeba proteus*.

Fig 1.12
The structure of *Amoeba*

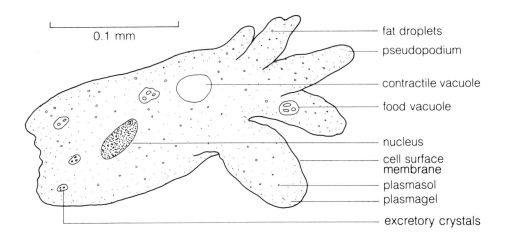

0.1 mm

fat droplets
pseudopodium
contractile vacuole
food vacuole
nucleus
cell surface membrane
plasmasol
plasmagel
excretory crystals

1.3.4 Locomotion

The cytoplasm of *Amoeba* can be observed to stream and **pseudopodia** are formed. These are processes which protrude from the cell surface and then withdraw. Amoeboid movement involves a colloidal change within the cytoplasm from sol to gel at the anterior end of the pseudopodium and from gel to sol at the posterior end. The exact mechanism is not known and may well involve the use of ATP. *Amoeba* is a bottom-dweller and moves along surfaces in this way. A fine pellicle surrounds the cell surface membrane, this creates friction with the surface and helps *Amoeba* to move along.

1.3.5 Nutrition

Amoeba feeds on a wide variety of pond microorganisms such as small algae, live ciliates and flagellates. The presence of food stimulates the formation of a cup-like pseudopodium which, by invagination of the membrane, traps the prey. The food cup finally closes and the prey is taken into the cell with some water as a food vacuole or **phagosome**. This feeding method is called **phagocytosis**. The food vacuoles are moved around the cytoplasm and enzymes are secreted into them to digest the food. At first, the vacuoles show an acid reaction, which gradually becomes alkaline as the food particle is broken down. Eventually, the soluble food products are absorbed into the cytoplasm and any undigested food residues are passed to the cell surface to be left behind in the water as the *Amoeba* moves on. *Amoeba* may also take in water droplets containing soluble nutrients during **pinocytosis** or 'cell drinking'; this is another characteristic membrane activity. This differs from phagocytosis in that the membrane invaginates forming a narrow channel. At the base of this channel, small fluid-containing vesicles are pinched off.

1.3.6 Water balance

Freshwater and some marine amoebae have one or many **contractile vacuoles**. These are usually spherical, and they can be seen to fill and then empty their contents to the outside. The membrane around the contractile vacuole has the same structure as the cell surface membrane.

1.3.7 Reproduction

When *Amoeba* reaches its optimum size of about 0.1 mm diameter, it becomes spherical and mitosis takes place. This process of **binary fission** occurs every two or three days if conditions are favourable. Sexual reproduction is rare in *Amoeba* but some species do show **hologamy**. This is where two individuals fuse together and then the cell divides, usually by multiple fission.

1.3.8 Amoeba and disease

Amoeba does not form cysts. However, the closely related *Entamoeba* species, which may be found as a harmless commensal in the human large intestine, does form resistant cysts. Cysts are formed when the organism secretes a layer of mucilage around the cell to protect it from adverse conditions. *Entamoeba hystolitica* causes the disease of amoebic dysentery and can be very serious because it is difficult to diagnose and does not respond to antibiotics. The cysts are passed on in the faeces of infected people and may contaminate drinking water. It is more common in Third World countries.

Some species of *Amoeba* have been implicated in the spread of Legionnaires' disease. This is a severe form of pneumonia first recognised in 1976 in Philadelphia and is so-called because 182 American Legion delegates were infected, leading to several fatalities. It has since been found to be carried in water-cooled air conditioning systems. The organism responsible is the bacterium *Legionella pneumophila* and is very difficult to isolate and culture. This is because it is a parasite of free-living amoebae. In warm conditions, these may proliferate in water and are spread in droplets of water vapour which are inhaled into the lungs.

1.3.9 Class Sporozoa

Example: *Plasmodium vivax*

All sporozoans are parasitic and typically have a resting spore, or a stage derived from the spore, which contains minute infective **sporozoites.**

Plasmodium species are the protozoan parasites responsible for producing the disease **malaria.** The structure of the parasite varies during the different stages of its life cycle (fig 1.13). Malaria is transmitted by the bite of an infected female mosquito who must feed on blood before laying her eggs. The sporozoites are found in the saliva of the mosquito and are injected into the human as it feeds.

Sporozoites are very small: about 10 μm long and 1 μm in diameter. They are motile and have a surface **pellicle** made up of two membranes. Below the pellicle is a layer of **microtubules** which run along the length of the organism. At the anterior end is an **apical ring** and several organelles including some called **rhoptries.** These stiffen the anterior end and secrete enzymes which help the sporozoite to penetrate the host cell membranes. The sporozoites move with the aid of the

Fig 1.13
Some stages in the life cycle of *Plasmodium* (based on electron micrographs)

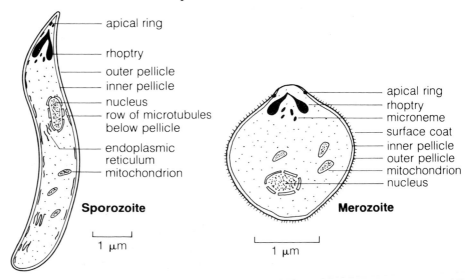

apical ring
rhoptry
outer pellicle
inner pellicle
nucleus
row of microtubules below pellicle
endoplasmic reticulum
mitochondrion
Sporozoite
1 μm

apical ring
rhoptry
microneme
surface coat
inner pellicle
outer pellicle
mitochondrion
nucleus
Merozoite
1 μm

17

microtubules sliding over each other and work their way through the host's tissues into the blood capillaries. They are carried by the bloodstream and are attracted to liver cells. Within a few minutes the blood itself is clear of sporozoites which penetrate and develop inside the liver cells, feeding by phagocytosis. They undergo cell division to form **merozoites**.

Merozoites are pear-shaped and about 1.5 μm in length. They have a double membrane pellicle and are surrounded by a surface coat of cell membrane identical to the host cell membrane. This protects them from detection by the human immune system. They also have an apical complex and are able to invade further liver cells or red blood cells (erythrocytes). When inside an erythrocyte a merozoite feeds on cytoplasm and haemoglobin by phagocytosis. It enlarges until it almost fills the host cell and then divides by a process called **schizogony** forming between eight and 24 **schizonts** which mature into merozoites. These are released into the bloodstream when the erythrocyte bursts and each invades a further cell, thus heavily parasitising the blood.

Further details about malaria, the disease and its control can be found in section 10.8.

1.3.10   *Class Ciliata*

Example: *Paramecium caudatum*

Paramecium is found in fresh water enriched by decaying vegetation. It is cultured easily in hay infusions. The cell body is elongated with a blunt anterior end and a tapering posterior (fig 1.14). The cytoplasm is enclosed in a semi-rigid **pellicle**, perforated by many cilia arranged in longitudinal rows. Each cilium arises from a basal body or **kinetosome**. Fibrils join the kinetosomes of adjacent cilia and form a complex network of fibrils, the **kinetodesmata**. These co-ordinate the beating of the cilia.

1.3.11   *Structure of* Paramecium

Inside the pellicle, the cytoplasm is divided into a clear outer ectoplasm and an inner granular endoplasm (fig 1.14). **Trichocysts** are specialised organelles situated in the ectoplasm and act as a means of attachment during feeding, or as weapons of defence. The contents of a trichocyst can be discharged to the outside in a few milliseconds. The discharged trichocyst has a long thread-like shaft with a barb at the end (fig 1.15). The shaft is not visible before discharge, and may be formed during discharge.

Many ciliates also have **mucigenic bodies** present below the outer membrane which discharge a thick slimy material that may form a protective covering or cyst.

Fig 1.14
The structure of
Paramecium

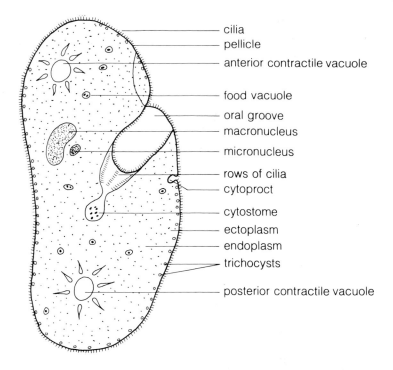

- cilia
- pellicle
- anterior contractile vacuole
- food vacuole
- oral groove
- macronucleus
- micronucleus
- rows of cilia
- cytoproct
- cytostome
- ectoplasm
- endoplasm
- trichocysts
- posterior contractile vacuole

Fig 1.15
The action of the
trichocyst in *Paramecium*

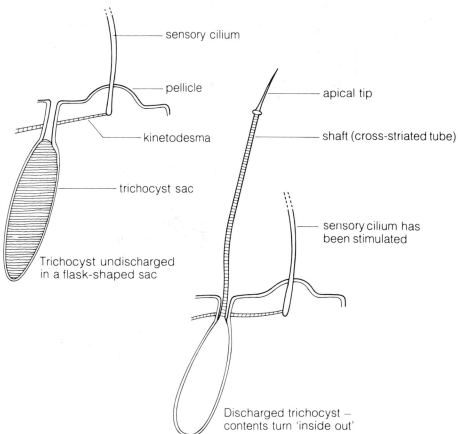

- sensory cilium
- pellicle
- kinetodesma
- trichocyst sac

Trichocyst undischarged
in a flask-shaped sac

- apical tip
- shaft (cross-striated tube)
- sensory cilium has
been stimulated

Discharged trichocyst –
contents turn 'inside out'

1.3.12 Locomotion and sensitivity

The cilia beat together in a coordinated fashion which is called **metachronal rhythm**. Each cilium has an effective power stroke and a passive recovery stroke, like an oar (fig 1.16). The movement is so fast that all you can see is a flickering at the edge of the *Paramecium*.

Fig 1.16
Metachronal rhythm of cilia in *Paramecium*

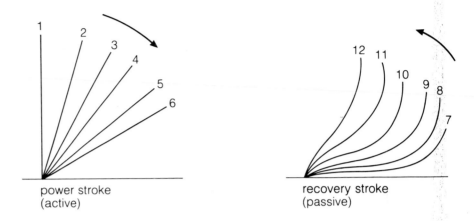

power stroke
(active)

recovery stroke
(passive)

This arrangement of cilia gives *Paramecium* a spiral course, and at the same time it rotates about its long axis. It is notable that some of the cilia are longer and stiffer than the others and are not so important in movement. These cilia are thought to have an important sensory function. The cilia can suddenly reverse their action; this is known as the avoidance reaction.

Paramecium samples the water ahead. This can be observed by placing a drop of Indian ink in the water. If a small amount of a chemical is placed in the centre of a drop of water it will slowly diffuse outwards. If a *Paramecium* is present, it swims about and gives an avoidance reaction whenever it enters a zone less favourable than the one it is in. Thereby it finds the area most favourable to it.

Paramecia are sensitive to temperature changes. If the temperature is even throughout, paramecia are found to be evenly distributed. If, however, a temperature gradient is set up across a Petri dish, the organisms are found to collect in the region of temperature (optimum) most favourable to them.

1.3.13 Nutrition

At the anterior end is a shallow ciliated **oral groove**. This forms a short **gullet** with a mouth or **cytostome** at the end in the endoplasm. A wide variety of microorganisms are swept into the gullet by the action of the cilia. At the cytostome, phagocytosis takes place and food vacuoles are pinched off. These can be observed to move through the endoplasm along a definite route (fig 1.17).

Fig 1.17
The path taken by food vacuoles through the cytoplasm of *Paramecium*

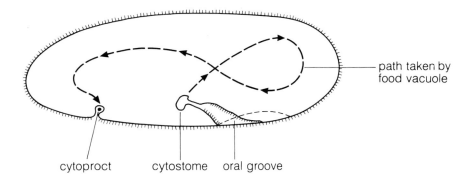

path taken by food vacuole

cytoproct   cytostome   oral groove

Using an indicator (such as universal indicator) it is possible to show the change in pH of the vacuole contents from acid to alkaline during digestion. Finally the food vacuole reaches the **cytoproct** where the undigested remains are passed to the outside. The soluble products of digestion have already been absorbed into the cytoplasm from the vacuole. Ciliates store food as glycogen and fat droplets in the endoplasm.

1.3.14   Osmoregulation

Paramecium has two **contractile vacuoles**, one at the posterior end, the other at the anterior. They empty through a canal which passes through the pellicle. In *Paramecium*, there are many collecting ducts surrounding the vacuole, though in other ciliates it is not as complicated as this.

1.3.15   Reproduction

Paramecium shows both sexual and asexual reproduction.

Asexual reproduction is by **binary fission**. There are two nuclei, a small rounded **micronucleus** and a larger **macronucleus**. The micronucleus divides by mitosis into two daughter nuclei which move to opposite poles of the cell. The macronucleus, which has increased in size, divides by fission but no spindle is set up. Instead, it seems to simply constrict, then cleaves in two. After this the cytoplasm cleaves and two identical daughter cells are formed.

Sexual reproduction is known as **conjugation**. Two individuals come together and stick to each other, joined by their oral grooves where the cilia seem to secrete a sticky substance. The two fused ciliates are called conjugants and they can remain attached for several hours. A complex series of nuclear divisions and exchanges then takes place (fig 1.18). Sexual reproduction is important for variation, though its frequency does vary from species to species.

**Fig 1.18
Sexual reproduction in
*Paramecium***

1 Oral surfaces fuse together

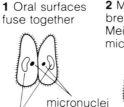

macronuclei
micronuclei

2 Macronucleus breaks down. Meiosis of micronucleus

3 Three of the four micronuclei break down

4 Remaining micronucleus divides

5 Nuclei are exchanged

6 Zygotic nuclei form

7 Zygotic nuclei divide

8 Zygotic nuclei divide again

9 Three nuclei disappear. Four become macronuclei, one becomes a micronucleus

10 Binary fission now takes place

11 Finally, each divides again, forming four new cells from each original conjugant

1.3.16 *Autogamy*

This is a type of reproduction that involves the same type of nuclear behaviour as in conjugation, except that no genetic material is exchanged between individuals. However, it does produce some degree of reorganisation of genetic material (fig 1.19).

**Fig 1.19
Autogamy in *Paramecium***

1 Micronucleus divides

2 Macronucleus breaks down. Micronucleus divides again

3 Zygotic nucleus forms

4 Zygotic nucleus divides

5 Two nuclei become micronuclei, two become macronuclei

6 Binary fission takes place

two 'daughter' paramecia

1.3.17 The economic importance of protozoa

Many ciliates are saprobionts and are vital in the recycling of organic wastes, particularly in sewage treatment (chapter 9). Parasitic forms, such as *Entamoeba* and *Plasmodium*, may cause loss of life. Malaria can be devastating to the economy of developing countries, incapacitating millions of workers every year (section 10.8).

Question   1   Summarise, with examples of protozoa:

(*a*)   the means of locomotion;
(*b*)   the means of reproduction;
(*c*)   nutrition.

1.4 Phylum Euglenoidea

Example: *Euglena viridis*

Euglena is often found in fresh and salt waters and on damp soil, particularly in areas with a high concentration of organic nitrogen, such as in farmyard puddles and slurry pits.

1.4.1 Structure

The cell is long and slender with a blunt anterior end and a pointed posterior. There is a flexible **pellicle** forming the outer covering layer, and this spirals around the cell (fig 1.20). At the anterior end there is a funnel-like **cytostome** and a short canal leading into a **reservoir**. The reservoir has a contractile vacuole on its inner surface with several smaller vacuoles leading into it. A **stigma** or 'eye spot', containing the light-sensitive pigment carotene, lies to one side of the gullet. There are two flagella of different lengths which arise from the base of the reservoir. One flagellum is whip-like and used for locomotion; this comes out through the cytostome. The second is smaller and lies inside the reservoir, close to the base of the long flagellum. Both have the 9 + 2 arrangement of microtubules typical of eukaryotes (fig 1.21). Each flagellum has a **basal granule**. In the cytoplasm are many mitochondria, a nucleus, and food granules of **paramylum**, a starch-like polysaccharide. The shape and number of chloroplasts varies with the species. They contain **pyrenoids** which store paramylum.

1.4.2 Locomotion

Waves of contraction can be observed passing from the base of the flagellum to the tip; this creates a force that pulls the cell through the water. The waves spiral along the flagellum and as the *Euglena* moves forward, it follows a helical path, rotating about its own axis (fig 1.22).

Fig 1.20
Structure of *Euglena viridis*

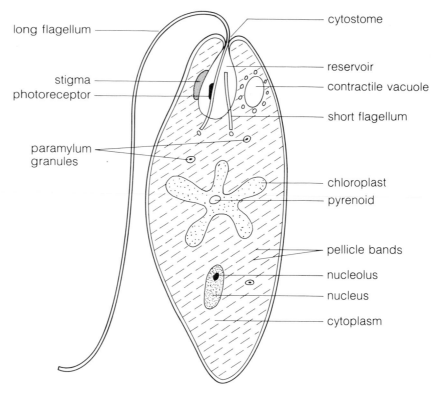

Fig 1.21
**Cross-section of flagellum
in *Euglena*, × 200 000**

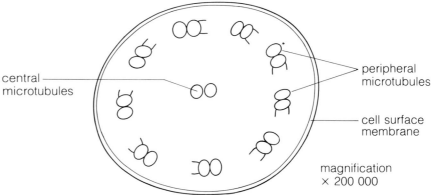

9 + 2 arrangement of microtubules, typical of eukaryotic cells.

The microtubules are linked by membranes containing enzymes which can release energy from ATP and cause the microtubules to slide over each other.

A basal body anchors each flagellum firmly in the cell.

The flagellum uses energy from ATP and the movement produced is very rapid.

Another form of locomotion is known as **euglenoid movement**. This is produced by alternate contractions and relaxations of the flexible pellicle. The pellicle bands articulate with each other and this produces a slow creeping movement.

Fig 1.22
The action of the flagellum
and euglenoid movement
in *Euglena*

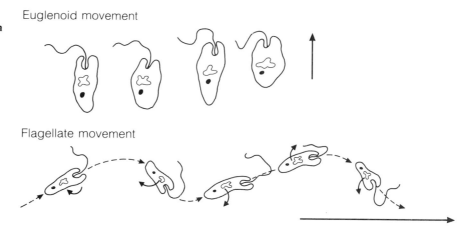

1.4.3 Sensitivity

Euglena normally swims towards a light source with its long axis parallel to the light rays. This is a **phototaxic response** and is controlled by a photoreceptor at the base of the longer flagellum working with the stigma. When the stigma casts a shadow on the photoreceptor, for example when the light rays are at right-angles to the body, *Euglena* changes direction and swims parallel to the light once more.

1.4.4 Nutrition

When light is present, *Euglena* is **photoautotrophic**. It does, however, depend on certain growth factors such as vitamins B_1 and B_{12} being available; without them, growth can not take place. If *Euglena* is kept in the dark for a long time, the photosynthetic pigments break down and nutrition becomes **heterotrophic**, provided that soluble organic nutrients are available. On returning to light, it becomes green again and photosynthesis resumes. Many species of *Euglena* show **phagocytosis** and take in solid food particles through temporary openings in the pellicle.

1.4.5 Reproduction

In favourable conditions, *Euglena* multiplies rapidly by longitudinal **binary fission**. The nucleus undergoes mitosis. The cytoplasm then undergoes longitudinal cleavage forming two identical daughter cells. Very rarely the cell encysts: the flagella are lost and the cell secretes an outer covering of mucilage. Within the cyst, the cytoplasm undergoes **multiple fission** forming many daughter cells which develop flagella when the cyst bursts.

1.5 Phylum Chlorophyta (green algae)

Example: *Chlorella vulgaris*

Chlorella vulgaris is a unicellular green alga which is commonly found in freshwater ponds. Each cell is spherical with a thin cellulose cell wall enclosing clear cytoplasm (fig 1.23). There is a large, cup-shaped chloroplast with a pyrenoid where starch is stored.

Fig 1.23
The structure of *Chlorella*,
× 3000

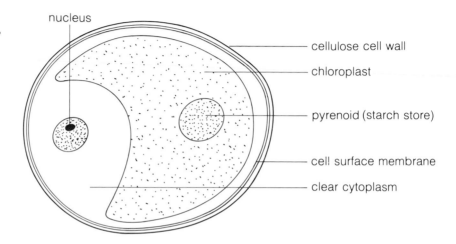

nucleus

cellulose cell wall

chloroplast

pyrenoid (starch store)

cell surface membrane

clear cytoplasm

In favourable conditions, which are slightly alkaline water enriched with nutrients and plenty of decaying organic matter, growth is very rapid. *Chlorella* has been extensively used in biological research since it is relatively easy to culture. It has been used to investigate photosynthesis and is currently used in investigations into alternative food as a single cell protein.

1.6 Kingdom Fungi

Fungi are **eukaryotic** organisms with a cell wall usually of **chitin**. They are not photosynthetic and derive their nutrients by absorption of organic nutrients and are therefore **heterotrophic**. Fungi are usually **filamentous**, or thread-like. The individual threads are called **hyphae** and they branch profusely, often fusing together to form a tangled mass of branched hyphae, the **mycelium**. Individual hyphae are surrounded by rigid cell walls and grow only at their tips. It is this form of **apical growth** that separates the fungi from almost all other organisms, even filamentous ones. They are aerobic or facultative anaerobes and are found almost everywhere.

1.6.1 Structure

Since fungi are eukaryotic, they have a distinct nucleus surrounded by a nuclear membrane with pores; chromosomes and a spindle appear during nuclear division. Mitochondria are found in the cytoplasm and there is extensive endoplasmic reticulum (ER). Ribosomes are found both free in the cytoplasm and attached to the ER. The cytoplasm also contains numerous vacuoles containing storage materials such as starch, lipid globules, and volutin (fig 1.24).

The protoplast is surrounded by a selectively permeable, phospholipid unit membrane. The cytoplasm is at its most dense at the tips of the hyphae, the older parts often being metabolically inactive, with large vacuoles in the cytoplasm. In septate species, there are pores in the cross-walls to allow substances in solution, including nuclei, to move freely from one section to another.

Fig 1.24
Diagram of the tip of a typical fungal hypha (based on electron micrographs)

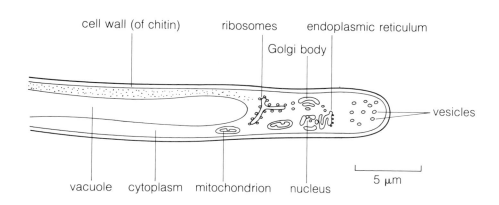

1.6.2 Fungal growth

The growth of hyphae is very rapid under favourable conditions. Each hypha grows at the tip and divides repeatedly along its length, locating food supplies and growing away from its own waste products (figs 1.25 and 1.26).

Fig 1.25
Growth of a mycelium.
(a) One day's growth of a fungal colony from a single spore on a malt agar plate.
(b) Part of the colony shown enlarged and alternately shaded to show how the hyphae extend over one hour

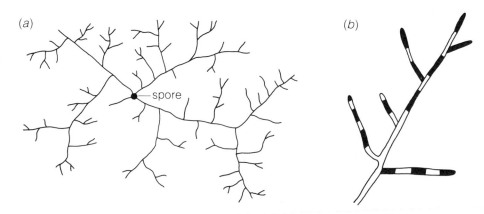

27

Fig 1.26
Conditions required for
fungal growth

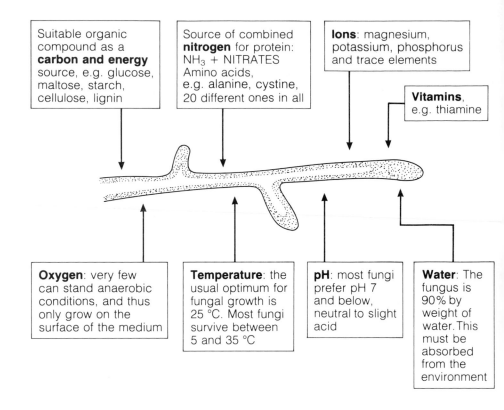

Suitable organic compound as a **carbon and energy** source, e.g. glucose, maltose, starch, cellulose, lignin

Source of combined **nitrogen** for protein: NH_3 + NITRATES Amino acids, e.g. alanine, cystine, 20 different ones in all

Ions: magnesium, potassium, phosphorus and trace elements

Vitamins, e.g. thiamine

Oxygen: very few can stand anaerobic conditions, and thus only grow on the surface of the medium

Temperature: the usual optimum for fungal growth is 25 °C. Most fungi survive between 5 and 35 °C

pH: most fungi prefer pH 7 and below, neutral to slight acid

Water: The fungus is 90% by weight of water. This must be absorbed from the environment

1.6.3   Phylum Oomycota (oomycetes)

Examples: *Phytophthora infestans*, *Pythium* spp.

The hyphae are **aseptate** with no cross-walls. The cytoplasm contains many nuclei enclosed within a common cell wall, usually made of **chitin**. Sometimes other wall polymers are present, such as mannan and glucan.

Asexual reproduction is by motile spores with two flagella. These are formed inside a **sporangium** which may be on a special hypha called the **sporangiophore** (fig 1.27).

Sexual reproduction occurs by fusion of a male **antheridium** with a female **oogonium** to produce a sexual spore (**oospore**) which acts as a resting stage and germinates by a germ tube or by producing zoospores to produce a new diploid generation.

1.6.4   Phylum Zygomycota (zygomycetes)

Example: *Mucor hiemalis*

The hyphae are aseptate with a large well-developed branching mycelium.

Asexual reproduction is by non-motile spores, formed in a sporangium borne on a sporangiophore (fig 1.28).

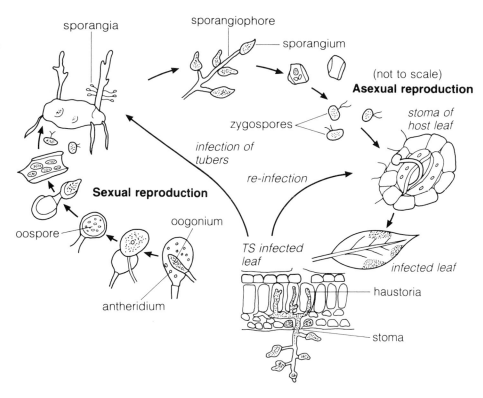

Fig 1.27
The life cycle of
Phytophthora infestans, the
cause of late-blight in
potatoes

sporangia

sporangiophore

sporangium

(not to scale)

Asexual reproduction

zygospores

*stoma of
host leaf*

*infection of
tubers*

re-infection

Sexual reproduction

oospore

oogonium

infected leaf

antheridium

*TS infected
leaf*

haustoria

stoma

Fig 1.28
Asexual reproduction in
Mucor

Stages in sporangiophore growth during spore formation

Growth of sporangiophore

aerial hypha
grows up out
of mycelium

rapid
growth

sporangium
forming

Development of sporangium

columella
forming

spores

mature
sporangium

Spore release and dispersal

Sporangia drop off as sporangial
wall dissolves.
Spore mass is saturated with water.
Spores usually dispersed in water
droplets in damp, humid conditions.
(This is wet spore dispersal.)

Sexual reproduction is by conjugation involving the fusion of sex organs called **gametangia**. The resulting diploid cell develops into a spiny-walled **zygospore**, which acts as a resting stage and can then divide by meiosis to form a new vegetative generation.

1.6.5 *Phylum Ascomycota (ascomycetes)*

Examples: *Penicillium notatum, Saccharomyces cerevisiae*

All ascomycetes have septate hyphae.

Asexual reproduction is by non-motile spores (**conidia**) formed on hyphae or on special hyphal branches called **conidiophores**, but *not* within a sporangium.

Sexual reproduction in the ascomycetes is very complex and there are several different methods by which sexual union is achieved. However, in all cases, the male gamete is borne in a structure called the **antheridium**. If the antheridium makes contact with the **ascogonium**, which contains the female gamete, the cell walls break down and fusion of the two nuclei takes place. A diploid ascus is formed and a fruiting body, or **ascocarp**, may develop to enclose several **asci** (fig 1.29*a*). Meiosis occurs in the ascus, followed by mitosis to release eight haploid **ascospores**, which act as resting cells and later germinate to produce a new generation.

The only exception to this is sexual reproduction in yeast which only occurs occasionally. A yeast cell undergoes meiosis to give four haploid ascospores in an ascus. These are released and divide by mitosis. They fuse randomly, each haploid cell acting as a gamete, to give a diploid zygote. This continues to grow and divide asexually by budding (fig 1.29*b*).

Fig 1.29
(*a*) Sexual reproduction in most ascomycetes (not drawn to scale). (*b*) Sexual reproduction in yeast (*Saccharomyces cerevisiae*)

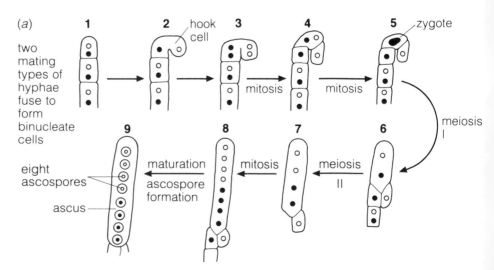

(b)

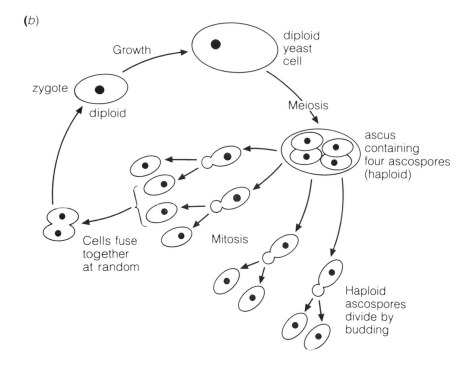

Yeasts, for example *Saccharomyces cerevisiae*, are ascomycetes and are industrially important fungi. They have been used for centuries in the making of bread, the brewing of beer and in winemaking. They are unicellular, eukaryotic organisms, differing from other fungi in that the cell wall is composed largely of polymers of mannan and glucan (fig 1.30).

**Fig 1.30
Section through
Saccharomyces (yeast) cell
(based on electron
micrographs)**

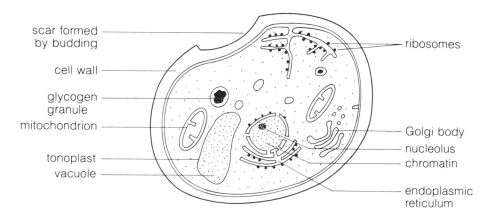

1.6.6 *Phylum Basidiomycota (basidiomycetes)*

Examples: *Agaricus campestris, Puccinia graminis*

All have septate hyphae.

Asexual reproduction is usually absent. Sexual reproduction is usually by the fusion of vegetative hyphae of two 'compatibility' groups. The nuclei do not fuse, and the fungus exists for most of its life as a **dikaryon,** with two types of nucleus in its hyphae (fig 1.31). Later, a complex fruiting body is formed. This **basidiocarp** contains many **basidia** in which the nuclei fuse and meiosis takes place. Four haploid **basidiospores** form from each basidium which germinate to form a new haploid mycelium, completing the life cycle.

The mushroom, *Agaricus,* is cultivated for food on a large scale. There are many other fungi which are nutritious and edible, although some are notoriously poisonous (fig 1.32).

Fig 1.31
The life cycle of a
generalised basidiomycete

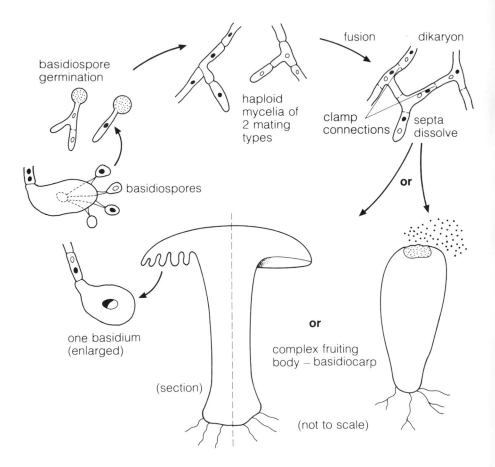

Fig 1.32
Some examples of fungi.
(*a*) Scanning electron
micrograph (SEM) of
Saccharomyces cerevisiae
(brewers' yeast) (× 8000).
(*b*) *Agaricus* sp. (edible
mushrooms).
(*c*) *Penicillium
chrysogenum*, a mould
used to produce the
antibiotic penicillin.
(*d*) *Aspergillus oryzae*.

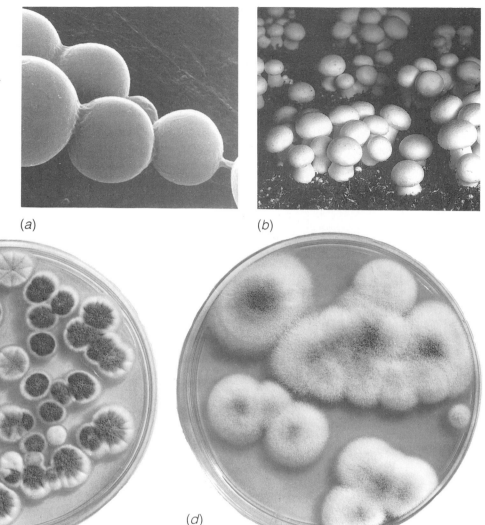

(a) (b)

(c) (d)

1.6.7 Phylum Deuteromycotina (deuteromycetes) imperfect fungi

Examples: *Fusarium graminearum, Candida albicans*

Asexual reproduction is by conidia as in the ascomycetes.
Sexual reproduction is rare or even unknown.
Fusarium is now of economic importance in the manufacture of a
new food product called mycoprotein (section 5.1). *Candida* is a
parasitic fungus which causes the disease thrush in humans
(section 10.7).

1.6.8 Fungal spores

At some stage, **spores** are produced on a specialised part of the
mycelium. The spores are dormant structures, but many are short-lived.

33

They have little resistance to desiccation, UV light or predators. Vast numbers of spores are produced and dispersed. If they do not land in favourable conditions, and are not destroyed, they remain dormant. In favourable conditions, a spore quickly swells, a germ tube grows out and the hypha elongates rapidly and soon branches. This process is called **germination** (fig 1.33).

Fig 1.33
The stages in the germination of a fungal spore

1 Most fungal spores are unicellular; some contain two or more nuclei. They are spherical or ovoid with a diameter of 5–50 µm.

2 The first stage of germination involves water uptake; large fluid-filled vacuoles appear in the cytoplasm.

3 The cytoplasm contains soluble food reserves, such as mannitol and trehalose, and also insoluble reserves, glycogen and oil. The insoluble reserves are broken down by enzymes once water is present as a solvent.

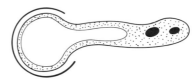

4 The outer wall breaks as the germ tube grows out of the spore, and a second inner wall is laid down.

1.6.9 The economic importance of fungi

Table 1.6 gives some examples of useful and harmful fungi.

Table 1.6
The economic importance of fungi

Some useful fungi	
Fungus	*Use*
Penicillium notatum	antibiotic penicillin
Penicillium chrysogenum	antibiotic penicillin
Penicillium griseofulvum	antibiotic griseofulvin
Penicillium roquefortii	cheese-ripening
Penicillium camemberti	cheese-ripening
Aspergillus fumigatus	antibiotic fumagillin (used against amoebic dysentery)
Aspergillus niger	citric acid production
Fusarium graminearum	mycoprotein production
Candida spp.	single-cell protein from waste hydrocarbons
Saccharomyces cerevisiae	brewing, baking, winemaking
Saccharomyces carlsbergensis	brewing
Agaricus campestris	food (mushroom)

Table 1.6 *(Cont.)*

Some harmful fungi

Fungus	Host	Disease
Phytophthora infestans	potato	potato blight
Rhizopus stolonifer	fruit	soft rot
Erysiphe spp.	cereals	powdery mildew
Ceratocystis ulmi	elm	Dutch elm disease
Claviceps purpurea	rye	ergot (infected rye can be fatal if eaten due to toxic alkaloids produced by the fungus)
Puccinia graminis	wheat	rusts
Trichophyton spp.	humans	athletes foot, ringworm
Candida utilis	humans	oral/vaginal thrush

Details of human diseases are to be found in chapter 10 and plant diseases in chapter 12.

Questions

1 What are the main characteristics of the fungi?

2 What are the main distinguishing features of

(a) ascomycetes;
(b) basidiomycetes;
(c) zygomycetes?

3 What features do the fungi

(a) have in common with higher plants and other eukaryotes;
(b) have different from higher plants?

4 Explain the meaning of the following terms:

(a) hypha,
(b) mycelium,
(c) heterothallic,
(d) septum,
(e) coenocytic,
(f) clamp connection,
(g) bud,
(h) basidium.

1.7 Viruses

Viruses are described as being **akaryotic**, which means without a cellular structure. They are all obligate parasites and can only reproduce when inside other living cells. They are about 50 times smaller than bacteria, ranging from 20 nm to about 300 nm and therefore cannot be seen with a light microscope. They were known to be infective agents able to pass through filters which retained bacteria as early as 1892. However, their structure was shown by extensive studies using the electron microscope.

Fig 1.34
Some examples of viruses.
(*a*) Transmission electron micrograph (TEM) of tobacco mosaic virus (× 560000). (*b*) TEM of a group of adenoviruses, the cause of the common cold (× 560000). (*c*) TEM of the SP105 bacteriophage, isolated from the bacterium *Bacillus subtilis* (× 165000).

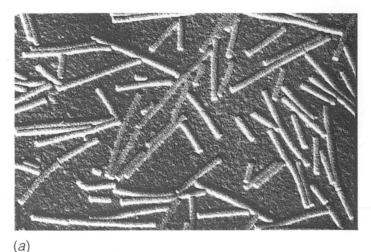

(*a*)

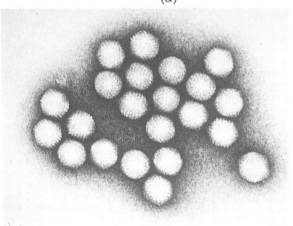

(*b*)

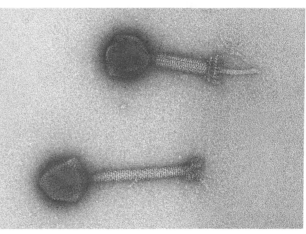

(*c*)

1.7.1 Structure of viruses

Viruses consist of a core containing genetic material, either DNA or RNA, which is surrounded by a protective coat of protein called a **capsid** made up of sub-units called **capsomeres** (fig 1.35). Some viruses have an envelope of lipoprotein around the capsid.

Fig 1.35
A generalised virus

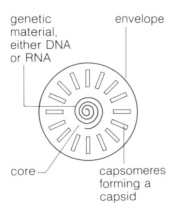

genetic material, either DNA or RNA

envelope

core

capsomeres forming a capsid

1.7.2 Shapes of viruses

There are three basic viral shapes as shown in table 1.7. These are polyhedral, helical and complex.

Table 1.7
Shapes of viruses

Polyhedrons	Helices
Capsomeres arranged into multi-faceted shapes. Icosahedron is the most common, with 20 triangular faces, 12 corners and 30 edges, e.g. adenovirus. The herpes virus has 162 capsomeres and has an envelope as a protective covering.	Conical capsomeres arranged helically in capsid in which RNA is embedded forming a nucleocapsid. Virions appear as hollow rods. Some may have an outer envelope. E.g. tobacco mosaic virus, myxovirus.

Herpes virus

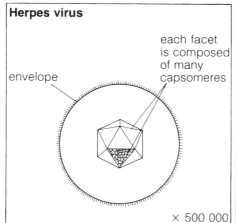

envelope
each facet is composed of many capsomeres
× 500 000

Tobacco mosaic virus

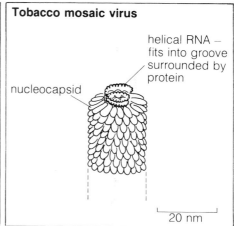

helical RNA – fits into groove surrounded by protein
nucleocapsid
20 nm

Complex	Bacteriophage (also complex)
More complex structure than other groups. Vaccinia (smallpox) virus has outer double membrane and inner core with DNA. Rabies virus is bullet-shaped with complex surface projections and a helical nucleocapsid.	Viruses that attack bacteria. Many have a distinct icosahedral head and a helical tail. E.g. T2 bacteriophage which infects *Escherichia coli*.

Vaccinia virus

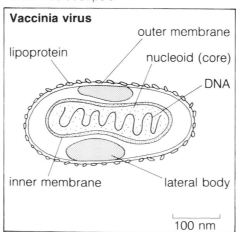

outer membrane
lipoprotein
nucleoid (core)
DNA
inner membrane
lateral body
100 nm

Bacteriophage e.g. T$_2$

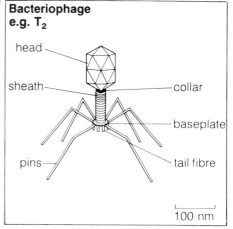

head
sheath
collar
baseplate
pins
tail fibre
100 nm

1.7.3   The life cycle of a virus

The life cycle of a bacteriophage virus, such as T2, is shown in fig 1.36.
   A similar life cycle is thought to occur in most viruses. However, they have different ways of penetrating animal, plant and bacterial cells because animal cells do not have a wall.

Fig 1.36
The lytic cycle of a
bacteriophage virus

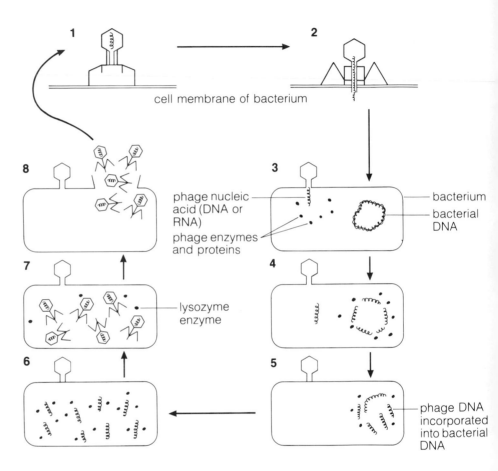

cell membrane of bacterium

phage nucleic
acid (DNA or
RNA)

phage enzymes
and proteins

bacterium

bacterial
DNA

lysozyme
enzyme

phage DNA
incorporated
into bacterial
DNA

1 Bacteriophage tail fibres attach to specific receptor sites on bacterial cell membrane.

2 Tail fibres bend and baseplate is anchored by pins to cell surface. Tail sheath contracts and hollow spike is pushed into cell aided by enzymes.

3 Nucleic acid is injected into bacterium with enzymes and viral proteins.

4 Phage enzymes break down bacterial DNA and phage DNA is incorporated.

5 Phage DNA takes over

6 Phage DNA replicates and codes for new viral proteins.

7 New phages are assembled; lysozyme enzyme made by phage DNA.

8 Cell lysis (bursting) due to build-up of lysozyme. Phages released (up to 1 000) to infect other bacteria.

Time for lytic cycle is approximately 30 minutes.

Some viruses do not replicate once inside the host cell but instead their nucleic acid becomes incorporated into the DNA of the host cell. The virus is then known as a **provirus** since it is inactive and the host cell is said to be **lysogenic**, since it is capable of lysis once the virus becomes active (fig 1.37).

Fig 1.37
The lysogenic cycle of a bacteriophage virus

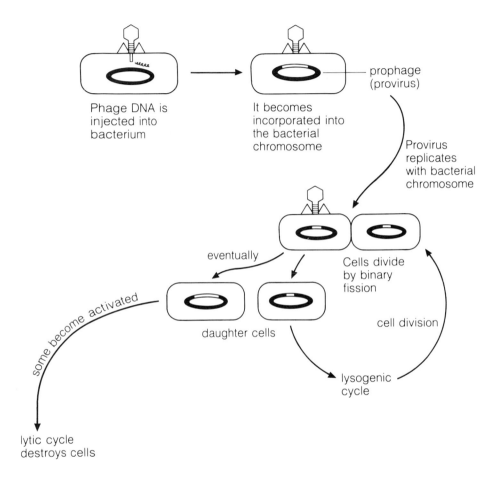

Phage DNA is injected into bacterium

It becomes incorporated into the bacterial chromosome

prophage (provirus)

Provirus replicates with bacterial chromosome

Cells divide by binary fission

cell division

eventually

some become activated

daughter cells

lysogenic cycle

lytic cycle destroys cells

1.7.4 *A one-step growth curve for a bacteriophage*

Viruses replicate following the lytic cycle and the main features of this can be demonstrated by plotting a 'one-step growth curve'. A broth culture of bacteria is mixed with a suspension of compatible bacteriophage particles, such as *E. coli* with the T2 phage. Quantities are chosen so that the bacteria are in considerable excess. The mixture is incubated for a little while, to allow the phages to become adsorbed on to the bacterial cell walls. The mixture is then greatly diluted and incubated. Samples of known volumes are taken at intervals and plated onto agar. The uninfected bacteria will grow as a lawn, but infected bacteria will fail to grow and leave a clear area in the bacterial lawn

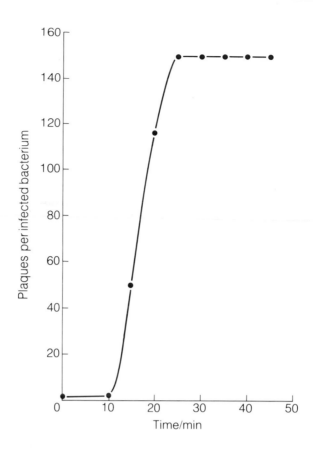

Fig 1.38
A one-step growth curve for a bacteriophage virus

known as a 'plaque'. A growth curve is obtained (see fig 1.38). Initially, the plaque count is constant; this is the latent phase following adhesion of phages on to bacterial cells. As these infected bacteria begin to lyse, and new phage particles are released, the plaque count rises abruptly until all the infected cells lyse. This is called the burst period. After this lysis has occurred, the plaque count remains approximately constant, since the diluting procedure ensures that few of the released phages will become adsorbed on to uninfected bacterial cells. The average number of new phage particles released from each infected cell is called the burst size.

1.7.5 Viruses as disease-causing agents

Since viruses are always parasitic they usually cause some symptoms of disease in their host. They are of economic importance because of the loss of human and animal life caused by some types, or the inability to work due to the many less virulent types (table 1.8). Plant viruses cause tremendous losses in cultivated crops particularly in areas of monoculture (table 1.9). Animal and plant diseases are considered further in chapters 10 and 12 respectively.

Table 1.8
Some viruses causing
human disease

Virus	Structure	Genetic material	Disease
Herpes simplex			
type 1	icosahedral enveloped	double-stranded DNA	cold sores
type 2	icosahedral enveloped	double-stranded DNA	genital herpes
Varicella zoster	icosahedral enveloped	double-stranded DNA	chickenpox
Adenovirus	icosahedral non-enveloped	double-stranded DNA	pharyngitis conjunctivitis
Variola major	complex	double-stranded DNA	smallpox
Hepatitis B	icosahedral enveloped	double-stranded DNA	serum hepatitis
Parvovirus	icosahedral non-enveloped	single-stranded DNA	viral gastroenteritis
Poliovirus	icosahedral non-enveloped	single-stranded RNA	poliomyelitis
Rhinovirus	icosahedral non-enveloped	single-stranded RNA	common cold
Rubella virus	icosahedral enveloped	single-stranded RNA	German measles (rubella)
Mumps virus	helical enveloped	single-stranded RNA	mumps
Influenza virus	helical enveloped	single-stranded RNA	influenza
Rabies virus	bullet-shaped helical, enveloped	single-stranded RNA	rabies

Table 1.9
Some viruses causing plant
disease

Virus	Shape	Genetic material	Vector	Symptoms
Tobacco mosaic, tomato mosaic, cucumber green-mottle	elongated	RNA	mechanical contact, grafts, fungus	yellow-brown mottled patches on leaves
Cauliflower mosaic	spherical	DNA	aphids	yellow mottled leaves, poor growth
Tobacco ringspot, tomato ringspot	spherical	RNA	seedborne nematodes	ring-like patches, brown-white on leaves
Barley yellows dwarf, soybean dwarf	spherical	RNA	aphids	stunted growth, yellow leaves
Tomato spotted wilt	spherical enveloped	RNA	thrips	wilting leaves, discoloured spots on leaves
Turnip yellow mosaic	spherical	RNA	beetle	yellow mottled patches on leaves
Potato X virus, narcissus mosaic	elongated	RNA	mechanical contact or damage	mottled leaves, poor growth
Tobacco rattle	elongated	RNA	nematodes	dry, brown papery leaves
Beet yellows, wheat yellow leaf, beet yellow stunt	elongated	RNA	aphids	stunted growth, yellow leaves

1.7.6   *Viroids*

Viroids are the smallest known agents of infectious disease. They consist of small single strands of RNA and so far have only been found in plants. **Potato spindle tuber viroid** (PSTV) was the first viroid to be identified using the electron microscope. Its RNA is in the form of rods or closed circles about 50 nm long. There is no protein capsid associated with it. In infected cells, PSTV is found in the nucleus where it appears to interfere with gene regulation. Infected tissue contains certain proteins in larger quantities than in healthy tissue. It has been suggested that PSTV may have originated from the genetic material of the host which has become altered in some way.

Questions

1   Name the three main viral shapes and give an example of each.

2   Compare the lytic and lysogenic cycles.

3   Do you consider viruses to be alive? Give reasons to justify your answer.

4   Define the following terms: viroid, capsomere, nucleocapsid.

5   Research the ways in which viruses are cultivated.

6   Describe five features which distinguish viruses from other groups of organisms.

7   What is, and where would you find, each of the following?

(*a*)   endospore   (*d*)   capsid
(*b*)   zygospore   (*e*)   murein (mucopeptide)
(*c*)   oospore

2 Biotechnology

2.1 What is biotechnology?

Biotechnology is the application of biological systems, organisms or processes in manufacturing or service industries. It is a composite science, involving microbiology, genetics, biochemistry and engineering.

While biotechnology is a recent term, it is based on ancient technology. The brewing of beer appears to have begun in Babylon, before 6000 BC. The Ancient Egyptians brewed several kinds of beer by about 3000 BC, and their skills were passed on via the Greeks to the Romans. Breadmaking is another ancient technology. Remains of the Swiss lake settlers, who lived 10 000 years ago, show that they had developed the ability to make a kind of bread. From tomb paintings of Ancient Egypt we can tell that they had highly developed breadmaking skills and, around 100 BC, the Romans could buy bread in over 250 breadshops in the streets of Rome. Cheese, wine, yogurt and vinegar have been made for centuries. More recently, in 1897, the Buchner brothers isolated enzymes from yeast, laying the foundations of enzyme technology. The discovery of antibiotics in 1929, and their large-scale production during the Second World War, created great advances in fermentation technology.

However, the latter half of the twentieth century has seen great advances in biology. It has become the most diversified of the natural sciences. Since the 1950s there have been many technical advances, for example the electron microscope, and these have led to a proliferation of biological discoveries. In the last 20 years more than 20 Nobel prizes have been awarded for discoveries in this area. Perhaps the greatest contribution to modern biotechnology has been about 40 years' research into DNA. At the time, most of this research was thought to be of purely academic interest, but genetic manipulation is now a central theme in biotechnology. It is this which has transformed centuries of traditional technologies into modern industrial processes. Already, the modern science of biology has made a great contribution to the quality of human life, but biotechnology promises far more than this. Modern biotechnology offers a variety of new industries, such as mining with microbes, new methods of fuel production, new pharmaceuticals, new ways of using industrial wastes and new food production techniques. It attempts to solve the greatest problems facing the modern world, such as the energy crisis, the food shortage, pollution and the threat of disease. Biotechnological industries generally use cheap, often waste, substrates, operate at low temperatures and consume little energy. Microorganisms are often used, which can be genetically manipulated. Since microorganisms are highly versatile, with rapid growth rates, the potential for new industries is enormous.

In 1979 *The Economist* stated that biotechnology may 'launch an industry as characteristic of the 21st century as those based on physics and chemistry have been of the 20th'. It is certainly considered to have at least as much commercial promise as the microelectronics revolution, and probably more. Biotechnology is an exciting and fast-growing area, offering enormous benefits to humankind with its potential to solve many of the perplexing problems faced by the world today.

2.2 Principles of biotechnology

The cells' enzymes are used for **primary metabolism**, which means generating energy and biomass, and degrading substrates, or for **secondary metabolism**. Secondary metabolism occurs at specific points in the life cycle rather than throughout the life of the organism. It is associated with changes in the organism, such as spore formation or aging. Examples of secondary metabolites are antibiotics, terpenoids, polyketides and acetylene (propene).

The biotechnologist is able to modify the normal metabolism of the cell, so that the particular product required is made in maximum amounts (fig 2.1).

Fig 2.1
Biotechnology exploits the chemistry of the cell to produce the chosen product

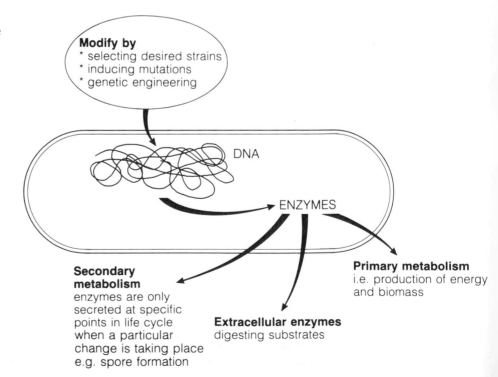

The cell's DNA can be altered by screening microorganisms and selecting those with the best qualities. Sometimes mutation is induced (perhaps by radiation) and favourable mutations are detected by screening procedures. A more reliable, modern method is **genetic engineering**, whereby the required gene is inserted in the cell's genome. (This is discussed in chapter 3.)

The biochemistry of cells relies on a sequence of enzymes arranged in a metabolic pathway. It is obvious that the enzymes must be regulated. A common regulatory mechanism in cell metabolism is **negative feedback**. For instance, fig 2.2 shows an imaginary metabolic pathway. A build-up of product D inhibits the enzyme that catalyses the conversion of A to B, avoiding wasteful production of B, which is not needed by the cell at that point.

Fig 2.2
Negative feedback

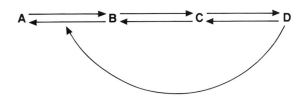

Biotechnologists seek to understand these regulatory mechanisms and exploit them for maximum yields of desired metabolic products. An example occurs in yeast as shown in fig 2.3. Yeast can metabolise glucose along two alternative pathways to produce either glycerol or ethanol. If sulphite is added, this will combine with the ethanal (acetaldehyde), blocking the ethanol pathway, so more glycerol is produced. This process was used by the Germans to produce glycerol in the First World War to make a number of explosives such as nitroglycerine.

Fig 2.3
The production of glycerol
by yeast

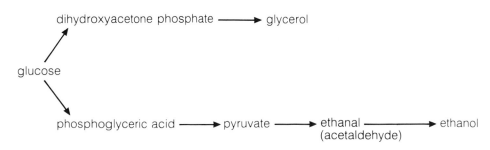

There are various fermentation pathways in different microorganisms. These can be used to produce a range of alcohols and organic solvents (fig 2.4).

Fig 2.4
The production of alcohols and organic solvents

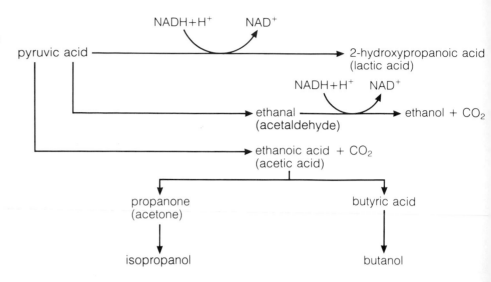

Questions

1 The text states that microbial enzymes can be used by the biotechnologist to generate **biomass, primary metabolites, secondary metabolites,** or the cell's **degradative enzymes** may be exploited directly. Explain what the terms in bold type mean.

2 How can biotechnologists maximise the yield of a microbially produced substance?

2.3 Methods of fermentation

2.3.1 *Solid substrate fermentation*

This is probably the oldest method of fermentation, and involves growing microorganisms on a solid or semi-solid substrate. Examples are: growing mushrooms on compost, breadmaking, cheese production, sauerkraut and tempe kedele (fermented soybean curd) production. Non-food examples include methanogenesis from sewage, sludge and other waste.

2.3.2 *Aqueous fermentation*

This refers to fermentation in a substrate which has a high water content. There are two methods of aqueous fermentation, batch fermentation and continuous fermentation.

Batch fermentation   This is carried out in a **closed** fermenter (fig 2.5). The microorganism is put into the fermenter with a nutrient medium. Then it is left for the fermentation to take place. The product is separated from the spent microorganisms and other waste products at the end. While the process is going on, nothing is added to the vessel

Fig 2.5
A section through a batch fermenter

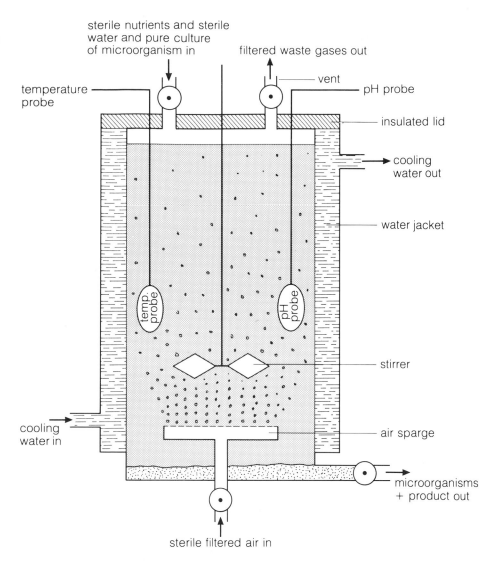

sterile nutrients and sterile water and pure culture of microorganism in

filtered waste gases out

temperature probe

vent

pH probe

insulated lid

cooling water out

water jacket

temp. probe

pH probe

stirrer

cooling water in

air sparge

microorganisms + product out

sterile filtered air in

and nothing is removed, except for the venting of waste gases. A typical growth curve for a batch fermentation is shown in fig 2.6.

Note that all nutrients are depleted at the end of the fermentation. During a batch fermentation, environmental factors are constantly changing, although temperature is usually controlled. The phase of exponential growth lasts for only a comparatively short time.

A variation on a batch fermentation is a **fed-batch process**, where nutrients are added at intervals during the fermentation. Advantages of a batch culture are:

(1) it is easy to set up and control the environmental factors;
(2) vessels are versatile, they may be used for different processes at different times enabling a manufacturer to meet market demands more easily;

47

Fig 2.6
Graphs showing changes taking place during the fermentation (batch) of beer

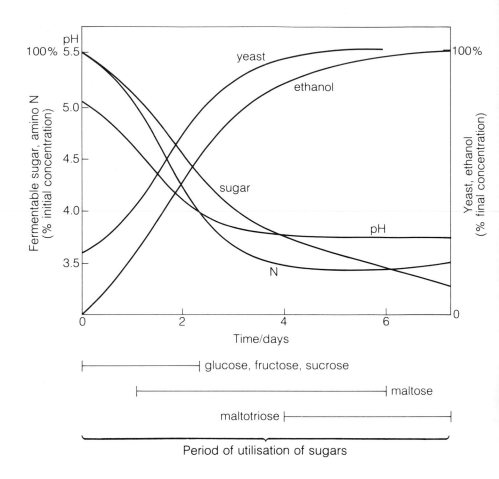

(3) should a culture become contaminated, only one batch is lost, so the cost to the manufacturer is minimised.

Continuous fermentation Continuous fermentation takes place in **open** fermenters. Nutrients are added continuously, at a steady rate, to exactly balance the amount of product being removed. This maintains the microorganisms in an **exponential** phase of growth. It is vital to monitor the environmental factors, that is pH, oxygen levels, nutrient concentration, accumulation of products, and to keep these constant.

Advantages of continuous fermentation are:

(1) smaller vessels are needed because the process is more productive, with the microorganisms being maintained in exponential growth;
(2) theoretically, this greater productivity is more cost-effective.

However, there are disadvantages.

(1) In practice, it is very difficult to monitor all the environmental factors and the system can become unbalanced. Should a

continuous fermentation break down there is considerable waste, which is costly.

(2) There can be practical problems, like foaming, clumping of cells and microbial growth blocking inlets.

2.4 Setting up an industrial process

It is not always straightforward to adapt a laboratory process to a profitable and efficient industrial process. In doing this, there are three stages involved:

Basic screening The chosen microorganism is cultured in small laboratory vessels to check its characteristics and find the optimum conditions for its growth.

Pilot plant The microorganism is cultured in a small-scale fermenter, 5–200 dm³ (litres) in volume. This is done to find out the optimum operating conditions, which may not be the same as they were for very small-scale growth.

Plant scale The microorganism is grown in a massive industrial fermenter, thousands of decimetres cubed (litres) in volume.

Questions

1 Make a table to summarise the features of the different methods of fermentation and their relative advantages and disadvantages.

2 What shape would you expect for a growth curve of a microorganism grown in a continuous fermenter?

2.5 Microbial nutrition

Organisms need nutrients to generate energy and synthesise cell materials. These nutrients must be obtained from their environment. A culture medium must contain all the necessary nutrients in sufficient amount, but microorganisms have varied requirements. Their general needs can be summarised, as in table 2.1.

All living things can be classified into one of four nutritional categories on the basis of their carbon and energy sources (table 2.2). Microorganisms, particularly bacteria, are extremely versatile, with representatives in all four categories.

2.5.1 *Carbon requirements*

Photoautotrophs and chemoautotrophs use carbon dioxide as their carbon source. Other nutritional groups need an organic carbon source. Microorganisms are so varied, that there is no naturally produced

**Table 2.1
Requirements for the
growth of microorganisms**

	Constituent	Functions
From water (a major component of any culture medium)	hydrogen	component of cellular water and organic cell materials
	oxygen	component of cellular water, organic cell materials, electron acceptor in aerobic organisms
Major nutrients	carbon	component of organic cell materials
	nitrogen	component of proteins, nucleic acids, coenzymes
	sulphur	component of some amino acids and coenzymes
	phosphorus	component of nucleic acids, phospholipids, coenzymes
Macronutrients (always included as salts in culture media)	potassium	major inorganic cation, cofactor for certain enzymes
	magnesium	important cellular cation, cofactor for many enzymes, including those involving ATP, binding of enzymes to substrates, component of chlorophylls
	calcium	important cellular cation, cofactor of some enzymes
	iron	component of cytochromes and some other conjugated proteins, cofactor of certain enzymes
Micronutrients (often present in adequate amounts as contaminants)	manganese	cofactor for some enzymes, sometimes replaces magnesium
	cobalt	component of vitamin B_{12} and coenzymes derived from it
	copper zinc molybdenum	inorganic components of special enzymes

NB Some microorganisms have special needs not covered by this table. For example, diatoms need silica for their cell walls which are impregnated with silica. Sodium is needed by blue-greens and photosynthetic bacteria.

organic compound that they cannot use as a carbon and an energy source. However, individual microorganisms may be extremely versatile in their carbon requirements, whilst others can be highly specialised. Some *Pseudomonas* species are able to use more than 90 organic compounds as their sole carbon and energy source. By contrast, certain cellulose-digesting bacteria can only use cellulose.

2.5.2 *Nitrogen and sulphur*

Some microorganisms can fix atmospheric nitrogen, for example *Rhizobium*. Most photosynthetic organisms assimilate these as nitrates and sulphates; many non-photosynthetic bacteria and fungi can do this too. Some microorganisms need the ammonium ion as their nitrogen source, rather than nitrate, such as *Nitrosomonas*.

Table 2.2
The nutritional categories of living organisms

Energy source	Carbon source	
	Inorganic	*Organic*
Chemical	**Chemoautotrophs** These organisms use carbon dioxide and other simple inorganic materials as their carbon source. They obtain their energy from oxidation or reduction reactions. Examples: some bacteria such as *Thiobacillus*, *Nitrobacter*, and *Nitrosomonas*.	**Chemoheterotrophs** These organisms use complex organic materials for their carbon and energy sources. Examples: most bacteria, Fungi, Protoctista and all higher animals.
Light	**Photoautotrophs** These organisms use energy from sunlight to fix carbon dioxide which is their carbon source. Examples: all green plants, Cyanobacteria, and some bacteria: the green sulphur bacteria, e.g. *Chlorobium*, and the purple sulphur bacteria, e.g. *Chromatium*. 	**Photoheterotrophs** These organisms use sunlight as their energy source, but complex organic materials as their carbon source. Examples: the purple non-sulphur bacteria, e.g. *Rhodospirillum*.

Certain microorganisms cannot assimilate sulphate, and therefore need sulphide or an organic compound containing sulphur, such as cysteine. The nitrogen and sulphur requirement is often met by organic nutrients, such as amino acids or peptones. These can also form the carbon and energy source.

2.5.3 Growth factors

These are substances which a microorganism cannot synthesise from simpler substances and are needed in small amounts as precursors for organic cell materials. They can be subdivided into three groups:

(1) amino acids, needed for proteins;
(2) purines and pyrimidines, needed for nucleic acids;
(3) vitamins, needed for prosthetic groups or active centres of certain enzymes.

2.5.4 Oxygen

All cells contain oxygen in the form of water and water is provided in all culture media. However, many organisms also need molecular oxygen for aerobic respiration. Obligate anaerobes, on the other hand, may be killed or inhibited by molecular oxygen.

2.6 Culture media

A culture medium must contain a balanced mixture of the required nutrients, at concentrations sufficient to allow a good growth rate. If a nutrient is in excess, it can inhibit growth or even be toxic. Often one nutrient is present in limiting quantities, to check the total growth rate of the culture and therefore keep the microorganisms healthy. Usually a **mineral base** is made, containing all the possible nutrients in inorganic form. To this can be added a carbon source, energy source, nitrogen source and growth factors, to suit the organism being cultured. A medium composed entirely of nutrients whose chemical composition is known exactly, such as potassium sulphate or tryptophan, is called a **synthetic medium**. A medium which contains some ingredients of unknown chemical composition, such as malt extract, is called a **complex medium**. Complex media are very good for growing a wide range of microorganisms, or when the exact nutritional requirements of a microorganism are not known. A medium may be satisfactory for initial growth, but microorganisms change the pH of the medium as they grow, because their metabolic waste products accumulate. To counteract this, buffers are often added.

As well as providing a satisfactory culture medium, factors such as light, oxygen and carbon dioxide are often necessary to meet the needs of individual microorganisms.

2.6.1 Selective media

Selective media are suitable for the growth of a specific organism. This means that if you inoculate it with a mixed culture, only the specific organism the medium was designed for will be able to grow on it:

other types of microorganism will be suppressed. Such media are very specialised and are useful in diagnostic work, for example, in hospital or veterinary laboratories. A faecal sample, containing an assortment of microorganisms, can be used to inoculate selective media. If any bacteria grow in a medium which is selective for salmonellae, then the doctors are alerted to the presence of a pathogen among the many normal bacteria and can prescribe a suitable drug.

Questions

1 The following is a recipe for **nutrient broth,** a medium used to culture bacteria.

10g meat extract ⎫ dissolve in 1 dm³
10 g peptone   ⎬ (litre)
5 g NaCl   ⎭ tap water

The pH is adjusted to pH 7.4 using molar sodium hydroxide or molar hydrochloric acid, then the medium is dispensed to suitable containers and autoclaved.

 (*a*) Is this a synthetic or complex medium? Explain.
 (*b*) What is the carbon source?
 (*c*) What is the nitrogen source?
 (*d*) Why is tap water used instead of distilled water?
 (*e*) Why is it necessary to adjust the pH?

2 Below are two recipes for fungal media. Read the recipes, then answer the questions below.

Potato dextrose agar

 (*a*) Wash 200 g of sound potato tubers. Slice and boil in tap water until soft.
 (*b*) Crush the boiled tissue in water. When cool, strain through muslin.
 (*c*) Make up to 500 cm³ with distilled water. Add 20 g glucose.
 (*d*) Melt 20 g plain agar in another 500 cm³ water. Mix with potato and glucose solution. Dispense to containers and autoclave.

Czapek–Dox medium

0.01 g zinc sulphate ⎫
 0.5 g magnesium sulphate
 2 g sodium nitrate
 0.5 g potassium chloride   all in
 0.01 g ferrous sulphate   1 dm³
 1 g potassium phosphate   (litre)
 30 g sucrose   water
 0.005 g copper sulphate
 15 g plain agar ⎭

For each of the two media, state the following.

    (*a*) Whether it is a synthetic or complex medium, and explain.

    (*b*) Explain the nutritional function of each ingredient.

    (*c*) Given a fungus which will grow equally well in both media, which medium would you choose to investigate:

        (i)   the nutritional requirements of the fungus?

        (ii) the conditions necessary for spore formation?

        (iii) the effect of pH on the growth of the fungus?

        (iv) the range of carbon sources which the fungus is able to utilise?

        (v) the effect of temperature on the growth rate of the fungus?

In each case, explain clearly your reasons for choosing that particular medium.

2.7   Growth in bacteria

As bacteria are so small, it is usual to study the growth of populations of bacteria rather than individuals. Growth rate is usually measured as the increase in cell numbers in a measured period of time.

    Most bacteria multiply by binary fission, which means that one cell divides into two daughter cells. In this way, the cell numbers double every generation. If conditions are ideal, some bacteria can divide every 20 minutes, although this situation is rare under normal conditions. Population growth studies are essential in biotechnological industries using microorganisms on a large scale, such as brewing, or producing antibiotics and single cell protein. By studying the growth of microorganisms, the ideal conditions and growth requirements can be found. If microorganisms are cultured in optimum conditions, maximum yield of the product can be obtained.

    There are two ways of measuring cell numbers in a bacterial population.

    (1) A **total cell count** gives the total number of cells present, whether living or dead.

    (2) A **viable count** takes into account only living cells since these are the only cells capable of dividing.

2.7.1   *Methods of counting*

Total counts   These are made by sampling the culture (usually in liquid medium) at known time intervals and counting the number of cells in a known volume using a counting chamber such as a haemocytometer. Total counts may also be estimated using a colorimeter. The increasing number of cells will make the culture medium more turbid (cloudy). The turbidity can be measured using a colorimeter and this can be compared to a range of standards.

Viable counts   The culture is sampled at known time intervals, and a known volume of sample is diluted with sterile distilled water (usually 10^{-1}, 10^{-2}, 10^{-3}, 10^{-4}, 10^{-5} and 10^{-6}). Each dilution is plated onto sterile nutrient agar using aseptic technique. The plates are usually made in triplicate to increase accuracy. They are incubated until colonies are visible. Since each colony has arisen from a single microorganism, the number of microorganisms in the original sample can be calculated, taking dilution factors into account.

2.7.2   Constructing a growth curve

Fig 2.7 shows the growth of a bacterium in batch culture. Because cell numbers are so great, it is hard to plot a graph using actual cell numbers, therefore the $\log_{10}$ of the cell number is usually plotted.

Fig 2.7
Generalised growth curve
of a bacterial culture

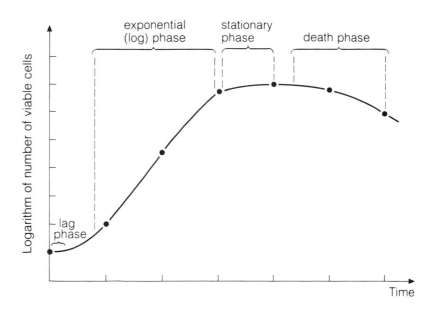

The lag phase   At first, there is very little increase in cell numbers. However, the cells do increase in size. Many factors influence the duration of the lag phase, for example:

(*a*)   if the bacteria are very inactive (e.g. in the spore stage) they may not divide until conditions are favourable;

(*b*)   the medium may be quite different from that on which the bacteria were growing previously, so they may need to produce new enzymes in order to digest the new nutrients;

(*c*)   the temperature and pH must be suitable for enzyme action.

The log phase (exponential phase) The bacteria multiply very rapidly because there is no factor limiting their growth. An ample supply of nutrients, oxygen and all other factors affecting growth are at an optimum, so that numbers double with each generation. For example, if the original inoculum is 10 000 bacteria/cm³:

after 1 generation $10\ 000 \times 2^1 = 20\ 000/cm^3$
after 2 generations $10\ 000 \times 2^2 = 40\ 000/cm^3$
after 3 generations $10\ 000 \times 2^3 = 80\ 000/cm^3$ etc.
after n generations $10\ 000 \times 2^n$

Therefore, $N = N_o \times 2^n$
  where N_o = original number of cells and N = number of cells after n generations

The stationary phase Here, the population remains stable. The 'birth' rate is approximately balanced by the death rate. Since this population study is using a batch culture, the amount of nutrients available will now be limiting. The available substrate will provide less energy than the population requires, so the growth rate is slowed down. Metabolic products may become toxic as they build up in the medium. There may also be a change in pH of the medium, inhibiting enzyme action. For example, *Lactobacillus* produces lactic acid from lactose during the souring of milk. Also, the oxygen content may become too low for microorganisms to survive.

The death phase Microorganisms are dying. Some undergo autolysis, temporarily yielding some nutrients for those microorganisms remaining alive, but the cell number falls rapidly.

2.7.3 Continuous cultures

Bacteria grown in batch culture eventually die, as already shown, due to such factors as nutrient depletion. In the laboratory, bacterial cultures can be maintained indefinitely in the exponential phase. This is done by continuing to supply fresh nutrients to the medium, and carefully removing excess microorganisms and toxic wastes at the same time. It is very difficult to achieve this in the laboratory, but there are many natural examples of continuous culture, the digestive system of the cow being perhaps the best example.

2.8 Growth of fungi

Unicellular fungi, such as yeasts, grow similarly to bacteria. Filamentous fungi, however, grow by elongation of their hyphae. Their form of growth varies according to the medium on which they are grown.

On a solid medium the fungal mycelium grows as an approximately circular colony across the surface of the medium. Usually the hyphae do not penetrate the medium very deeply because fungi are aerobic and rely on gaseous diffusion through the medium. Colony diameter is usually used as an index of growth.

On a stationary liquid medium the mycelium forms an approximately circular 'felt' or 'mat' on the surface. However, on a rapidly stirred liquid medium the fungus forms pellets of mycelium, which are approximately spherical, spread throughout the medium. To measure growth, the fungus can be filtered off, dried to constant mass, and the dry mass obtained.

2.8.1   Growth curve for a filamentous fungus

Fig 2.8 shows the growth curve of *Mucor hiemalis* growing in a liquid medium.

Lag phase   As with bacteria, there is a lag phase when no growth occurs. There are various reasons for this:

(a)   if a spore suspension is used as an inoculum, these will take time to germinate;

(b)   if a mycelial disc is used, there will be many damaged hyphae which will need repairing before they can grow;

(c)   in either case, new enzymes may need synthesising before the fungus can feed off the available nutrients.

Rapid growth phase   The colony diameter, or dry mass of the fungus, increases linearly with time. However, with a fungus growth is rarely

Fig 2.8
The growth in liquid medium of the filamentous fungus *Mucor hiemalis*

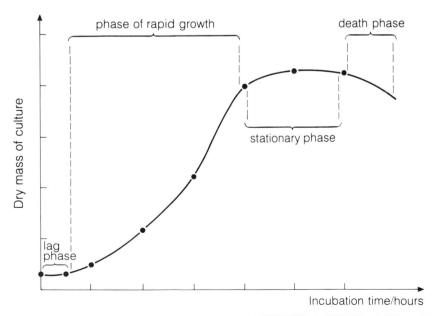

exponential. Like bacteria, fungi grow rapidly at this time due to a plentiful supply of nutrients and optimum conditions.

Stationary phase   Growth slows down, due to the accumulation of toxic wastes, lack of nutrients, or a physical barrier, such as the edge of the Petri dish. Sometimes, the hyphae in the centre of the mycelium undergo autolysis.

Death phase   The mycelium undergoes autolysis if the culture is maintained for a sufficiently long time.

2.9   Factors affecting microbial growth

2.9.1   Temperature

Microorganisms, like all living organisms, have an optimum temperature for maximum growth. They can be classified into three categories according to the temperature range in which they grow best.

Thermophiles have an optimum temperature above 40 °C. Thermophiles grow in hot springs, compost heaps, hot water heaters, tropical soils, hot tubs and so on. A bacterium has been found growing at 250 °C in the hot water streaming from a thermal vent in the ocean floor: the huge pressures at this depth prevent the cytoplasm from boiling, and the bacterial proteins have extra chemical bonds to protect them from destabilisation.

Mesophiles grow best between 20 and 40 °C. Most microorganisms fall into this category, including the human pathogens which are adapted to grow at 37 °C.

Psychrophiles (or cryophiles) grow actively at temperatures below 20 °C. These organisms grow in deep oceans, in the Arctic and Antarctic, and cause spoilage of refrigerated and frozen foods.

2.9.2   pH

Most bacteria grow best at a neutral pH of 7, preferring to grow in the range 6–8. Few bacteria can survive at pH values below 4. The human stomach has an extremely low pH which kills most bacteria. The skin and vagina in the adult are acid to protect against infection. However, some bacteria can grow at extremes of pH. *Thiobacillus thiooxidans* oxidises sulphur to sulphuric acid and can grow at a pH of 0.

Fungi can tolerate acid conditions although they grow best at pH 5–6. Fungi are very important in the decay of organic matter in acid soils.

Microorganisms tend to produce waste products that can rapidly alter the pH of the medium. For this reason, buffers are usually added to culture media.

2.9.3 Oxygen

Aerobes require molecular oxygen for their metabolism. **Facultative anaerobes** grow aerobically when oxygen is present, but have a less efficient, alternative mechanism so that they can also function in the absence of oxygen.

Microaerophiles require some oxygen, but are harmed if too much or too little is available. Many of these need elevated carbon dioxide levels. Microaerophilic conditions exist in some parts of the human body, for example in the large intestine.

Obligate anaerobes need an oxygen-free atmosphere for their growth. Some anaerobes can survive, although they will not grow, in the presence of oxygen; these are aerotolerant. The strict anaerobes are killed by even the slightest amount of oxygen.

2.9.4 Carbon dioxide

Some microorganisms prefer elevated carbon dioxide levels; these are called **capneic** organisms. Many human pathogens are in this category.

2.9.5 Osmotic potential

Microorganisms must have water available for growth. If the water potential of the medium is higher (less negative) than that of the microbial cell, the microorganism will take up water by osmosis. Fortunately, the rigid bacterial cell wall helps to resist cell lysis, but this can occur in microorganisms with more fragile cells. Similarly, if the osmotic potential of the environment is much lower (more negative) than that of the microorganism, water leaves the microbial cell by osmosis and the microorganism dies. This observation has been exploited in food preservation; high levels of either salt or sugar have been used for centuries to preserve food.

Some microorganisms are adapted to grow at very low osmotic potentials; these are called **halophiles**.

2.9.6 Light

Photoautotrophs require visible light as an energy source. Some other wavelengths can be used to kill microorganisms. Short wavelength ultra-violet light is often used to kill pathogens, for example in food shops and hospitals. X-rays can be used to sterilise surgical equipment such as Petri dishes.

2.9.7 Chemicals

Many chemicals inhibit microbial growth, such as antiseptics and disinfectants. Antibiotics also affect microbial growth; these fall into two types, the bacteriostatic which prevent bacterial replication, and the bactericidal, which kill the bacteria.

2.9.8 Nutritional factors

These are discussed in section 2.5. Lack of any of these nutrients will limit the growth of a microorganism. Each nutrient has an optimum value which will give maximum growth. If a nutrient is supplied at a sub-optimum level, there is often a linear relationship between the amount of substrate available and growth rate. This is the basis of a **bioassay**.

A bioassay is a valuable means of measuring the concentrations of substances like vitamins when these are very low. A test bacterium is selected which will only grow in the presence of the vitamin. When the vitamin has been used up, bacterial growth stops. The amount of bacterial growth will therefore be proportional to the concentration of the limiting vitamin, provided all other nutrients are available in excess. A standard curve is made, and from this the amount of vitamins in other substances can be assessed.

Questions

1 (a) Use the data in table 2.3 to construct a growth curve.
   (b) Label your graph and discuss the factors which control the growth rate at each stage.
   (c) Calculate the generation time for *E.coli* using the data from your graph.

Table 2.3
Growth of a population of *E. coli* in nutrient broth

Hours	No.s of viable cells/cm³ medium	Total no. of cells/cm³ medium
0	20 100	20 100
2	21 500	27 300
4	496 450	560 000
6	5 430 265	6 450 000
8	81 900 500	105 760 500
12	83 405 700	126 350 045
24	80 500 045	127 600 500

2 *Saccharomyces cerevisiae* is the yeast of beer fermentation. This is carried out in large, stainless steel, rectangular vessels cooled to 15 °C.
   Describe and explain the changes taking place within the fermentation vessel during the six-day period.

3 Differentiate between

   (a) batch and continuous cultures;
   (b) obligate aerobes, facultative anaerobes, obligate anaerobes and microaerophiles;
   (c) thermophiles, mesophiles and psychrophiles.

4 Account for the differences in the form of growth between a fungus grown on a stationary liquid medium and a fungus grown in an agitated liquid medium.

5 Explain fully how you could use a bioassay to estimate the level of vitamin B_{12} in a sample of cornflakes.

6 The graph in fig 2.9 shows the results obtained for a viable count of *E. coli* grown in liquid culture in three separate fermenters. Temperature and aeration were kept constant in all three cultures, and each contained a minimal medium necessary for the growth of the bacterium. However, each fermenter contained a different carbon and energy source.

Fermenter 1 contained glucose (1%)
Fermenter 2 contained lactose (1%)
Fermenter 3 contained a mixture of glucose and lactose (both 1%).

Samples were removed every 15 minutes from the culture, diluted using aseptic technique and plated out onto nutrient agar. The plates were labelled and incubated at 30 °C for 48 hours. The number of bacterial colonies were then counted to give an estimate of the number of viable cells in each culture.

(a) Comment on the shape of the glucose curve.
(b) Why is the lactose curve so different?
(c) Explain why the glucose and lactose curve has a 'step' between 100 and 120 minutes.
(d) Why is the eventual population so much greater in the glucose and lactose culture?
(e) What control mechanism must be operating in *E. coli*?
(f) How would this help *E. coli* to survive in its natural habitat?

Fig 2.9
Viable counts of *E. coli* in a culture containing glucose and lactose

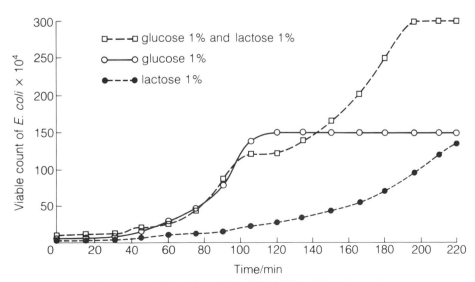

3 Genetic engineering

3.1 The gene: an introduction to genetic engineering

The **gene** is the basic unit of heredity: a piece of deoxyribonucleic acid (DNA) that codes for the production of a single protein. A single gene confers a particular characteristic that can be passed on from generation to generation.

Genetic engineering is a means of introducing new genes into cells. The resulting cells will therefore have new characteristics.

In the early 1970s, researchers found **restriction enzymes** in bacterial cells. These enzymes are part of the bacterium's natural defence mechanism and are released when any foreign nucleic acid enters the bacterial cell. For instance, when a virus invades a bacterium, it injects its own nucleic acid, either DNA or RNA. The bacterium produces restriction enzymes that cut the viral DNA or RNA into small fragments. Restriction enzymes are very specific and each recognises and cuts only one particular nucleotide sequence in the DNA.

Another useful property of restriction enzymes is their ability to produce a staggered cut. This means that the fragments produced from a double strand of DNA have single-stranded 'sticky ends' protruding. These single-stranded ends have a sequence of bases that can recognise and pair with one another. An example (shown in fig 3.1) is when the restriction enzyme EcoR1 is used, the fragments have the sequence 'AATT' on one end and 'TTAA' on the other. If the fragments are brought together, provided that the conditions are right, they will join together again and can be resealed by using another enzyme called a DNA ligase. This allows DNA from different sources to be combined, forming recombinant DNA. This will happen provided that the DNA fragments were cut originally by the same restriction enzyme.

3.2 Gene cloning

A particular gene can be inserted into the DNA of a virus, which is then used to introduce the gene into a culture of bacteria or other cells. The recombinant DNA is replicated as the cells divide, producing many copies of the gene.

Plasmids are also used to carry foreign genes into cells. Plasmids are circular strands of DNA which are found in many bacteria and are separate from the bacterial chromosome. The first plasmid to be

Fig 3.1
To show how 'sticky ends'
are produced

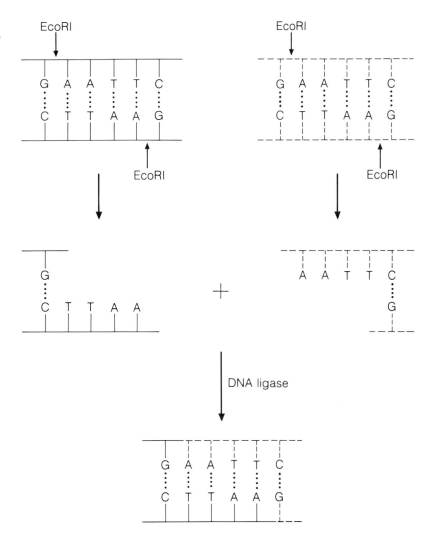

developed, as a vector for the transfer of foreign DNA into bacteria, was pSC1O1, discovered by Stanley Cohen at Stanford University.

The reproduction of 'foreign' genes in bacterial or other cells is called **gene cloning,** a clone being a group of cells, organisms or genes that are exact copies of each other (fig 3.2).

Genetic engineering has transformed industrial processes. One advantage is that microorganisms can be genetically engineered to produce high yields, without the time-consuming process of mutation and selection. Sometimes, the microorganism which synthesises the desired product is slow-growing, so genetic engineers can insert the appropriate gene into the genome of a fast-growing organism, such as *Escherichia coli.*

Recently, it has become possible to separate the growth phase from the production phase. The cells are allowed to grow and divide rapidly at first, without producing the required product. Once the correct cell

Fig 3.2
Diagram of gene cloning

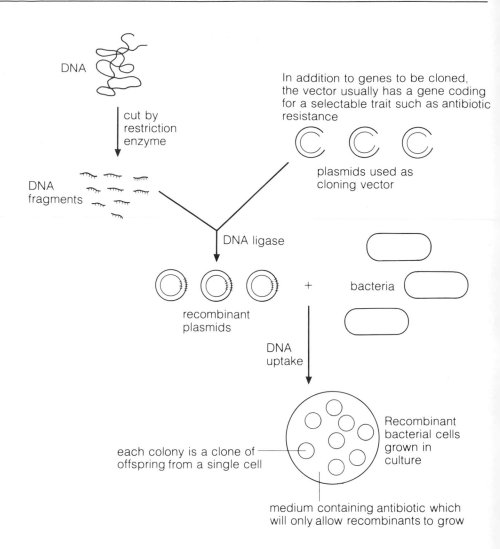

DNA

cut by restriction enzyme

In addition to genes to be cloned, the vector usually has a gene coding for a selectable trait such as antibiotic resistance

DNA fragments

plasmids used as cloning vector

DNA ligase

recombinant plasmids

+ bacteria

DNA uptake

each colony is a clone of offspring from a single cell

Recombinant bacterial cells grown in culture

medium containing antibiotic which will only allow recombinants to grow

density is reached, they can be genetically 'switched on' to produce the end-product by activating a key enzyme in the synthetic pathway. This is of particular use in fermentations where the end-product is toxic.

One problem with industrial-scale fermentations is that microorganisms produce a considerable amount of heat. Cooling the fermenter is expensive, so genetic engineers try to produce a thermophilic microorganism which will synthesise the desired product.

3.3 Applications of genetic engineering

Many **human proteins** can now be produced in culture, by introducing the necessary gene into the DNA of a yeast or bacterium. Among human proteins being made in this way are interleukins and interferon, both of which have an effect on the immune system and have potential in cancer therapy.

Human growth hormone is produced by the pituitary gland and regulates normal growth. Some children lack this hormone and are unable to grow properly unless treated with the hormone. Until recently, the hormone was prepared from animal pituitary extracts which made it expensive to produce and the supply was limited. Using genetic engineering techniques, the gene for human growth hormone, a protein, has been inserted into bacterial cells and produced on a large scale. Growth hormone produced this way is better than the animal hormone, since it is 'human' and it produces fewer side-effects.

Similarly, **human insulin** is now being produced on a large scale. This, too, has the advantage that the engineered product closely resembles human insulin and produces fewer side-effects than the insulin prepared from animal pancreatic extracts.

Scientists have found that they can produce mice that are twice the normal size by giving them a gene for growth hormone. The gene can be inserted into a mouse embryo which is then implanted into a host mother. Offspring from this mouse will carry the new gene. Scientists are now trying to repeat this with farm animals in the hope of improving meat and milk yields.

Research is also taking place into the production of industrial proteins, particularly fibres and adhesives. Silk is an extremely strong fibre but, at present, it can only be produced by silk moth larvae, which are expensive to farm. Scientists hope to insert the gene for silk into microorganisms and produce it more cheaply. Barnacles produce one of the strongest adhesives known. It is a protein and it may soon be possible to genetically modify the gene and insert it into appropriate microorganisms so that it could be manufactured industrially.

3.4   Improving crop plants by genetic engineering

For centuries, plant breeders have improved the yields of major food crops, such as grain, by selective breeding methods. More recently, plant breeders have induced mutations in selected plants by treating them with chemicals or radiation. This has produced better plants, but it is an unpredictable, lengthy and wasteful process. Genetic engineering means that desirable genes can be isolated and inserted into plants in a much more precise way. Genes can be isolated from a whole range of organisms and then inserted into the plant using a gene-transfer vector.

One widely used vector is the bacterium *Agrobacterium tumefaciens*. This bacterium causes a plant disease called crown gall, a form of cancerous growth, when it invades plant cells. It has a large Ti (tumour-inducing) plasmid that becomes incorporated into the genome of the infected plant cell. Genetic engineers use restriction enzymes to insert the required gene into the Ti plasmid, thereby introducing foreign genes into the plant. *Agrobacterium* has several strains so it is able to infect a wide range of plants. Some plant viruses are also being used to act as gene vectors.

At present, only single genes can be transferred, or very small groups. Examples of such characteristics are disease resistance and herbicide resistance (for example, resistance to the herbicide, glyphosate) (fig 3.3). Fields can be sprayed with the herbicide, but only the weed species will die, since the genetically engineered crop plants are resistant to it.

Fig 3.3
Gene transfer into plants

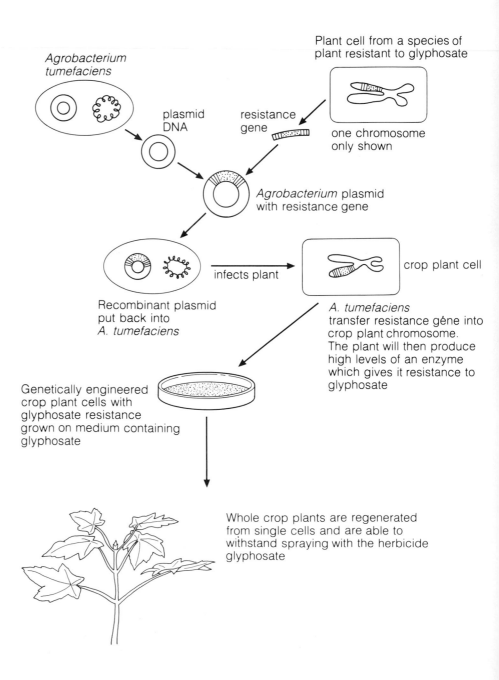

Plant cell from a species of plant resistant to glyphosate

Agrobacterium tumefaciens

plasmid DNA

resistance gene

one chromosome only shown

Agrobacterium plasmid with resistance gene

Recombinant plasmid put back into *A. tumefaciens*

infects plant

crop plant cell

A. tumefaciens transfer resistance gene into crop plant chromosome. The plant will then produce high levels of an enzyme which gives it resistance to glyphosate

Genetically engineered crop plant cells with glyphosate resistance grown on medium containing glyphosate

Whole crop plants are regenerated from single cells and are able to withstand spraying with the herbicide glyphosate

3.5 Breeding disease-resistant plants

Virus-resistant plants are now being produced by gene transfer. *Agrobacterium* has been used to produce tomato and tobacco plants with increased resistance to the tobacco mosaic virus. It should be possible soon to produce many more crop plants that are resistant to virus disease. It may also be used to improve resistance to the many fungal and bacterial diseases of plants by inserting genes which code for a substance toxic to the pathogen or for an enzyme which blocks an essential metabolic pathway.

3.6 Breeding insect-resistant plants

New strains of insect-resistant plants are now being produced. In Britain alone, millions of pounds a year are spent by farmers and growers in trying to control the tremendous amount of damage caused to crop plants by insect pests. This is apart from the effect that the widespread impact of spraying of potentially toxic insecticides has on the environment.

The bacterium *Bacillus thuringiensis* produces spores which contain a natural insecticide. If the spores are eaten by many kinds of leaf-eating caterpillars, or the larvae of flies and mosquitoes, the crystals release proteins that are broken down by digestive enzymes into toxic proteins. Only organisms with the correct enzymes are susceptible, so it is much safer to use than most insecticides. Useful insects, birds and most other wildlife are unaffected. *B. thuringiensis* does not survive well in the environment, so genetic engineers cloned more-resistant bacteria carrying the appropriate gene. This was not found acceptable to many people, who are concerned about releasing genetically engineered organisms into the environment. Therefore, plants have been engineered which carry the gene for the toxin. The toxin gene from *B. thuringiensis* is inserted into the Ti plasmid and thereby into a tobacco plant.

Questions

1 Construct a model or some other visual aid to explain simply to a non-scientist what genetic engineering is.

2 What are the following, and why are they important?

    (*a*) Restriction enzyme
    (*b*) Sticky ends
    (*c*) Recombinant DNA
    (*d*) Plasmid

3 There has been concern recently about the release of genetically engineered strains of bacteria into the environment during trials of producing a natural insecticide. What concerns do you think were expressed?

4 Some of the present and potential uses of genetic engineering have been mentioned. What future uses of the technique do you envisage?

5 In the future, clinicians hope to be able to cure certain hereditary diseases in humans that are caused by defective genes by giving the affected person new copies of good genes. What diseases have the potential of being treated in this way?

3.7 DNA fingerprinting

DNA fingerprinting is a revolutionary technique which can be used in forensic science, immigration disputes, or indeed at any time when family relationships need to be established with certainty. The process was developed by Jeffreys at Leicester University in 1984.

A gene is a length of DNA which carries the code for a particular protein. However, between genes are regions of DNA which do not code for proteins. They sometimes carry repetitive sequences of bases called **hypervariable regions**. Jeffreys noticed that the hypervariable regions of individuals vary considerably, yet there are marked similarities between the hypervariable regions of individuals who are related. He went on to synthesise a **DNA probe**, which is a small double-stranded DNA copy of a repetitive sequence from the hypervariable regions. This probe could then be used to produce a 'genetic fingerprint' of an individual (fig 3.4).

DNA can be extracted from a variety of sources, such as blood, semen or hair roots, so long as the sample contains nucleated cells. The DNA is cut into small sections by incubating it with a **restriction enzyme** (fig 3.5). The DNA sample is then subjected to **gel electrophoresis**. This separates out the pieces of DNA in such a way that the shorter fragments move further through the gel than the longer fragments. At this point, the DNA pieces are invisible. The DNA pieces are transferred from the gel to a nylon membrane, using a technique known as **Southern blotting**. The DNA probe, which has had a radioactive marker attached to it, is now applied to the nylon membrane. The probe bonds with the specific sequence it recognises, but not to other parts of the DNA. Thus it locates the hypervariable regions. To make the pattern visible, the membrane is placed in contact with X-ray film. The radioactive marker attached to the probe causes fogging of the film, and a pattern rather like a supermarket bar code is produced. This pattern is unique to every individual.

3.8 Single-locus probes

The technique already described uses a **multi-locus probe**, so-called because it binds to the DNA in many places. More recently, **single-locus probes** have been developed. They are fifty times more sensitive

Fig 3.4
A DNA fingerprint

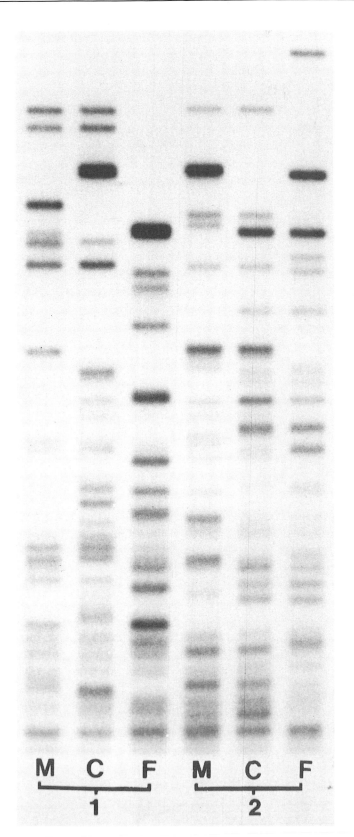

M C F   M C F

1   2

Fig 3.5
Making a genetic
fingerprint

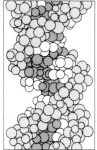

1 Computer representation of DNA (deoxribonucleic acid) molecule. Genetic information, unique to each individual, is coded by a sequence of nucleic acids

2 DNA can be extracted from blood, semen, hair roots and other body tissues

3 Strands of DNA are cut into fragments using a restriction enzyme

4 Fragments of DNA are separated using gel electrophoresis

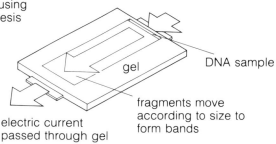

gel

DNA sample

fragments move according to size to form bands

electric current passed through gel

5 Bands are transferred to a nylon membrane like ink blots

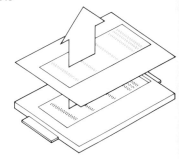

6 Radioactive 'probe' combines with bands on the membrane

7 Radioactive image is exposed on to X-ray film creating permanent 'fingerprint'

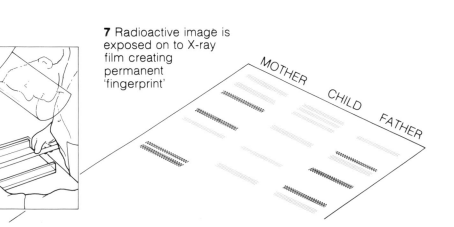

MOTHER   CHILD   FATHER

8 Bands in child's fingerprint are inherited from both parents. A comparison between mother's and child's DNA fingerprint reveals which bands must have come from the father

than multi-locus probes and can be used on very small DNA samples. It is this great sensitivity which makes the new probes so useful in forensic investigations and they can show a clear profile pattern when as little as 10^{-8} g of DNA is present. They are also proving successful in cases where the DNA is partially decomposed. This is more likely to happen in forensic cases, where warm temperatures and damp conditions will accelerate the breakdown of DNA.

Single-locus probes bind to the DNA molecule at one location only and give a pattern of just two bands per individual. There are two bands because an individual has pairs of homologous chromosomes (two sets of chromosomes, one set from the father and one set from the mother) (fig 3.6).

Fig 3.6
Single-locus probes

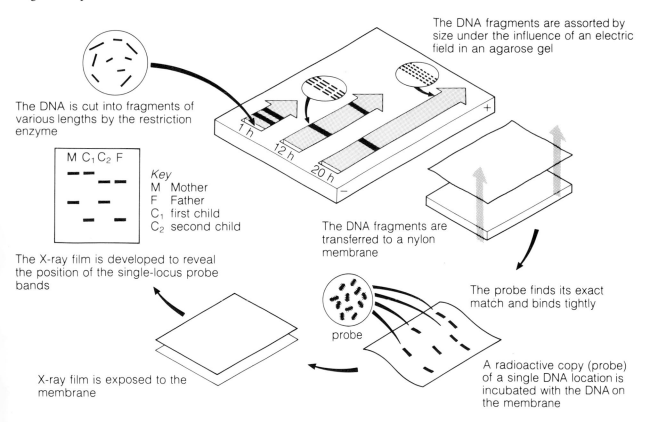

The DNA is cut into fragments of various lengths by the restriction enzyme

The DNA fragments are assorted by size under the influence of an electric field in an agarose gel

Key
M   Mother
F   Father
C_1 first child
C_2 second child

The X-ray film is developed to reveal the position of the single-locus probe bands

The DNA fragments are transferred to a nylon membrane

The probe finds its exact match and binds tightly

probe

X-ray film is exposed to the membrane

A radioactive copy (probe) of a single DNA location is incubated with the DNA on the membrane

Table 3.1 shows some of the present applications of DNA fingerprinting.

**Table 3.1
The applications of DNA fingerprinting**

Application	Probe	Notes
forensic science e.g. murder, rape	single-locus	used on very small samples of blood (0.05 cm³), semen (0.005 cm³) or hair roots to positively identify culprit
immigration applications, paternity disputes	multi-locus	if at least 10 bands match, then chances are over a million to one certain that individuals are very closely related
confirming animal pedigrees	multi-locus	used to confirm parentage of pedigree animals with certainty
identification of human remains	single or multi-locus	if DNA can be extracted, dead bodies may be positively identified by comparing bands with those of living relatives
detecting remission of bone marrow transplants	single-locus	used to detect the presence of donated cells' DNA; if original cancerous cells reappear, then this can be detected early
locating genes causing inherited disease	single-locus	used now to locate cystic fibrosis genes or other genetic defects; used in diagnosis and studies of inheritance
identification of cell lines	single or multi-locus	used in tissue culture to check that a pure cell line has not mutated nor become contaminated
animal and plant breeding	multi-locus	used to research breeding programmes and locate individual genes for required traits
breeding endangered species	multi-locus	used to advise on which animals should be paired to avoid inbreeding in limited populations; has been used with success in Californian condors

4 Plant and animal cell culture

4.1 Mammalian cell culture

An important part of modern biotechnology is the ability to grow mammalian cells and tissues in culture. For some time, it had been known how to keep excised organs alive for a period of hours, by keeping them in balanced salt solutions. However, this was only of limited use. Modern media can keep cells alive indefinitely, so that they can be used in research or for their biosynthetic potential.

4.1.1 How mammalian cells are cultured

Primary cells are obtained from fresh mammalian tissue, for example heart and liver. The protease enzymes **collagenase** and **trypsin** are used to separate the individual cells by digesting the connective tissue between them. These cells may be put in a culture medium and grown, but they retain their differentiated characteristics for only a short time, up to 24 hours, then they rapidly lose their characteristics and become **undifferentiated**. They lose specific functions such as the synthesis of digestive enzymes or hormones. These primary cells have a **finite life** of only about 30 divisions. They are also **attachment-dependent**. This means that they need to be in contact with the surface of the tissue culture vessel, and grow as a monolayer. They stop growing when they touch each other; this is known as **density-arrest**. They are also **serum-dependent** and will not grow unless serum is present in the medium. Primary cells showing these characteristics are known as **untransformed** cells. Human skin fibroblasts, from skin explants, are examples of such a culture, although most kinds of tissue can be used.

    Cell lines are cells which will grow indefinitely in culture. An example is **HeLa cells** which have been cultured continuously since 1953. HeLa cells, originally derived from a tumour in a woman called **Helen Lane**, will outgrow many other cells and they are frequent contaminants of other mammalian cell cultures. They are said to be **transformed** or immortalised; they sometimes lose the requirement for attachment, they have a minimal serum requirement, and the cell cycle does not arrest. Some other examples of these cells are HL60 (leukaemia) and A431 (cervical carcinoma).

4.1.2 Conditions for cell culture

Primary cells used for mammalian tissue culture are larger than microbial cells and divide less frequently. The lower division rate for mammalian cells means that sterility is essential to prevent contaminating microorganisms from outgrowing the mammalian cells.

Unlike microorganisms, mammalian cells require complex culture media which are very expensive. They require a controlled environment, a constant 37 °C, and about 5% carbon dioxide. The carbon dioxide is vital as a buffer, since the cells do not grow in alkaline conditions. The attachment requirement of many mammalian cell cultures is a characteristic not shared by most microorganisms.

4.1.3 The applications of mammalian cell culture

Cancer research Cancer-causing viruses and chemicals have the ability to transform cells from the **untransformed** primary culture, which die after a limited number of divisions, into **transformed** cells. This is applied in research to identify viruses which may cause cancer. A monolayer of primary cells is cultured, then a liquid containing the virus under investigation is spread over the top of the culture and incubated (fig 4.1). If a cancer-causing or transforming virus is present, areas will be seen where cells grow on top of each other. These are called **transformation foci**. By counting the number of foci, it is possible to assess the number of transforming virus particles in the original sample.

An **oncogene** is a gene which causes cancer. If a gene is suspected of oncogene activity, it can be inserted into the genome of a fibroblast and cultured. If the gene is an oncogene, transformation foci appear. These cells in the foci can be cloned and the presence of the oncogene demonstrated in the cell's genome. These studies are often carried out using a partly transformed cell line which does show density-arrest. Partly transformed cells are just like untransformed cells except that they are easier to grow because their nutritional requirements are not so fastidious, for example they do not need serum. The density-arrest can be overcome if an oncogene has been inserted. Oncogenes are often normal genes which code for a particular protein. In certain types of cancer it is thought that tumours are caused by the gene regulation mechanism being at fault. It can be useful to find out which protein a suspect oncogene codes for. The protein being tested can be microinjected into single cells, which, over 24 hours, become temporarily transformed if the protein does prove to be an oncogene product.

Carcinogens are substances suspected of causing cancer. Possible carcinogens can be spread over cell cultures, then the culture examined for transformation foci. These are clearly visible and result from oncogenes in the cells being activated by the carcinogen.

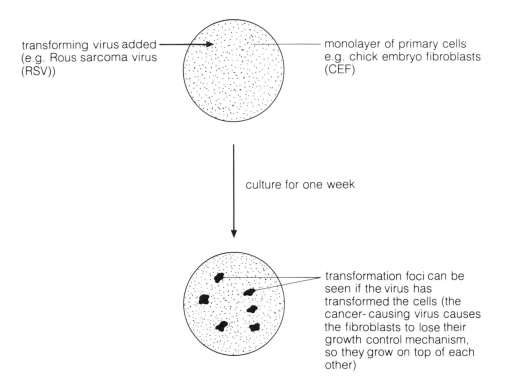

Fig 4.1
Assay for transforming
viruses

transforming virus added
(e.g. Rous sarcoma virus
(RSV))

monolayer of primary cells
e.g. chick embryo fibroblasts
(CEF)

culture for one week

transformation foci can be
seen if the virus has
transformed the cells (the
cancer- causing virus causes
the fibroblasts to lose their
growth control mechanism,
so they grow on top of each
other)

Virus cultivation Cell cultures can be used to grow viruses for vaccine production. Cells are cultured to form a monolayer in a suitable vessel, then the virus is inoculated into the medium. The viruses will infect the cells by the normal lytic cycle, leaving clear areas or **plaques** as new viruses are released into the medium. The viruses can be harvested from the medium and treated. The virus may then be inactivated using chemicals such as phenol, if a dead vaccine is required (such as for prevention of influenza). If a live or attenuated vaccine is required (such as that for prevention of polio or measles), it may be subcultured repeatedly to reduce its pathogenicity.

Cell cultures can also be used to screen for the presence of a virus in a sample of fluid. The cell culture is grown as a monolayer as described above, and a sample of fluid added to the medium. If plaques develop, this indicates that a virus was present. The number of plaques indicates the number of viruses in the original sample.

4.1.4 *Monoclonal antibody production*

Lymphocytes, which secrete antibodies, will not divide in culture. However, large quantities of specific antibody molecules, synthesised from one gene (and hence one cell), would be very useful. Cesar Milstein and Georges Kohler found a solution in 1975, when they fused normal antibody-producing cells with cells from cancerous tumours called **myelomas**. All cells from a given myeloma are identical, having

75

descended by mitotic division from the same parent cell. They can also be grown in culture.

In order to obtain a cell line that made the antibody that they wanted, Kohler and Milstein injected mice with red blood cells from sheep. These red cells have surface antigens and the mice produced B lymphocytes in response (fig 4.2). They then extracted these B lymphocytes and fused them with myeloma cells using a **fusogen**, such as polyethylene glycol (which has a high molecular mass). Very few B lymphocytes hybridise with myeloma cells, and unfused B lymphocytes will die. The resulting **hybridoma** cells were then cloned. Since all hybrids of the same clone produce the same antibody, they were called **monoclonal antibodies**. Unfused myeloma cells could survive along with the hybridised cells, but a special medium is used that will only support the growth of the hybridoma cells. The hybridoma cells can secrete antibody, like the original B lymphocytes, but in addition, they can be cloned, grown in suspension, and they divide rapidly.

However, of all the hybridoma cells, very few will secrete the antibody needed. It is necessary to clone the cells and test them to see whether any of the surviving hybridomas secretes the desired antibody. The medium is diluted and divided so that an average of one cell only is added to each of the wells on a multi-well culture dish (fig 4.2). After about a week, each well will contain about 10 000 identical hybridoma

**Fig 4.2
Monoclonal antibody
production**

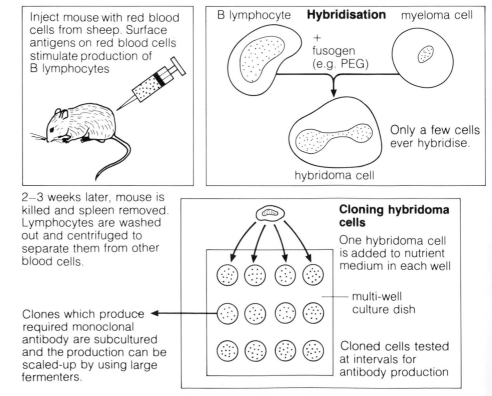

Inject mouse with red blood cells from sheep. Surface antigens on red blood cells stimulate production of B lymphocytes

B lymphocyte   **Hybridisation**   myeloma cell
+
fusogen
(e.g. PEG)

Only a few cells ever hybridise.

hybridoma cell

2–3 weeks later, mouse is killed and spleen removed. Lymphocytes are washed out and centrifuged to separate them from other blood cells.

Cloning hybridoma cells

One hybridoma cell is added to nutrient medium in each well

multi-well culture dish

Clones which produce required monoclonal antibody are subcultured and the production can be scaled-up by using large fermenters.

Cloned cells tested at intervals for antibody production

cells. A tiny sample is tested from each one to see whether the desired antibody has been produced. If it is found, cells from that well will be cloned, on as large a scale as possible, to produce gram quantities of monoclonal antibodies.

4.1.5 Applications of monoclonal antibodies

Monoclonal antibodies have a number of applications.

Testing for specific antigens An example of this is in pregnancy testing kits, based on antibodies to human chorionic gonadotrophin.

Purifying antigens Examples of these are enzymes or interferon.

'Magic bullets' anti-cancer drugs Monoclonal antibodies have been developed which bind specifically with cancer cells. Drugs are bonded to the monoclonal antibodies so that they are targeted specifically to cancer cells. This minimises any side-effects and prevents damage to healthy cells.

Diagnosis of infectious diseases Monoclonal antibodies can detect antigens, such as viruses or bacterial toxins, in samples of body fluids. They are now in use for the rapid diagnosis of the sexually transmitted disease (STD) gonorrhoea. It was difficult to distinguish between the STD caused by the bacterium *Neisseria gonorrhoeae* and that caused by a protozoan parasite called *Chlamydia* which does not respond to antibiotics. Doctors had to culture the bacterium from a swab which takes about two days. *Chlamydia* can only be cultured in living cells and it therefore takes several days to complete the test. New tests, which use monoclonal antibodies, have been developed that can give a positive diagnosis in only 20 minutes. This allows the correct treatment to be given almost immediately.

Manufacture of passive vaccines Monoclonal antibodies to combat a pathogen can be injected directly into the patient's blood, or they may be used to suppress a patient's own immune system, for example following an organ transplant.

Questions

1 Explain the meaning of:
   (*a*) primary cell;
   (*b*) cell line;
   (*c*) transformed cell;
   (*d*) density-arrest.

2 Tabulate the differences between an untransformed cell line and a transformed cell line.

3   Briefly summarise the applications of animal cell culture.

4   How far does animal cell culture present an alternative to the use of animals in medical research? Explain your answer.

5   What is meant by a 'monoclonal antibody'? Make a list of some of their applications.

4.1.6   Biosensors

Sensitivity is one of the characteristics of living things. In order to survive, they must be able to respond to changes in the environment, to detect food or to avoid toxic chemicals. Biological sensory systems can be extremely sensitive. 'Sniffer' dogs are able to detect explosives, while sharks can detect small amounts of blood from hundreds of metres away.

Scientists are working on making artificial biological sensory systems that can be used to detect the presence of certain chemicals. Some are already available, in the form of the 'dipstick' type of pregnancy-testing strips that are available over the counter at most chemists. During pregnancy, a hormone called human chorionic gonadotrophin (hCG) is released from the placenta. This is excreted in the urine during pregnancy. In one version of the test, monoclonal antibody to hCG is labelled with blue latex and incorporated into the surface coating of a dipstick. This is dipped into a sample of urine and if there is hCG present, it binds to the antibody and is drawn up the dipstick with the urine until it meets a second fixed row of antibodies and forms a blue line across the stick. This is a positive test. If there is no hCG, then the blue labelled antibody moves on up the stick and a higher line indicates a negative test. Fig 4.3 shows another kind of pregnancy testing kit which is currently available on the market.

Biosensors, therefore, contain a **biological recognition layer**, and recent developments are towards incorporating such a layer into a probe which could then convert the response into an electrical signal (fig 4.4a). This type of reaction takes place all the time in the olfactory cells of the nose, but it is very difficult to produce such a sensitive artificial sensor.

Many biological recognition layers have been tried, such as antibodies, microbes and enzymes. There has been some success with enzymes. A biosensor has been developed to detect the level of glucose in blood. This is of particular use to diabetics who have to constantly monitor their blood glucose level. One such biosensor uses the enzyme glucose oxidase which catalyses the reaction between glucose and oxygen in solution to form gluconic acid and hydrogen peroxide. The enzyme is incorporated into a disposable probe which clips into the electrical device, about the size of a pen. The tip of the probe is dipped into a drop of blood. If the glucose level is high, hydrogen peroxide is

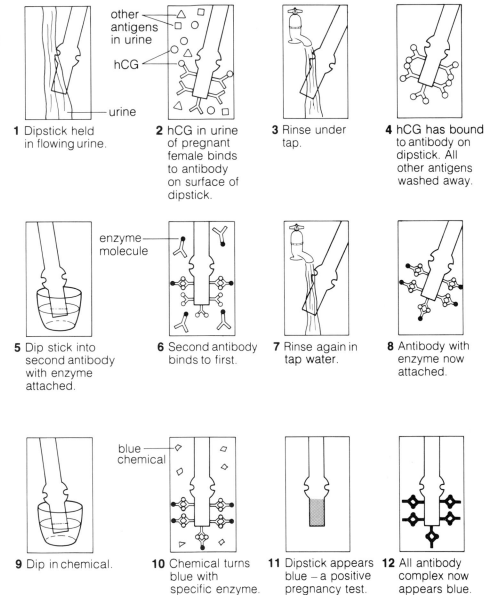

Fig 4.3
Monoclonal antibodies in use in a pregnancy testing kit

other antigens in urine

hCG

urine

1 Dipstick held in flowing urine.

2 hCG in urine of pregnant female binds to antibody on surface of dipstick.

3 Rinse under tap.

4 hCG has bound to antibody on dipstick. All other antigens washed away.

enzyme molecule

5 Dip stick into second antibody with enzyme attached.

6 Second antibody binds to first.

7 Rinse again in tap water.

8 Antibody with enzyme now attached.

blue chemical

9 Dip in chemical.

10 Chemical turns blue with specific enzyme.

11 Dipstick appears blue – a positive pregnancy test.

12 All antibody complex now appears blue.

(not to scale)

produced. This liberates electrons, which flow through a microchip generating an electrical current. This can be measured and displayed on a digital scale. The current is relative to the amount of glucose there is. It can also give warning of low blood glucose levels (hypoglycaemia). This makes it easier for a diabetic to calculate the dose of insulin needed.

Probes are also being developed with the enzyme immobilised on the surface of a silicon chip, a so-called **biochip**. When a positive charge forms on the surface of the chip, due to the gluconic acid produced, electrons flow and this signal can be processed. The advantages are that the probe can be used over and over again and the biochips are not easily damaged. It is also able to respond to and process the signal. It may soon be possible to implant a small glucose biosensor under the skin. This could control the release of insulin into the bloodstream automatically. The device would therefore act as an 'artificial pancreas'.

Food, such as meat, may look fit enough to eat but may have been kept for too long in unsuitable conditions and may contain too many potentially harmful microorganisms such as *Salmonella*. Until recently, there was no immediate test of food freshness. The culture and identification of contaminating microorganisms can take several days. A biosensor probe has been developed for use in the food industry to detect the numbers of microorganisms in meat. It consists of a sharp metal probe containing a biosensor which can be inserted into the meat. This is able to respond to the concentration of a range of different sugars in the meat. There is a correlation between the sugar concentration and the number of microorganisms which feed on the sugars. If the reading is above a certain level, then the meat is unsafe for human consumption. This technique has many future applications and may be used to test the freshness of a wide range of food products.

Fig 4.4
Biosensors

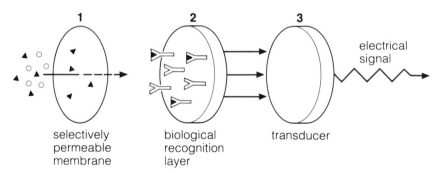

1 — selectively permeable membrane

2 — biological recognition layer

3 — transducer

electrical signal

(a) *The parts of a biosensor*

1 The substance to be detected passes through the membrane.

2 The substance binds to the recognition layer which may contain antibodies or enzymes; a reaction takes place.

3 The product of the reaction passes to a transducer and this produces an electrical signal.

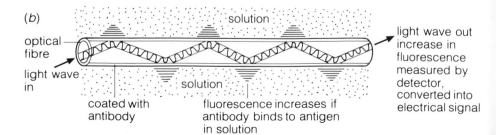

(b)

optical fibre

light wave in

light wave out
increase in fluorescence measured by detector, converted into electrical signal

solution

coated with antibody

fluorescence increases if antibody binds to antigen in solution

It has the advantage of giving an immediate result, vital in today's 'fast food' industry. It should soon be available for use in food preparation areas and supermarkets and will lead to a higher level of food safety.

A different approach involves the use of the latest optical fibre technology. Antibodies can be tagged with fluorescent molecules and deposited on the surface of an optical fibre. When light travels along the fibre it is reflected back off the outer layer as in fig 4.4*b*. At the points of internal reflection, some of the light energy is transmitted outwards and when it meets the antibody layer some of the light is deflected back into the fibre as fluorescence. The fluorescence increases when the antibody binds with its antigen. The intensity of light resulting can be detected by a sensor and converted into an electrical signal. This enables the presence of antigens to be detected in a sample of body fluid. Alternatively, the optical fibre could be coated with antigen and used to detect the presence of antibody. In the future, it should be possible to obtain an immediate indication of the presence of antibodies such as those produced in response to the HIV virus.

Modern medicine relies heavily on tests carried out in laboratories, but this process can take days. The development of biosensors to detect changes in body fluids would make 'bedside' diagnosis rapid and convenient.

Biochips can also be used to monitor changes in the environment. Many microorganisms respond to the presence of heavy metals and organic toxins. It may soon be possible to produce a whole range of biosensors incorporating different microorganisms, in order to monitor drinking water for example.

Question   1   Imagine that you are a scientist working for a company that makes biosensors. Make a three-dimensional model of a biosensor which a salesman could use to explain the technique to a customer with very little scientific knowledge.

4.2   Plant tissue culture

Since the 1970s, many horticultural and agricultural uses for this technique have been found. Plant tissue culture is now a very important part of biotechnology. This technique involves the regeneration of whole plants from individual cells or small pieces of plant tissue.

Plant cells can be grown in culture as follows.

(*a*)   Their cell walls can be removed and the protoplasts grown in a liquid medium, just like fungal or bacterial cultures (fig 4.5). The biosynthetic potential of the cells can be exploited readily, their genome can be manipulated, or the cells may be redifferentiated to produce many embryos.

(*b*)   Pieces of plant tissue, called **explants,** are grown on a solid medium. These develop in various ways, depending on the constituents of the medium

4.2.1 Plant tissue culture methods

A number of different methods are used in plant tissue culture. They are summarised in figs 4.6–4.11.

4.2.2 Transplanting plantlets

Many factors control the success of transplanting these plantlets and their survival:

(a) the quality of their root systems;
(b) environmental factors, such as temperature and humidity;
(c) water supply;
(d) soil factors, such as pH and mycorrhizal associations.

Before transplanting, micropropagated plants must be properly hardened off to withstand the lower temperatures and higher light intensities outside the culture vessels. Micropropagated plants have very thin cuticles, so they must be kept in extremely moist conditions at first. Usually, hardening off takes place in a protected environment, such as a greenhouse, with high light intensity, warm ambient temperature, high humidity and adequate ventilation. After a few weeks, the plants can be transferred to individual pots and later to outdoor conditions. Individual species vary considerably in their hardening-off requirements, so this must be established for each species. Success rates of up to 70% have been achieved.

Fig 4.5
Protoplast suspensions

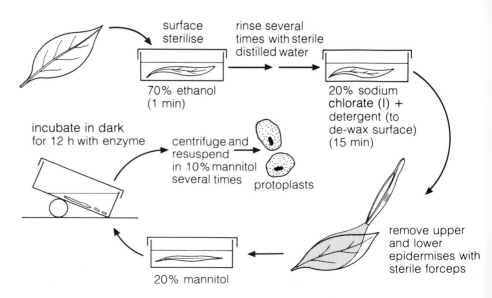

Fig 4.6
Callus cultures

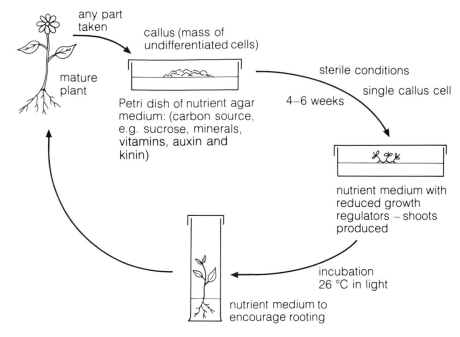

plant surface-sterilised

any part taken

callus (mass of undifferentiated cells)

mature plant

Petri dish of nutrient agar medium: (carbon source, e.g. sucrose, minerals, vitamins, auxin and kinin)

sterile conditions

single callus cell

4–6 weeks

nutrient medium with reduced growth regulators – shoots produced

incubation 26 °C in light

nutrient medium to encourage rooting

Fig 4.7
Embryogenesis

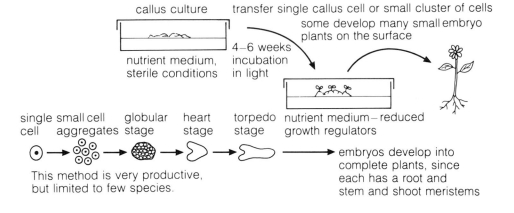

callus culture

transfer single callus cell or small cluster of cells

some develop many small embryo plants on the surface

nutrient medium, sterile conditions

4–6 weeks incubation in light

nutrient medium – reduced growth regulators

single cell | small cell aggregates | globular stage | heart stage | torpedo stage

This method is very productive, but limited to few species.

embryos develop into complete plants, since each has a root and stem and shoot meristems

Fig 4.8
Meristem cultures

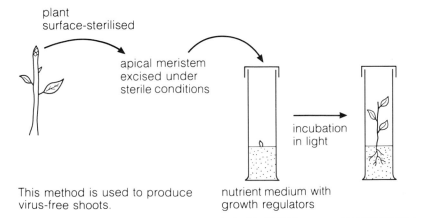

plant surface-sterilised

apical meristem excised under sterile conditions

incubation in light

This method is used to produce virus-free shoots.

nutrient medium with growth regulators

Fig 4.9
Axillary shoot culture

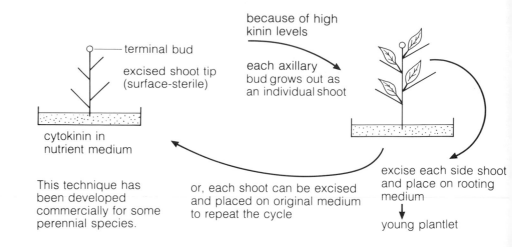

terminal bud

excised shoot tip
(surface-sterile)

because of high
kinin levels

each axillary
bud grows out as
an individual shoot

cytokinin in
nutrient medium

excise each side shoot
and place on rooting
medium

young plantlet

This technique has
been developed
commercially for some
perennial species.

or, each shoot can be excised
and placed on original medium
to repeat the cycle

Fig 4.10
**Adventitious bud and
embryo culture**

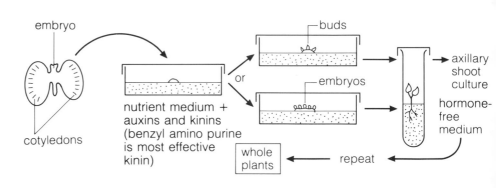

embryo

cotyledons

nutrient medium +
auxins and kinins
(benzyl amino purine
is most effective
kinin)

buds

embryos

or

axillary
shoot
culture

hormone-
free
medium

whole
plants

repeat

Fig 4.11
Micrografting

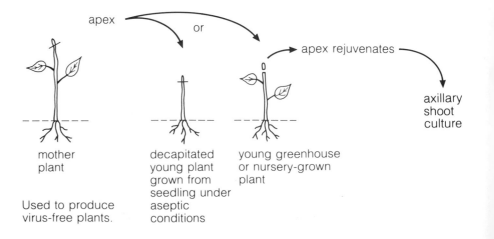

apex

or

apex rejuvenates

axillary
shoot
culture

mother
plant

decapitated
young plant
grown from
seedling under
aseptic
conditions

young greenhouse
or nursery-grown
plant

Used to produce
virus-free plants.

4.2.3 Uses of plant cell and tissue culture

Micropropagation   Micropropagation is not always easy to achieve; some species respond better than others. However, the technique, although expensive and time-consuming, has a number of useful applications. Some valuable trees, such as hybrids or polyploids, are infertile and need vegetative propagation and tissue culture is much faster. Kew Gardens is an example of a place where these methods are used to increase numbers of rare and endangered plant species.

Breeding disease-free plants   Micropropagated plants are disease-free and so more desirable for exchange of plant material between countries, since they eliminate the need for quarantine. Plant breeders have sometimes been surprised to find that when certain plants have been propagated using meristem culture and are therefore virus-free, they grow far more vigorously than before. The plants have not shown any sign of disease, but nevertheless must have been virus-infected. An example of this is the King Edward variety of potatoes.

Creation of new hybrids   Protoplasts can be encouraged to fuse, creating new hybrids which may prove to be valuable crop plants. Tomato/potato hybrids have been made experimentally, but these are not commercially useful.

Transformation by selected gene transfer   Desirable genes can be inserted into the plant cell, which means that new hybrids can be produced with such qualities as drought resistance or herbicide resistance. One new area of research is in producing trees with characteristics that will enable them to thrive in the higher carbon dioxide levels expected over the next 50 years or so, due to the greenhouse effect.

Production of secondary plant products   Plants produce many useful secondary products, such as digitalis (a heart drug) from the foxglove, codeine (a painkiller) from the opium poppy, spearmint (a flavouring) from mint, and pyrethrin (an insecticide) from chrysanthemum. At present, many of these products are imported, so climate, transport difficulties and political instability affect supply. Although research is still at a very early stage, it is theoretically possible to grow protoplast cultures in vast fermenters (just like microbial cells) to produce these products on a large scale. Problems occur because protoplasts are so fragile, but immobilising them might protect them.

4.2.4 Transformation of plant cells

Individual genes can now be transferred into the plant protoplast by **cloning**. There are various methods.

The Ti plasmid occurs in the bacterium *Agrobacterium tumefaciens*, which will pass on part of this plasmid to the plant cell genome. The transferred part of the plasmid is called T-DNA. New genes can be inserted into the T-DNA and these will then be transferred to the plant. Some viruses are also being used as cloning vectors. One example is cauliflower mosaic virus (CMV). This is an unusual virus since it is one of the few to have double-stranded DNA. CMV has been used to transfer new genes to Brassicae.

Naked plasmids are often taken up by plant cells, from their medium, by the process of transformation. If the plasmid carries a gene, this will also be taken up by the plant cell.

The above process of transformation can be enhanced by **electroporosity**. An electrical potential difference is applied across the plant cell culture. This disrupts the membranes slightly, creating tiny pores through which the DNA in the medium can enter the cells.

It should be pointed out that much of the DNA taken up by the plant cells is broken down by the cell's nucleases. Only a small percentage of the DNA taken up by plant cells actually becomes incorporated in the plant cell's genome.

Techniques like these are being used to produce transformed cells with remarkable new characteristics. For example, the bacterium *Salmonella* has resistance to the herbicide glyphosate. If the gene for glyphosate resistance can be transferred to barley protoplasts, a new strain of barley could be developed with herbicide resistance (section 3.4). Herbicide-resistant turnips have already been produced.

Other useful qualities which could be incorporated into transformed plants are drought-resistance, for crops in the Third World, or plants which fix their own nitrogen and can therefore tolerate poor soil.

4.2.5 Plant cell culture media

A commonly used medium is that of Murashige and Skoog (M and S medium) described in table 4.1.

It is important that the nutrient medium contains the correct balance of plant growth hormones, particularly auxins and kinins. The effect of auxin and kinin on growth is shown in fig 4.12.

4.2.6 Animal tissue culture media

Animal cells have very complex nutritional requirements, even more so than bacteria, fungi and plant cells. In a living animal, the cell obtains all the substances for its survival from the tissue fluid surrounding it. The composition, pH and solute potential of the fluid is maintained by a complex homeostatic mechanism involving many other organs, such as the liver and kidney.

Table 4.1
Murashige and Skoog
plant cell culture medium

Nutrients	Ingredient	Concentration mg dm^{-3}
macronutrients	ammonium nitrate	1650.0
	potassium nitrate	1900.0
	calcium chloride	440.0
	magnesium sulphate	370.0
	potassium dihydrogen phosphate	170.0
chelated iron	sodium EDTA	37.3
	iron[II] sulphate	27.8
micronutrients	boric acid	6.2
	manganese sulphate	16.9
	zinc sulphate	8.6
	potassium iodide	0.83
	sodium molybdenate	0.25
	copper sulphate	0.025
	cobalt chloride	0.025
organics	sucrose	20 000.0
	inositol	100.0
vitamins	thiamine	0.1

Auxins and kinins are added in appropriate quantities to the above
medium in order to stimulate the organogenesis required.
It is made up to 1 dm³ with glass distilled water.
For a solid growth medium, agar is added.

Fig 4.12
Control of morphogenesis

Whether callus tissue, shoots or roots develop, depends on the levels of auxins and
kinins in the medium.

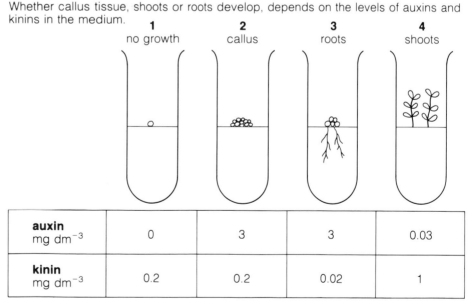

	1 no growth	2 callus	3 roots	4 shoots
auxin mg dm^{-3}	0	3	3	0.03
kinin mg dm^{-3}	0.2	0.2	0.02	1

To cultivate animal cells *in vitro*, the medium must:

(a) **provide nutrients**, as carbohydrates, amino acids, lipids, mineral
salts and vitamins;

(b) **have buffering capacity** to maintain the pH at around 7.0–7.3
despite the fact that living animal cells produce acid; the buffers
must be non-toxic;

(c) **be isosmotic** with the usual tissue fluid to avoid osmotic problems;

(d) **be sterile**, since microorganisms would find the conditions ideal for rapid multiplication and would quickly outgrow and destroy the living animal cells.

There are two categories of media for animal tissue culture, these are:

(a) **natural**: derived from body fluids and animal tissues;

(b) **synthetic**: precise mixtures of substances dissolved in pure water.

Natural media

Serum Blood is collected aseptically from an animal (such as horse, calf or human) and is allowed to clot. It is then centrifuged to remove cells and debris and the clear supernatant is transferred to sterile containers. Serum may be frozen using liquid nitrogen and stored at $-20\,°C$. Foetal serum is often used because it contains no antibodies (gamma globulins). Human foetal serum may be obtained from the umbilical cord and placenta after birth. Calf foetal serum is also used.

Animal plasma Fresh blood is collected aseptically and centrifuged immediately, to spin down the cells. The clear supernatant is used and has advantages in that it provides nutrients and contains a high concentration of the blood protein fibrin, which forms a firm clot and acts as a support medium for the animal cells. Chicken plasma is used extensively because it has a high concentration of fibrin.

Embryo extract This was derived from chick embryos and was widely used during the early days of tissue culture. It is rarely used today.

Collagen Although collagen provides few nutrients, it has been used with some success because it does physically support the cells *in vitro*. It is quite difficult to prepare and is not widely used.

Synthetic media

Balanced salt solutions These were first developed by Ringer in 1883 who used a solution of sodium chloride, potassium chloride and calcium chloride to keep the excised heart of a frog beating for several hours. In 1895 Locke changed the concentration of these salts to suit the mammalian heart and in 1910 Tyrode produced a complex mixture of salts and glucose with sodium hydrogen carbonate as a buffer.

Modern balanced salt solutions are used to culture animal cells. Examples are Hank's medium and Earle's medium. The composition of these is shown in table 4.2.

Table 4.2
Examples of modern
balanced salt solutions
used for the culture of
animal cells

Ingredients	Hank's medium (mg dm^{-3})	Earle's medium (mg dm^{-3})
sodium chloride	8000	6800
potassium chloride	400	400
calcium chloride	185	264
magnesium sulphate	200	200
sodium dihydrogen phosphate	0	140
disodium hydrogen phosphate	60	0
sodium hydrogen carbonate	350	1680
glucose	1000	1000
phenol red	17	17

Balanced salt solutions:

(a)   provide inorganic ions which are essential to the life of all cells;
(b)   have buffering capacity and are thus able to maintain the pH at around 7.2–7.4;
(c)   provide an aqueous environment with the correct solute potential;
(d)   have phenol red indicator which is not toxic to cells when used at low concentration and is used to indicate if there is a significant change of pH.

Complete synthetic media   Balanced salt solutions will maintain the life of animal cells for several hours. However, if a medium is to be capable of maintaining life for a longer period and to allow for growth and division, then a more complex medium is required. A great deal of research is taking place to find complete media which will provide all the necessary ingredients. Now available are a wide range of synthetic media to which a small proportion of a natural medium (usually serum) must be added. An example of a synthetic medium is **Eagle's minimal essential medium** which is based on a balanced salt solution to which amino acids and vitamins are added. The composition of Eagle's medium is shown in table 4.3.

Table 4.3
Eagle's minimal essential
medium

Ingredients	mg dm^{-3}	Ingredients	mg dm^{-3}
Based on a balanced salt solution (Earle's or Hank's) plus:			
L-arginine HCl	126.4	L-cysteine	24.02
L-glutamine	292.3	L-histidine HCl	41.90
L-isoleucine	52.5	L-leucine	52.5
L-lysine HCl	73.06	L-methionine	14.9
L-phenylalanine	33.02	L-threonine	47.64
L-trytophan	10.2	L-tyrosine	36.22
L-valine	46.90	D-Ca pantothenate	1.0
choline chloride	1.0	folic acid	1.0
N-inositol	2.0	nicotinamide	1.0
pyridoxal HCl	1.0	riboflavin	0.10
thiamin HCl	1.0		

Eagle found that if any single component of the medium was omitted, the animal cells degenerated and died. The complete medium with the electrolytes and glucose supplied by a balanced salt solution, together with 5–10% serum, was sufficient for the successful propagation of animal cells *in vitro*. The medium must be renewed at regular intervals, depending upon the metabolic rate of the cells being cultured and on the total volume and composition of the medium.

Sometimes, antibiotics are added to animal tissue culture media. Penicillin and streptomycin have been used at concentrations non-toxic to living animal cells but adequate to inhibit the growth of many bacteria which may accidentally contaminate the culture. Recently, gentamycin has been used. This is a broad-spectrum antibiotic which is able to inhibit the growth of bacteria and particularly that of mycoplasmas which are commonly found to be contaminants of animal tissue cultures. However, provided that aseptic procedures are very strictly followed, antibiotics are not usually needed.

Sterilisation of animal tissue culture media Balanced salt solutions may be sterilised by **autoclaving**, but the sodium hydrogen carbonate may need to be replaced by bubbling carbon dioxide aseptically through the sterilised solution. Few media used for animal tissue culture can be sterilised by heat, and **filtration** is the only practical method for sterilising the majority of natural and synthetic media. Several types of filter are available. One of the most widely used is a membrane filter with a pore size of about 0.2 μm in diameter. This will trap any contaminating bacteria, although viruses may still pass through. Balanced salt solutions and synthetic media are readily available from commercial sources, pre-sterilised and ready for use.

Questions

1 Make a table to compare the different plant tissue culture methods. State what each method is useful for.

2 Explain why it is particularly vital in plant tissue culture that sterility is maintained at all times.

3 Compare the growth curve of a callus culture (fig 4.13) with that of a protoplast suspension (fig 4.14). Give reasons for any differences you notice.

4 It is stated that 'protoplasts may be grown in a liquid medium, just like fungal or bacterial cultures'. How far is this a fair comparison? (Clue: compare their structures and growth curves.)

5 Briefly explain the following terms.

(*a*) Micropropagation
(*b*) Transformation
(*c*) Protoplast

**Fig 4.13
Growth curve of callus
cultures**

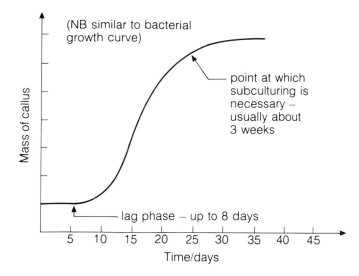

(NB similar to bacterial growth curve)

point at which subculturing is necessary – usually about 3 weeks

lag phase – up to 8 days

**Fig 4.14
Growth curve of
protoplast suspension**

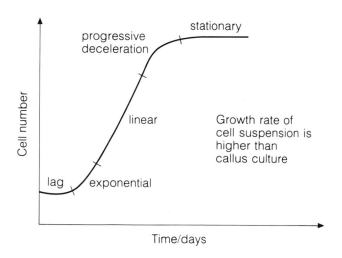

stationary

progressive deceleration

linear

Growth rate of cell suspension is higher than callus culture

lag

exponential

Time/days

(d) Callus
(e) Meristem
(f) Plasmid
(g) Explant

6 List the uses of plant cell and tissue cultures. Can you foresee any future developments?

7 In the recipe for M and S medium, why are the following included?

(a) Sucrose
(b) Ammonium nitrate
(c) Thiamine

8 Compare the composition of media used for plant tissue culture with those used for animal cell culture. Why is the plant medium much simpler?

9   To maintain sterility, autoclaving is used wherever possible. However, the pectinase/cellulase enzymes used in the preparation of a protoplast suspension cannot withstand autoclaving. Suggest ways of making the enzyme solution sterile.

10 Why are the 13 amino acids in Eagle's minimal essential medium all L-isomers?

11 Why are folic acid, n-inositol, nicotinamide, pyridoxal and riboflavin added to Eagle's medium?

12 A small quantity of animal serum is usually added to the complete synthetic medium. Suggest what other substances may be present in serum which are vital to the growth of animal cells.

5 Microorganisms and food production

5.1 Single cell protein

Microorganisms can be grown on a whole range of cheap or waste materials, harvested, and then purified or processed to provide food for either humans or livestock. If the foodstuff produced is a protein, the product is called **single cell protein** (SCP). Many microorganisms are suitable for this process, including algae, blue-greens, fungi and bacteria.

5.1.1 *Examples of substrates available*

The **cheese industry** produces large amounts of whey, and much of this is wasted. Whey contains both protein and lactose, but some yeasts can grow on this waste to produce high grade protein and certain vitamins. The product is used to supplement cattle feed.

The **sugar-refining industry** produces molasses. At present, some of this waste is fermented and distilled to produce rum and some is fed directly to cattle. However, yeast can be grown on molasses to give very high yields of products such as ethanol or single cell protein.

Sulphite liquor is a waste product from the **wood-pulping industry**, containing low levels of sugar. Fungi can grow on this, although newer wood-pulping methods have led to less sulphite liquor waste.

The **oil industry** burns off considerable quantities of natural gas while producing oil, because it is uneconomic to use the gas. In the future it could become economic to liquefy and store the gas for conversion to **methanol**, which would support bacteria and yield high value protein. In oil distillation straight-chain alkanes, a rather waxy product, are produced as a waste. They are not useful in other industries, but they can be used as a substrate for **yeasts** which then form animal feed.

5.1.2 *Advantages of using microorganisms to produce SCP*

(1) Microorganisms have very rapid growth rates. If conditions for growth are kept at an optimum, some microorganisms can double their biomass every 20 minutes.

(2) They can exploit a great variety of substrates, particularly wastes and other low value substances.

(3) The genetic characteristics of microorganisms can be manipulated fairly easily and they can readily be screened for desirable characteristics, such as high growth rate or oil content.

(4) Microorganisms have a fairly high protein content with a good proportion of essential amino acids.

(5) It is comparatively easy to grow microorganisms in fermenters, making their growth independent of climate or political considerations. They also require very little land area.

5.1.3   Problems encountered with SCP

(1) SCP is often contaminated with the substrate, as total purification is not feasible. This creates a problem where the substrate is toxic, such as sewage or methanol. This problem can be overcome by adding an extra stage in the food chain, that is, the toxic substrate is used to grow organism A. Organism A is then used as a substrate for organism B, which is then harvested to yield SCP. This is safer, but as the food chain is longer, the process is less efficient.

Alternatively, a product may be produced from the toxic waste which is then used as a substrate for SCP. An example of this is when sewage is converted to methane by methanogenic bacteria. The methane is then used as a substrate for single-cell protein.

(2) Prokaryotic microorganisms used for SCP production have high nucleic acid content. This happens particularly where production is by continuous fermentation, since growth is exponential. Nucleic acid content is about 15% of dry mass of bacteria, but only about 4% in meat and fish. Excess nucleic acid in human diets leads to health problems such as kidney stones, and can cause nausea, vomiting and diarrhoea. Using chemical methods or enzymes to reduce nucleic acid levels is prohibitively expensive, so prokaryotic SCP is best used either as a human food supplement or for feeding farm animals. Eukaryotic SCP, based on algae and fungi, does not cause such problems as the nucleic acid content is much lower.

(3) Scientists must choose the species of microorganism carefully, as there should be no risk of pathogens being present. *Pseudomonas* is a useful bacterium which grows on various hydrocarbons and methanol. However, some related pseudomonads are pathogens and scientists are concerned that if the organism undergoes a genetic change it could cause disease. One way to avoid this is to totally denature the microorganism during some stage of SCP processing.

5.1.4 Examples of SCP production

'**Pruteen**' is an animal feed supplement, which is high in protein, manufactured by ICI. It is made from methanol using a bacterium, *Methylophilus methylotrophus* as shown in fig 5.1. It is produced by continuous fermentation, which means the rate of addition of new substrate must exactly balance the rate of removal of product.

Fig 5.1
Pruteen manufacture

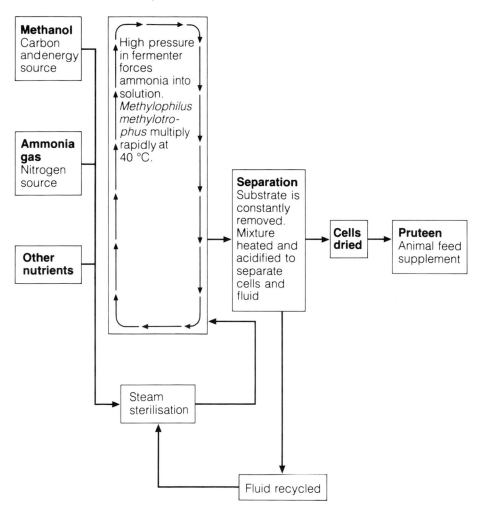

Marlow Foods produce a product called '**Mycoprotein**' by using a filamentous fungus, *Fusarium graminearum*, grown in continuous fermenters. The substrate is a glucose solution, together with oxygen nitrogen and minerals. As the fungus is filamentous, the product contains fibres which can be aligned to make a meat substitute. It is available in ready meals in major supermarkets throughout the country (fig 5.2).

Pekilo is an animal foodstuff rich in protein and vitamins. It is made in continuous fermenters by growing the filamentous fungus

Fig 5.2
Some mycoprotein
products

Paecilomyces varioti on carbohydrate wastes, such as sulphite liquor, molasses, whey and waste fruit.

Spirulina is a blue-green alga which has been grown for many years as SCP. Because it is photosynthetic, it grows in ponds needing only carbon dioxide and inorganic ions. Dried *Spirulina* has high nutrient value and can be fed to animals. It is gaining popularity as a health food.

'**Toprina G**' was a protein food additive produced by BP, using the yeast *Candida lipolytica* in continuous fermenters. The substrate was straight-chain alkanes. However, BP had to stop production as the process was not economically viable.

A low-technology process for making SCP from fruit waste in Belize has been developed by Tate and Lyle. Fruit wastage can be high and waste fruit is not very useful as animal feed since it has a low protein content. In Tate and Lyle's process, the fruit waste is minced and ammonium salts and minerals added. This can be fermented by a fungus over 24 hours to give a high protein product. A portion of the batch is kept back to inoculate the next batch.

Questions 1 Copy table 5.1 and fill in the blank spaces.

Table 5.1

Type of organism used	Species	Substrates	Type of fermentation	Product	Use
bacterium				Pruteen	
	Candida lipolytica				
		fruit waste	batch		
blue-green					
				Pekilo	
					meat substitute

2 What is meant by single cell protein?

3 Give examples of substrates used for SCP production. Why are these substrates widely available, cheap, waste products?

4 Why are microorganisms so suitable for SCP production?

5 What problems are encountered in SCP production? Suggest ways in which these can be overcome.

6 Continuous fermentation is not easy to achieve and currently batch processes are more popular in industry. Suggest why SCP production seems particularly suited to continuous production.

7 Sketch a diagram to show the process by which you think Tate and Lyle produces SCP from fruit waste in Belize. What features of the process make it suitable for use in the Third World?

5.2 Wine making

Crushing The harvested grapes are crushed to form the **must**. Traditionally the grapes are not pre-treated, but in some areas, such as California, sulphur dioxide is used to treat the must so that any natural yeasts present are killed.

Inoculation Traditionally, the natural yeasts present on the grape skins are allowed to ferment the sugars in the must. A complex succession of yeasts develop, dominated by the true wine yeast, *Saccharomyces cerevisiae* var. *ellipsoideus*. Sterilised musts need to be inoculated with this yeast.

97

Fermentation This takes several days. The must from both red and white wine grapes is white and results in a white wine. Red wines are fermented with the grape skins still present. As the sugars are converted to ethanol and carbon dioxide, the ethanol dissolves the red pigments from the grape skins and gives a red wine. For white wine the skins are removed.

Secondary fermentation, fortification and pre-fermentation treatment Many wines, especially red wines, undergo a spontaneous secondary fermentation during the first year, the **malo-lactic fermentation**. This process converts malic acid, present in the grapes, to lactic acid and carbon dioxide, reducing the acidity of the wine. This fermentation is carried out by a variety of lactic acid bacteria, such as *Pediococcus*, *Leuconostoc* and *Lactobacillus*. **Sparkling wines** (**champagne types**) undergo a **second alcoholic fermentation**. Sugar is added, and the carbon dioxide produced carbonates the wine.

Sherries are fortified with alcohol to about 15% and exposed to air. This develops a heavy surface growth of certain yeasts which produce the characteristic sherry flavour.

Some European sweet wines, for example French Sauternes, have pre-fermentation microbial treatment. Before the grapes are picked, they are naturally infected with the fungus *Botrytis cinerea*. This infection causes water loss, therefore increasing sugar content. In addition malic acid is destroyed, so the grapes are less acid. The must from these grapes is very sweet and is fermented by glucophilic yeasts, which rapidly ferment the glucose leaving residual fructose. Thus the product is a very sweet dessert wine.

Questions

1 If yeasts are already present on the skin of the fruit used for wine-making, why should some wine-makers sterilise the must and then inoculate with yeast?

2 How would the colour of a rose wine be produced?

3 Explain why a mature wine will taste quite different from a new one.

5.3 Beer manufacture

Malting Barley grains are soaked in water for 2–3 days, drained, then incubated at 13–17 °C for 10 days. This causes the grain to germinate, producing amylase enzymes which convert the stored starch to maltose. The temperature is raised to 40–70 °C to stop germination by denaturing enzymes. Malting is often carried out by specialist maltsters and the malt sent by road to the brewery.

Milling   Grains are roasted at 80 °C, then cracked open by passing between rollers. The crushed malt is called grist.

Mashing   The grist is mixed with hot brewing water at 62–8 °C in a large vessel called a mash tun. The mash stands for about two hours.

Sparging   The mash passes into a lauter tun. A sugary liquid, called **wort** is drained off. The grain is sprayed with hot liquor to wash the sugars out of the grains, which act as a filter. The spent grain is left behind and sold for cattle fodder.

Boiling   Large coppers are used to boil the wort for several hours to concentrate it. Hops are added to give the characteristic bitter flavour of beer. A small amount of sugar is also added. The boiled wort is then separated from the spent hops, which are sold for hop manure.

Cooling   The wort is passed through heat exchangers to cool it to a suitable temperature for fermentation.

Fermentation   Yeast is added to the cooled wort in the fermenting vessel. *Saccharomyces cerevisiae* is used for beer, and *S. carlsbergensis* for lager. Traditionally, lager yeasts are 'bottom fermenters' and beer yeasts 'top fermenters'. The newer varieties of beer yeasts are 'bottom fermenters', enabling breweries to use the same type of fermenter for either process. The yeast converts the sugars to ethanol and carbon dioxide in 2–5 days. The yeast is separated off. Some is used to inoculate the next batch and the rest is sold off for products such as yeast extract (Marmite). Sometimes the carbon dioxide is collected and sold.

Conditioning   Traditional beers are stored in barrels and allowed to 'condition'. Modern beers are filtered, pasteurised, standardised (brought to a standard colour and flavour) and canned or bottled.

Recently, there have been developments to produce both wine and beer by continuous fermentation methods. In these processes, the yeast is kept in its exponential growth phase, so the product is made much more quickly. This process is particularly popular for making lager, which can be made in about four hours instead of several days. However, although this process is more economical, the flavour and alcohol content are reduced.

Fig 5.3
Summary diagram of beer
manufacture

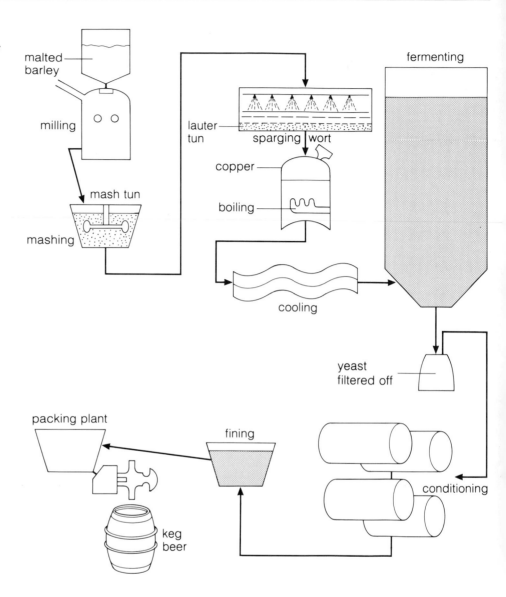

Questions

1 Explain what the following are, and how they are used in beer production.

    (*a*) Malt
    (*b*) Hops

2 What is the difference between a 'top-fermenting' and a 'bottom-fermenting' yeast?

3 Explain why beer or wine produced by continuous fermentation would have a lower alcohol content than its traditionally produced equivalent.

5.4   Cheese manufacture

5.4.1   Production of a hard cheese

Ripening of the milk   Milk is heated and a starter culture of bacteria is added to speed up the natural process of milk souring. The culture is made up of lactic acid bacteria, such as *Streptococcus lactis, S. cremoris* and *S. lactis* subsp. *diacetylactis*.

Renneting or coagulation   When the milk has reached the desired pH, it is kept warm and **rennet** added to coagulate it.

Cutting the coagulum   When the milk has set adequately, the **solid curd** is chopped up using special knives, releasing a lot of the **liquid whey** which is trapped inside the curd.

Scalding the curd   The curd is continuously stirred, while being scalded or heated to release more of the whey. Temperature and pH must be carefully controlled to maintain cheese quality and to avoid destroying the starter microorganisms.

Draining the whey   Stirring is stopped so that the curd settles. The whey is drained off and the curd chopped to release more whey.

Milling and salting   An electric mill is used to cut the blocks of curd into smaller pieces. Salt is added as a preservative and flavour enhancer.

Pressing   For most hard cheeses the salted curd is filled into moulds or hoops and pressed.

Ripening or maturing   Cheese is placed in a ripening room at a controlled temperature and humidity. Bacterial and enzymatic changes occur giving the cheese its characteristic flavour. During ripening most of the lactic acid streptococci are inhibited, but lactobacilli and others proliferate. All the lactose is converted to lactic and other organic acids. Proteins are converted to peptones and amino acids. Enzymes convert some of the fats to fatty acids and glycerol. Amines, aldehydes and ketones are also produced, adding to the cheese flavour. Finished cheese contains approximately 0.1% microorganisms by weight, that is about 10^8 organisms per gram.

Package

5.4.2   Blue cheeses

Blue Cheshire, blue Stilton and blue Wensleydale all have blue veins due to the mould *Penicillium roquefortii*. The cheese is pierced with stainless steel skewers which allows the air to penetrate and enables the

Fig 5.4
Butter manufacture

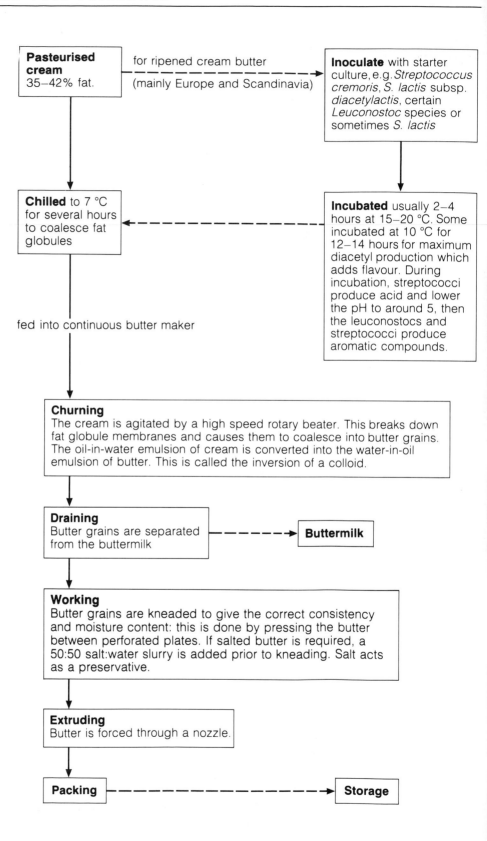

Pasteurised cream
35–42% fat.

for ripened cream butter
(mainly Europe and Scandinavia)

Inoculate with starter culture, e.g. *Streptococcus cremoris*, *S. lactis* subsp. *diacetylactis*, certain *Leuconostoc* species or sometimes *S. lactis*

Chilled to 7 °C for several hours to coalesce fat globules

Incubated usually 2–4 hours at 15–20 °C. Some incubated at 10 °C for 12–14 hours for maximum diacetyl production which adds flavour. During incubation, streptococci produce acid and lower the pH to around 5, then the leuconostocs and streptococci produce aromatic compounds.

fed into continuous butter maker

Churning
The cream is agitated by a high speed rotary beater. This breaks down fat globule membranes and causes them to coalesce into butter grains. The oil-in-water emulsion of cream is converted into the water-in-oil emulsion of butter. This is called the inversion of a colloid.

Draining
Butter grains are separated from the buttermilk

Buttermilk

Working
Butter grains are kneaded to give the correct consistency and moisture content: this is done by pressing the butter between perforated plates. If salted butter is required, a 50:50 salt:water slurry is added prior to kneading. Salt acts as a preservative.

Extruding
Butter is forced through a nozzle.

Packing

Storage

Fig 5.5
Yogurt manufacture

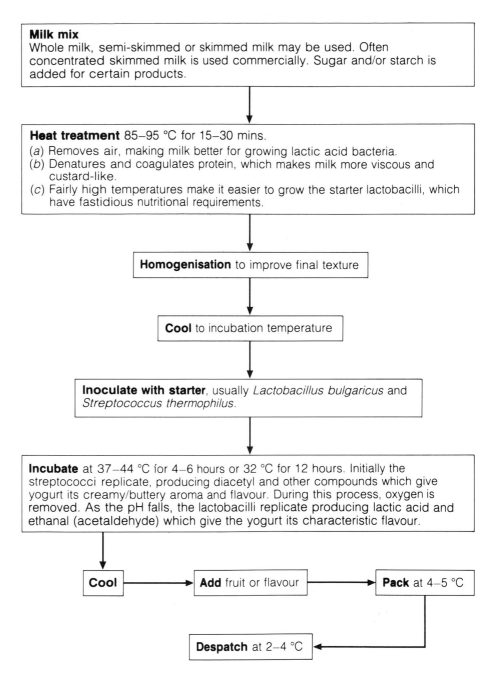

Milk mix
Whole milk, semi-skimmed or skimmed milk may be used. Often concentrated skimmed milk is used commercially. Sugar and/or starch is added for certain products.

Heat treatment 85–95 °C for 15–30 mins.
(a) Removes air, making milk better for growing lactic acid bacteria.
(b) Denatures and coagulates protein, which makes milk more viscous and custard-like.
(c) Fairly high temperatures make it easier to grow the starter lactobacilli, which have fastidious nutritional requirements.

Homogenisation to improve final texture

Cool to incubation temperature

Inoculate with starter, usually *Lactobacillus bulgaricus* and *Streptococcus thermophilus*.

Incubate at 37–44 °C for 4–6 hours or 32 °C for 12 hours. Initially the streptococci replicate, producing diacetyl and other compounds which give yogurt its creamy/buttery aroma and flavour. During this process, oxygen is removed. As the pH falls, the lactobacilli replicate producing lactic acid and ethanal (acetaldehyde) which give the yogurt its characteristic flavour.

Cool → **Add** fruit or flavour → **Pack** at 4–5 °C

Despatch at 2–4 °C

mould to grow faster. The blue colour is due to spore production by the mould. The mould produces enzymes which hydrolyse fats into fatty acids and ketones, which add to the flavour of the cheese.

Many blue cheeses have a wrinkled drying coat which supports the growth of many microorganisms, such as moulds, yeasts, streptococci and lactobacilli.

Fig 5.6
Cheesemaking: Once the curd has formed, it is cut mechanically to release the whey. The contents of the vat are scalded and stirred to firm the curd and release more whey.

5.4.3 Soft cheeses

These are unripened and unpressed, such as cottage cheese, so they have a much higher water content than hard cheeses. The curd is drained off slowly using gravity, and no pressure is applied.

5.5 Butter manufacture

Fig 5.4 shows the stages involved in making butter.

5.6 Yogurt manufacture

Fig 5.5 shows the manufacture of yogurt.

Questions

1 Cheese making is basically the same for all kinds of cheese, yet there is an enormous variety of cheeses on sale in shops. Which stages in the cheese-making process might be the source of these differences?

2 Explain the meaning of the following terms.

(*a*) Starter culture
(*b*) Incubation
(*c*) Homogenisation

3 Give five advantages, over more conventional methods, of the use of microorganisms as food producers.

6 Biological fuels

6.1 The need for biological fuels

The world has become increasingly dependent on non-renewable energy sources such as petrol. World oil supplies are predicted to run out in about 50 years' time. Scientists are working to overcome the crisis by finding alternative, preferably renewable, energy sources. Microbes offer one solution to this problem.

The use of biomass as an energy source is attractive, since it depends on energy from sunlight, which is unlimited. Therefore, biomass is called a **renewable energy source**. At present, a great deal of biomass is currently wasted in the form of agricultural, industrial and domestic waste. Microbes can make use of these wastes and at the same time help to solve waste disposal problems. In addition, 'low-tech' designs for fuel production are available for use in the Third World or on a small scale, where traditional energy-production methods are less applicable.

6.2 Raw materials

These include wastes and crops.

6.2.1 Wastes

Dry wastes which can be used as a source of biofuels include domestic refuse, agricultural and industrial wastes, straw and forest residues. There are also **wet wastes** including industrial effluent, animal wastes and sewage. The use of wastes as fuel can be highly cost-effective, since they are cheap to obtain and using them to make fuel saves the often high cost of disposal. However, wastes can be bulky and unpleasant or toxic to handle.

6.2.2 Crops

In the future, crops may be grown specially for energy production, perhaps on land unsuitable for growing foodstuffs. Sugar cane is already being grown in Brazil for this purpose. In the UK, forestry is likely to be the most attractive energy crop. New species of rapidly growing conifers are being developed for this purpose. The technologies used include fermentation, anaerobic digestion and combustion.

6.3   Ethanol production

Since ancient times, humans have produced ethanol by fermentation and it was first used as a motor car fuel as long ago as 1890. In the 1920s and 1930s cars were run on ethanol in some parts of the world and fuel shortages during the Second World War encouraged developments in this technology. At present, most industrial alcohol is made synthetically from by-products of the petrochemical industry.

However, many developing countries have always used traditional fermentation methods to make industrial alcohol, since cheap raw materials are available. The rising cost of oil is making this method more attractive to industrialised countries. Alcohol can be home-produced, thereby reducing import costs. A further advantage is that alcohol can be converted easily to ethene and similar compounds, that are basic raw materials in plastics manufacture. Brazil has made the greatest advances in this direction and are currently the world leaders in fuel alcohol, with production in excess of 11×10^9 dm³ (litres) per year. In the USA production has also been rising rapidly, to 3.3×10^9 dm³ (litres) in 1985.

Substrates include sugar cane, cassava roots, cellulose waste and corn (fig 6.1). Cassava roots contain starch which must be hydrolysed to sugars, and cellulose waste, such as timber and straw, needs quite complex pre-treatment with ligno-cellulase enzymes or chemicals.

Brazil is building over 500 fermentation and distillation plants and eventually aims to supply the country's entire petrol needs with ethanol. At present, alcohol production is similar to the traditional process but much research is taking place. It is hoped that more efficient, genetically engineered microorganisms will be developed and that newer fermenter designs and immobilised enzyme technology will improve efficiency. Distillation costs can be reduced by using a cheap fuel, and **bagasse** (the waste from sugar cane) has proved to be an economical fuel for raising steam for the process by combustion.

There is concern about increasing the volume of carbon dioxide in the atmosphere due to the burning of fossil fuels on a global scale. This may lead to the 'greenhouse effect', since rays of infra-red light from the Sun are trapped by air rich in carbon dioxide and the temperature of the atmosphere would rise. This could effect changing world weather patterns and sea levels could rise due to melting of glaciers and the polar ice caps. By using plants on a large scale to produce fermentable substances, a balance could be achieved, whereby carbon is recycled (fig 6.2). Therefore there would be no net effect on the carbon dioxide in the atmosphere if all our fuels were produced by renewable methods, using plants as the initial producers.

A range of microorganisms have been used in the production of ethanol, using many different carbohydrates as substrate. Traditionally, ethanol production has relied upon the use of yeasts, mostly

**Fig 6.1
A flow diagram showing
the production of ethanol
from corn**

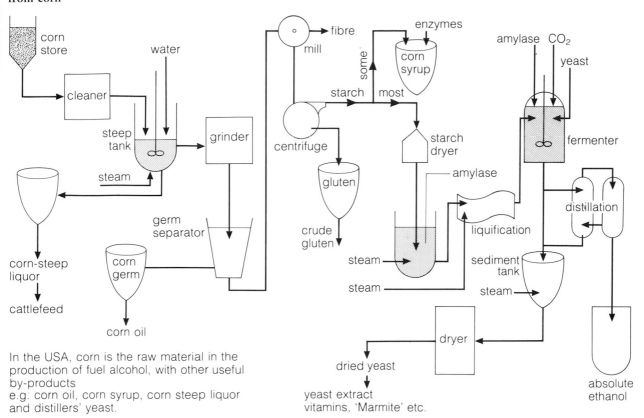

In the USA, corn is the raw material in the
production of fuel alcohol, with other useful
by-products
e.g: corn oil, corn syrup, corn steep liquor
and distillers' yeast.

Saccharomyces species. *Zygomonas mobilis* has been used in South America for many years in the production of tequila, and in Indonesia and Africa to make palm wine. However, its use in the western world is quite new. Recent research into *Zygomonas* has shown that it is more efficient than yeasts in converting sugar to ethanol. Another advantage of using *Zygomonas* is that glycerol, a major by-product in yeast fermentation, is only produced in trace amounts, giving a higher ethanol yield. The smaller *Zygomonas* cells have a higher surface area to volume ratio and thus take up sugar and give out ethanol more quickly. Its fermentation rate is faster than yeast and it has a greater ethanol tolerance limit.

A technique has been developed to produce ethanol using *Zygomonas* in a continuous culture process, rather than the more traditional batch culture methods. *Zygomonas* cells are immobilised on to an inert support medium and packed into a column with the substrate in solution flowing slowly past. This process shows a very promising method for ethanol production, particularly when oil supplies begin to run out.

Fig 6.2
Recycling carbon using 'renewable' fuel such as ethanol (simplified)

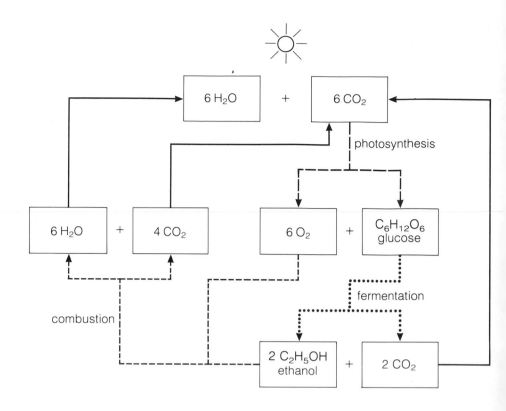

6.4 The production of methane

The rumen of ruminant animals, such as the cow, is a natural methane production system. This is a complex fermentation system with many different microorganisms involved. Attempts to set up similar processes in fermenters need precise monitoring, since it is not easy to imitate the natural process. However, methane production can be done on a very low technology scale, which is suitable for Third World countries.

Sewage Many sewage works have anaerobic digesters for sewage treatment. These digesters produce methane, which can be used to power the works.

Urban waste, landfill gas In recent years, a biofuels programme, with the backing of the Department of Energy, has concentrated on the production and use of gas formed when domestic refuse biodegrades in landfill sites. Refuse undergoes decomposition, under anaerobic conditions, to yield a mixture of gases containing large quantities of methane. One successful scheme is at Bidston Moss, Merseyside (fig 6.3).

Formerly a peat mossland, it has been used as a waste disposal site for over 50 years, receiving mostly domestic refuse for the past 10 years. The waste has been tipped to form a mound about 20 m thick.

**Fig 6.3
Plan of Bidston Moss
landfill site showing
collecting main and wells**

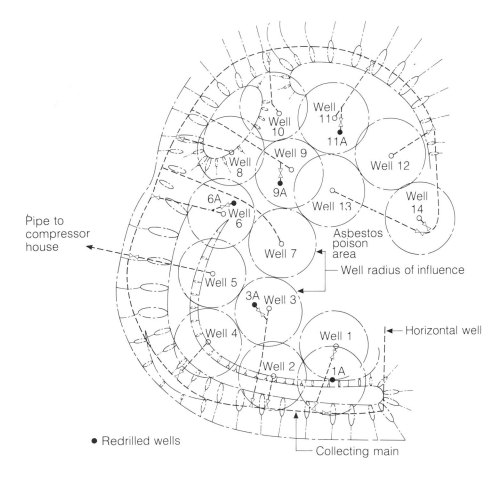

Vertical wells were drilled to collect gas from an area covering about 40% of the site. The gas is transported, via pipelines, to a header pipe which circles the site. The gas flow and yield are controlled by a series of valves. The gas is dried before being piped 2.5 km along a polyethylene pipe laid 1 m underground to a large factory complex where the gas is used to raise steam in a huge boiler. This site yields between 1–1.5 million therms of gas annually. At Bidston Moss, the scheme has proved to be economically viable due to the large volume of gas released and the convenient location of a customer. It has also helped to cut down on the unpleasant smells formerly released from the site, although the isolated, exposed position of the site adjacent to the River Mersey meant that it was never the subject of complaint. Other local authorities are liquefying landfill gas and using it to run their vehicles.

Biogas fermenters These have been used for hundreds of years in some countries. For example, in India, Pakistan and China, systems range from very small family schemes to quite large biogas plants. Animal dung and water are allowed to ferment in these in almost anaerobic conditions.

It may be possible to grow crops specially as a substrate for methane production. In addition, the wastes from methane digesters can be useful by-products. The residue is rich in such nutrients as ammonia and phosphates, so can be used as a soil conditioner or even animal feed. As well as methane, other fuels such as propanol and butanol can be made this way. Utilising digester wastes for soil conditioning increases the cost-effectiveness. However, while this is a useful small-scale process, it is unlikely to be commercially viable on a large scale because:

(a) methane can be produced far more cheaply from coal at present;
(b) natural gas is cheaper than microbially produced methane;
(c) there are many natural sources of methane;
(d) gas is expensive to store, transport and distribute at present;
(e) it is expensive and difficult to liquefy.

Agricultural wastes   Some farms now place animal manure and other crop residues into anaerobic digestion tanks. Here, the waste is fermented by microorganisms and the methane produced is collected, liquefied and used to power farm machinery. In some cases it may be used to fire boilers, which heat glasshouses and produce early crops of tomatoes, peppers and other vegetables.

6.5   The production of hydrogen

Hydrogen is produced by photosynthetic bacteria and in fermentation. Unfortunately, the efficiency is very low and considerable research is needed before microbial production of hydrogen, as a fuel, can be considered. However, there is an alternative use for microbial production of hydrogen: in biological fuel cells for production of electricity.

6.6   Microbial generation of electricity

As microorganisms respire, hydrogen is passed to certain coenzymes, which become reduced, for example NADH + H$^+$. These reduced coenzymes are energy-rich. In aerobic respiration, the hydrogen is passed on, via these coenzymes, to molecular oxygen, producing water. However, this pathway can be blocked by excluding oxygen and the reduced coenzymes will then give up their hydrogen, which splits into protons and electrons, to a mediator. Mediators are 'redox' reagents, which usually change colour when they are reduced, such as tetrazolium salts, resazurin, and methylene blue. Many of these are already used in tests to detect microbial activity, for example resazurin is used to check the microbial quality of milk. The mediator becomes reduced by accepting electrons from NADH + H$^+$. This reaction may be used to produce an electric current (a flow of electrons) in a microbial fuel cell, which is rather like a car battery. The reduced mediator passes its electrons to the anode and so to the external circuit.

Many different substrates can potentially be used in these cells, since microbes can utilise virtually anything. Less than 0.1 g of carbohydrate can power a watch for a year. Prototype microbial fuel cells can power a digital clock. Larger microbial batteries can be made; it may be possible in the future to fuel electric cars with waste carbohydrate in this way. Microbial fuel cells also contain no metallic parts and are largely biodegradable, which has environmental advantages. Research is taking place into using photosynthetic organisms in 'bio-solar' cells which would make direct use of the Sun's energy (fig 6.4).

Fig 6.4
Structure of a microbial fuel cell (expanded to show components)

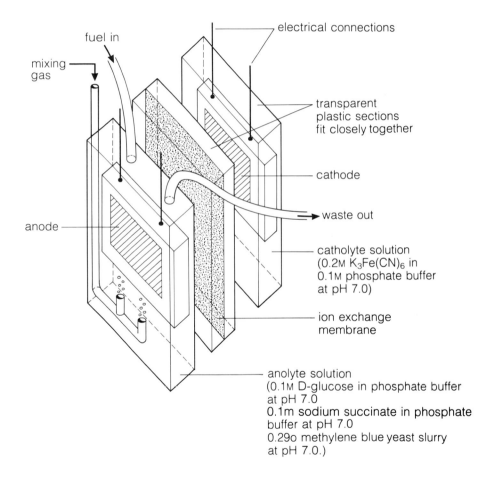

6.7 Organic solvents – propanone (acetone), butanol and glycerol

These important solvents can be made by batch fermentation from a range of carbohydrate-based raw materials, such as starches, cellulose, whey, molasses and sulphite liquor. Vitamins and a protein source are normally added. Waste from corn production is ideal, because it contains all these requirements. The organism used is *Clostridium*

**Fig 6.5
Pathway for the
production of organic
solvents and acids**

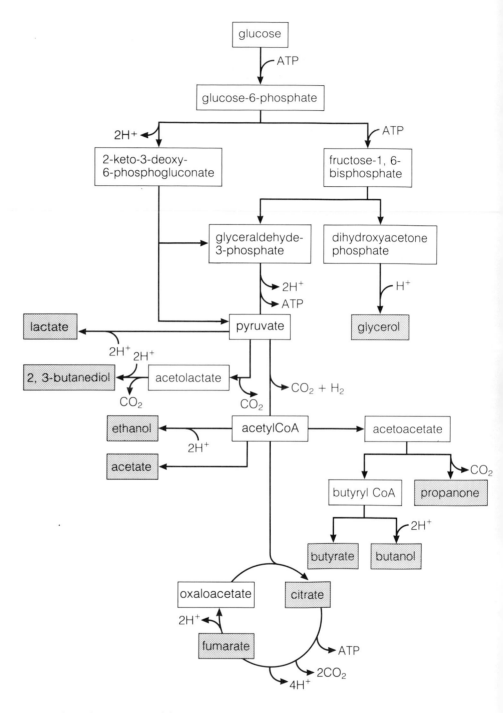

acetobutylicum, an obligate anaerobe which secretes amylase, so that
the raw materials do not need to undergo prior hydrolysis. Since
Clostridium is an anaerobe, it respires glucose following the normal
glycolysis pathway. However, in the absence of oxygen, acetyl coA is
converted to acetoacetate, then on to propanone and butanol (fig 6.5).
Eventually, the build-up of these solvents becomes toxic to the

Clostridium, but the microbial biomass produced can be used as animal feed, since it is high in B vitamins and protein.

Propanone (acetone) was used as a solvent in the First World War for the manufacture of the explosive cordite. It is now widely used as a solvent, for example in nail varnish remover, paint stripper and cleaning fluids.

Butanol is produced commercially by fermentation in South Africa, as a petroleum substitute, since the country has a shortage of petroleum as a result of international sanctions.

Glycerol is an important lubricant in the manufacture of pet food, baked goods, confectionery, icing, toothpaste, adhesives, cork board, cellophane and some kinds of paper. It is also used as an ointment base and moisturiser in many pharmaceuticals and cosmetics. As a solvent, it is used for extracts, flavourings and food colours. Esters of glycerol are important for explosives and propellants. In the First World War, glycerol was needed for explosives. The method by which it was made is discussed in section 2.2. Recently, yeasts have been found which can make glycerol without the need to use sodium sulphite or any other 'trapping' agent.

Questions

1   List the advantages and disadvantages of using biomass as a source of energy.

2   Design a simple biogas fermenter which could safely be used by a family in the Third World.

3   Explain why microbial fuel cells are anaerobic. Do you consider that these will have a useful role in the future? Justify your answer.

4   What environmental and ecological benefits are there in tapping landfill sites?

7 Further industrial uses of microorganisms

7.1 Antibiotics

Alexander Fleming's accidental discovery of penicillin in 1929 is well known. He found the mould *Penicillium notatum* contaminating a Petri dish of pathogenic bacteria and inhibiting their growth. He isolated penicillin but it was not until the Second World War that it was successfully produced on a large scale. At first, it was grown in static liquid culture in various flasks, shallow pans and milk bottles, but this process was highly inefficient and it was not possible to produce enough penicillin to meet demand. Later, a strain was developed which would grow submerged in the medium and give better yields. Modern production of penicillin uses a mutant strain developed in the laboratory.

An antibiotic can be defined as 'a chemical substance produced by a microorganism that, in dilute solution, can exert a growth-inhibiting effect on other microorganisms'. This definition is sometimes considered to be rather narrow since it leaves out the sulphonamides which are synthesised chemically, but operate similarly to other antibiotics.

Scientists are not sure why microorganisms produce antibiotics. It seems unlikely that they produce antibiotics to fight natural enemies, as so few species possess this ability and they are not produced until late in the microorganism's life cycle. Two theories have been proposed to explain antibiotic production.

(1) Antibiotics are secondary metabolites, so they may be produced to keep enzyme systems operative when the microbe has run out of nutrients and cell division is no longer possible. Normally, when the substrate has been used up, the enzymes of that particular pathway would be broken down. Then, if a new nutrient supply was found, there would be a delay while the necessary enzymes were produced. It has been suggested that making a secondary metabolite keeps the enzymes active, so that the microbe can quickly take advantage of any new food supply.

(2) Some scientists think that antibiotic production is a means of ridding the cell of toxic metabolic waste. Although not toxic to

the organism producing them, these substances could still be highly toxic to other microorganisms. If the toxin phenylacetic acid is added to a culture of *Penicillium*, penicillin production is increased. This observation supports this theory. It is of course, possible that both theories are correct since they are not contradictory.

7.2 The industrial production of antibiotics

The first stage of antibiotic production is screening for microorganisms which produce antibiotics (fig 7.1). Many such organisms have been found in soil, although other sources have been useful.

Once an antibiotic has been found, it must be tested to find its optimum production conditions (such as temperature and pH).

Fig 7.1
Antibiotic screening

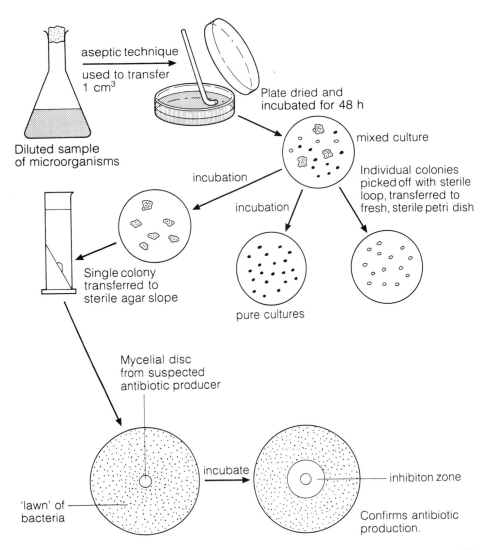

Chromatography and other techniques can be used to see whether one or more compounds are produced. This method also indicates whether the antibiotic is new, and its chemical structure may then be determined. Many new antibiotics are discovered every year, but very few are ever marketed because they must satisfy strict safety codes, and must be better at killing microorganisms than ones already in use. There are many microorganisms used in the commercial production of antibiotics. Examples include *Penicillium notatum* and *P. chrysogenum*, both used to manufacture penicillin, and *P. griseofulvum*, used to manufacture griseofulvin.

Commercial production of antibiotics is by **batch** or **fed-batch** culture. The antibiotic-producing microbe is cultured in a sterile medium in a vast fermenter (fig 7.2). It is grown under optimum temperature and pH conditions (as determined by the pilot study) so that the microbe grows and produces the antibiotic, which is secreted into the medium. The fermentation is monitored so that culture is stopped when maximum levels of antibiotic are present. The medium is then filtered off and the antibiotic extracted (fig 7.3). The spent microbes are sometimes used for animal feed.

Questions

1   Antibiotics are 'secondary metabolites'. What does this mean?

2   Why do some microorganisms produce antibiotics?

**Fig 7.2
Industrial fermenter in action. Only the top can be seen**

Fig 7.3
Antibiotic production

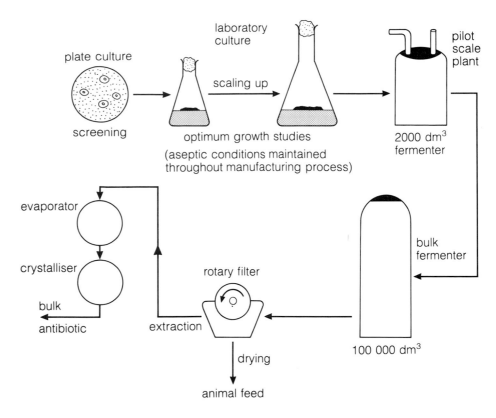

3   Do you think antibiotic production would be more efficient if a continuous fermentation system was used?

4   Suggest advantages and disadvantages of using antibiotic waste for animal feed.

5   Suggest techniques which might be used to extract antibiotics from the filtered medium.

6   In a test to find out whether a newly isolated organism X produces an antibiotic, the following procedure was carried out. First, organism X was inoculated on to an agar plate, along the line AB (fig 7.4). Four different known species of bacteria were inoculated along CD, EF, GH and IJ. The plate was incubated for three days. What results would you expect to see if X

   (a)   has antibiotic activity?
   (b)   does not have antibiotic activity?

7.3   Microbial mining

Some bacteria are useful in extracting metals from low-grade ores. This is because they are **chemoautotrophic** which means they derive their energy from inorganic chemicals. Bacteria of the genus *Thiobacillus* are used commercially to extract copper and uranium from otherwise

117

Fig 7.4
To find out if organism X
produces an antibiotic

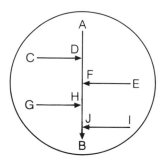

uneconomic reserves. Cobalt, lead and nickel may also be extracted in this way in the near future. The extraction process may require extremes of environmental conditions, such as heat and pH. Genetic engineering techniques are being used to confer acid- and heat-resistance on these microorganisms.

7.3.1 Copper mining

Thiobacillus ferrooxidans can oxidise insoluble chalcopyrites ore and convert it into the soluble salt, copper sulphate. Sulphuric acid is produced during this process, yet the organism is able to flourish in these conditions. Copper can be extracted by reacting the copper ions with scrap iron. This method is responsible for more than 10% of the copper produced in the USA.

7.3.2 Uranium mining

In uranium mining areas it has been found that water collects underground and these pools are a rich source of the radioactive mineral, since microorganisms on the rock face break down the low grade uranium ore. The natural process is enhanced by pumping the run-off water, containing such bacteria as *Thiobacillus ferrooxidans*, into the mine. The resulting run-off water is pumped out and is found to be rich in uranium ions. This means the metal can be economically extracted, and environmental damage minimised.

7.4 Bioaccumulation

Some microorganisms are able to accumulate metals and this property can be exploited both for extracting valuable metals from low-grade waste and for detoxifying wastes. Some bacteria, such as *Pseudomonas* sp., can accumulate metallic mercury. *Pseudomonas aeruginosa* accumulates uranium from effluents, while some *Thiobacillus* species accumulate silver.

Fig 7.5
Microbial mining

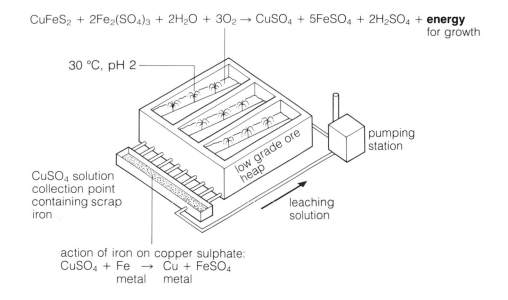

$$CuFeS_2 + 2Fe_2(SO_4)_3 + 2H_2O + 3O_2 \rightarrow CuSO_4 + 5FeSO_4 + 2H_2SO_4 + \textbf{energy}$$
for growth

30 °C, pH 2

pumping station

low grade ore heap

leaching solution

$CuSO_4$ solution collection point containing scrap iron

action of iron on copper sulphate:
$$CuSO_4 + Fe \rightarrow Cu + FeSO_4$$
metal   metal

7.5 The production of organic acids

7.5.1 Citric acid

This used to be obtained directly from citrus fruits, but batch fermentation methods have proved to be a cheaper and more convenient option. It is added to many food products, such as jams, jellies, drinks and sweets, as an antioxidant and flavour enhancer. It is also used in cosmetics and pharmaceuticals to adjust the pH. It is useful in electroplating, leather tanning and clearing metal-blocked pipes in the oil industry, since it has metal-binding properties. This property is valuable in detoxifying waste such as the run-off water from mines.

Citric acid is a Krebs (tricarboxylic or citric acid) cycle intermediate and made by many microorganisms, although the usual organism used in commercial production is *Aspergillus niger* (fig 7.6). The conversion of citrate to cis-aconitate is carried out by an enzyme which needs iron (Fe^{2+}) as an activator (fig 7.7). In the commercial fermentation, the substrate is kept extremely pure and deficient in iron to inhibit this reaction. Therefore, citric acid accumulates.

7.5.2 Production of ethanoic (acetic) acid, (vinegar)

Traditionally vinegar is made by the **Orleans process** (fig 7.8). Wooden vats are partly filled with wine, leaving a large air space. Acetic acid bacteria, such as *Acetobacter*, form a surface film. These turn the ethanol to ethanoic acid over a period of several weeks (fig 7.9). A high quality vinegar is obtained by this process.

The traditional method in Britain is to trickle cider or malt wort into a wooden tank loosely packed with wood shavings. Acetic acid bacteria

Fig 7.6
Flow chart for the
production of citric acid

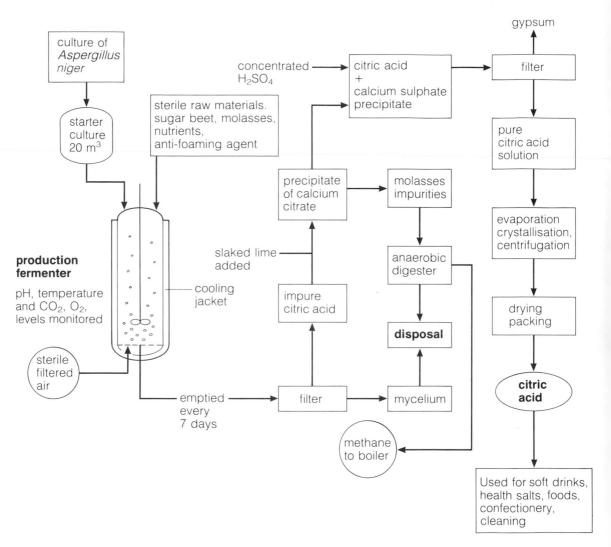

form a film on the shavings and air is circulated (fig 7.10). This is a much quicker method; vinegar is made in about four or five days.

Although these traditional methods are still popularly used, newer methods using **batch fermenters** are being developed. Ethanoic acid is also used in industry in the manufacture of plastics, rubber, acetate fibres, pharmaceuticals, dyes, insecticides and photographic materials. In Japan, it is used as a substrate for making amino acids. Ethanoic acid for commercial use is not made in the same way as vinegar. Two processes are being developed in the USA. Either cellulose may be converted to ethanoic acid by thermophilic bacteria, or hydrogen and carbon dioxide combined to give ethanoic acid by *Acetobacter woodii* and *Clostridium aceticum*.

Fig 7.7
The Krebs (tricarboxylic acid) cycle

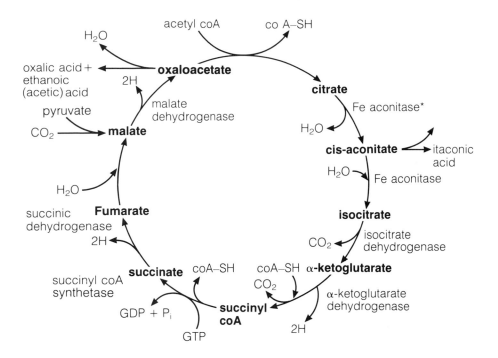

*This stage needs the cofactor iron (Fe). Therefore, to produce citric acid, steps are taken to block this reaction by removing iron ions from the fermentation mixture and prevent cis-aconitate forming. This greatly improves the yield of citric acid.

Fig 7.8
The Orleans process for vinegar manufacture

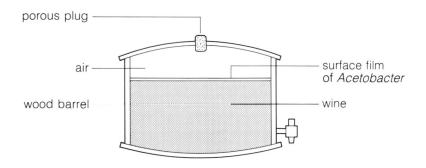

Fig 7.9
The conversion of ethanol to ethanoic acid

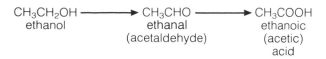

$$CH_3CH_2OH \longrightarrow CH_3CHO \longrightarrow CH_3COOH$$

ethanol   ethanal   ethanoic
(acetaldehyde)   (acetic)
acid

Fig 7.10
A quick vinegar generator

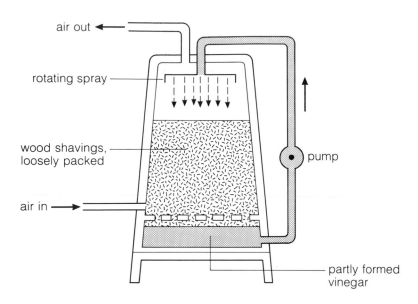

air out

rotating spray

wood shavings,
loosely packed

air in

pump

partly formed
vinegar

7.5.3 Itaconic acid

This is a metabolite of the Krebs cycle and is produced by *Aspergillus terreus*. It is useful in the plastics industry.

7.5.4 Lactic acid

This can be made from glucose using the bacterium *Lactobacillus delbrueckii*. It is used as an additive in such foods as soft margarine, carbonated drinks and confectionery. Lactic acid is also used as a preservative, acidifier, flavouring, or to enhance the anti-oxidant effects of other substances.

7.6 Amino acid production

Corynebacterium glutamicum and *Brevibacterium flavum* are bacteria which produce **glutamic acid** by fermentation, using glucose, ethanoic (acetic) acid, or *n*-paraffin fractions of petroleum as a substrate. This can be neutralised to produce **monosodium glutamate**, a common food additive used as a flavour enhancer which is popular in Chinese food. All monosodium glutamate used in food production is made by fermentation. Glutamic acid is synthesised in the bacterium from α-ketoglutarate, a Krebs cycle intermediate (fig 7.11). The glutamic acid pathway is encouraged by maintaining low levels of the enzyme α-ketoglutaratase. The bacterium is also deprived of the vitamin biotin, which makes the membrane more leaky, so that a greater yield of glutamate is secreted into the fermentation liquor. Alternatively,

Fig 7.11
The Krebs cycle in the
manufacture of glutamate

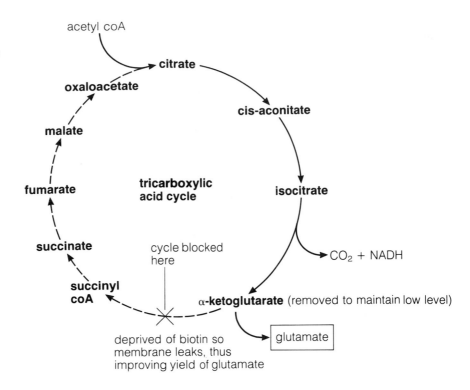

saturated fatty acids, detergent or penicillin may be added to make the membrane leaky.

Lysine and **methionine** are particularly important amino acids nutritionally, since most cereals are deficient in them. Most methionine is still made synthetically, but 80% of lysine is now made by bacterial fermentation. Organisms used are *Corynebacterium glutamicum* and *Escherichia coli*.

Glycine and **alanine** are used as flavouring agents. **Glutamine** and **histidine** are sometimes used to treat gastric ulcers, and **arginine** has been used for liver disorders. These can all be produced by fermentation. One advantage in making amino acids by fermentation is that of the two optical isomers, only one is biologically active. When amino acids are synthesised chemically, an even mixture of the two isomers is obtained, so only half the yield is useful. Fermentation will produce only the required isomer.

7.7 Single cell oil

Many microorganisms, especially filamentous fungi and yeasts, store large amounts of fats and oils. These can be grown on a variety of carbohydrate wastes. The process is not exploited industrially at present, but may have commercial applications as vegetable oils are

123

costly. However, the process needs further development and the efficiency is poor at present.

7.8 Biodegradable plastics

The bacterium *Alcaligenes eutrophus* can be grown on various waste carbohydrate substrates. It contains up to 80% by weight of polyhydroxybutyric acid, which can be processed to form a **biodegradable plastic**, marketed by ICI as **BIOPOL** (fig 7.12). Production occurs in a fermenter similar to that used for Pruteen. Currently, production costs are high, but as scale increases, costs will decrease. There is also the possibility that BIOPOL can be used to produce derivatives, such as drugs.

7.9 Steroids and hormones

There are several commercially important steroids, including cortisone, hydrocortisone, prednisone, dexamethasone, testosterone, oestradiol and spironolactone. Steroids are useful for:

(*a*) making contraceptives, such as oestradiol;
(*b*) treating hormone deficiencies;
(*c*) to treat skin diseases and allergies;
(*d*) to relieve pain and inflammation, for example the use of cortisone to treat rheumatoid arthritis.

Fig 7.12
Some BIOPOL plastic products

Chemical synthesis of sterols took 37 steps. It was then found that the fungus *Rhizopus arrhizus* could hydroxylate progesterone and produce cortisone in only 11 stages. Microorganisms have made steroid synthesis commercially viable, since the unit cost of production is now much lower.

Steroid synthesis starts with a source of sterols, which are complex alcohols. The usual sources of sterols are the waste from soybean oil production or the roots of the Mexican barbasco plant. The plant sterol in the substrate is converted to a steroid by mycobacteria, then another bacterium is used to modify it to the steroid required.

Peptide hormones can also be synthesised. The first peptide hormone made was **somatostatin**, a pituitary hormone. This inhibits the release of insulin and human growth hormone. It consists of only 14 amino acids, so genetic engineers were able to synthesise the correct DNA sequence for its synthesis. This DNA sequence was then inserted into the genome of *E. coli*. Later, human insulin and human growth hormone were developed.

7.10 Other pharmaceuticals

Interferons are antiviral chemicals, which also have some tumour-inhibiting properties. These used to be extracted from human fibroblast cells, but yields were minute. Recombinant DNA methods have now been used to synthesise interferons using a suitable bacterium, such as *Escherichia coli*. Some other anti-tumour pharmaceuticals are also made microbiologically. An example is **bleomycin**, a glycopeptide, made by *Streptomyces verticillus*. This drug has the ability to disrupt the DNA and RNA of tumour cells.

Question

Summary essay
(It may be necessary to use information from more than one chapter.)
Discuss the contribution of the use of microorganisms in helping the world population overcome the problem of diminishing natural resources.
You are free to write on any aspect of this topic but may wish to refer to food and fuel products and the recycling of scarce resources.

Total = 20 marks

JMB Option C July 1988

8 Enzyme technology

8.1 The production of enzymes

Although humans have used enzymes for thousands of years, without realising it, for making bread, beer, wine and cheese, the development of microbial enzyme technology is comparatively recent. Some of the industrial applications of enzymes are shown in table 8.1.

Table 8.1
Industrial applications of enzyme technology

Industry	Enzyme	How used	Difficulties
dairy industry	animal-derived rennin	cheese-making	rennin can only be taken from very young animals, as rennin production decreases with age
	microbial rennin	increasingly used as a substitute for animal rennin	
	lipases	ripening in blue cheeses by extracellular lipases from mould e.g. *Penicillium roquefortii*	
brewing industry	amylase and protease enzymes in barley grain	break down starch and proteins in barley grains to sugars and amino acids during malting and mashing stages	
	industrially produced amylase, protease, glucanase	used to break down proteins and polysaccharides in the malt by some breweries	
	betaglucanase	breaks down yeast cell walls so reduces cloudiness of beer	
	protease	breaks down yeast and improves clarity of beer	
	amyloglucosidase	breaks down sugars in production of low-calorie beer	
baking industry	proteases	lowers protein content of flour for biscuit production	
	alpha-amylase enzymes from yeast	break down starch in flour to sugars which can be used by yeast	
biological washing powders	mostly bacterial extracellular proteases	used for removing organic stains from washing	factory workers may become allergic; encapsulation of enzymes overcomes this
	amylases	mainly used in dishwasher detergent for removing starch residues	

126

Table 8.1 *(Cont.)*

Industry	Enzyme	How used	Difficulties
confectionery industry	alpha-amylases from *Bacillus subtilis*	to produce glucose syrup as a sweetener from waste potato starch; alpha amylases break down starch to dextrins	
	alpha-amylases from *Aspergillus niger*	hydrolyse dextrins to glucose. Enzymes are immobilised and production is continuous; enzymes function for 3 months and have replaced the older acid hydrolysis method	
agriculture and forestry	ligninases from *Sporotrichum pulverulentum*	most wood waste is not very useful as it contains lignocellulose which few organisms can utilise; ligninases make cellulose available for animal feed or as an industrial substrate	
textile industry	bacterial amylases	used to remove starch size from threads during weaving; these enzymes withstand working temperatures above boiling point	
leather industry	microbial trypsin	used to remove hair and excess tissue from hides and skin to make leather more pliable; trypsin used to be obtained from dung so microbial trypsin is preferred	
medical uses	trypsin	used to dissolve blood clots and to clean wounds	
	various	laboratory diagnosis	

Microorganisms have been found to be a valuable source of enzymes, for several reasons.

(a) Microorganisms produce a higher proportion of enzymes in relation to their body mass than most other organisms.

(b) Microorganisms are easy to manipulate genetically and can be subjected to gene transfer techniques.

(c) Product yield can be increased by means of strain selection, mutation, optimising growth conditions, and so on.

(d) Microorganisms are not influenced by season or climate and can be grown in suitable laboratories anywhere. This ensures independence of supply from world markets which may be subject to political influence.

(e) The enzymes of microorganisms show an enormous range of pH and temperature characteristics because microorganisms can occupy a great variety of habitats and extremes of conditions.

8.2 Industrial enzymes

Traditional enzyme technologies, such as beer-making and cheese-making, use the whole microorganism. However, recent developments have been to use **isolated enzymes**. This has several advantages.

(a) When whole organisms are used, some of the substrate is converted to microbial biomass. Using isolated enzymes, this does not occur so the chemical process is far less wasteful.

(b) Only one chemical process needs to be considered, so it is much easier to set up the optimum environmental conditions for that process.

(c) Only one enzyme is present, so there will not be wasteful side reactions.

(d) It is easier to isolate and purify the desired product.

Most industrial enzymes are **extracellular enzymes**, that is those which are secreted by the microorganism into its substrate. These enzymes can easily be extracted from the fermentation liquor. If intracellular enzymes are required, recovery is more complex, since the cells must first be disrupted and then the desired enzyme extracted from a mixture of a great many enzymes.

8.3 The industrial production of enzymes

Industrial microbiologists have many factors to consider when selecting microorganisms for enzyme production, as shown in fig 8.1. When the

Fig 8.1
Factors to consider when selecting microorganisms for enzyme production

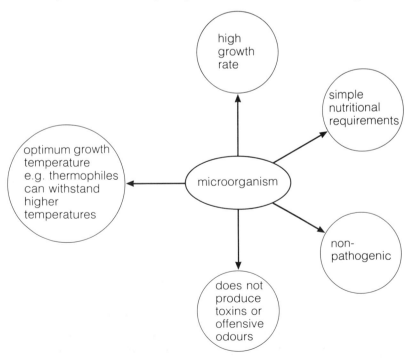

organism has been selected, genetic engineering may be used to produce a strain which gives a high enzyme yield with other useful properties, such as stability. Any less favourable characteristics, such as odour, can be selected against.

Substrates for industrial enzyme technology should be cheap, plentiful, and nutritionally safe. Commonly used substrates include whey, molasses, and waste starch from flour milling.

Enzymes are usually produced by **batch** fermentation, although it is sometimes found that better yields are obtained if different substances are added at various times during the fermentation. This is called a **fed-batch** process. There are several stages involved in the extraction of extracellular enzymes from the fermentation liquor:

(a) filtering off the microorganism;
(b) concentrating the enzyme by reducing the water content of the liquor; this is often done by **reverse osmosis**;
(c) removal of any contaminating microorganisms by filtration and addition of anti-bacterial agents to prevent contamination;
(d) quality control, to ensure uniformity of the product;
(e) packaging.

Fig 8.2
Extraction of extracellular enzymes

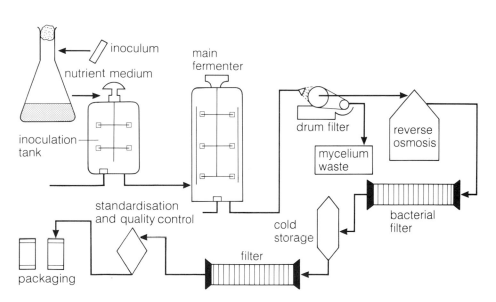

8.4 Immobilised enzymes

Recently, methods have been developed whereby enzymes are attached to insoluble materials which act as a support for the enzyme. The enzymes can then be held in place during the reaction, removed afterwards and used again. This is called **immobilisation** of the enzyme. Sometimes entire microbial cells are immobilised.

There are various methods for enzyme immobilisation (fig 8.3).
Enzymes can be **adsorbed** onto an insoluble matrix, such as collagen;
held inside a gel, such as silica gel; held within a semi-permeable
membrane; or trapped in a microcapsule, such as polyacrylamide beads.
These processes all involve a **physical** bonding of the enzyme. They are
not easy to carry out and tend to result in low enzyme activity.

Fig 8.3
The immobilisation of
enzymes

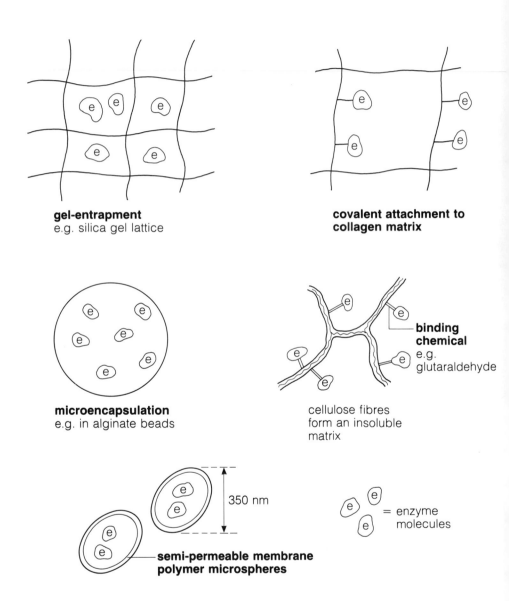

gel-entrapment
e.g. silica gel lattice

**covalent attachment to
collagen matrix**

microencapsulation
e.g. in alginate beads

**binding
chemical**
e.g.
glutaraldehyde

cellulose fibres
form an insoluble
matrix

350 nm

**semi-permeable membrane
polymer microspheres**

= enzyme
molecules

Enzymes can also be **chemically** bonded to the support medium.
Since the enzymes are covalently bonded, enzyme activity is high,
although preparing enzymes in this way is difficult.

8.4.1 Immobilised whole cells

Immobilised whole cells are useful because it is not necessary to start with a pure enzyme. Therefore, this is cheaper and quicker. Whole cells are immobilised in the same way as purified enzymes. Immobilised whole cells are being used increasingly for complex fermentations, such as waste treatment, nitrogen fixation, synthesis of steroids, semi-synthetic antibiotics and other medical products.

8.4.2 Advantages of using immobilised enzymes

(a) Enzymes can be recovered and used over and over again, which is particularly useful when the enzyme is expensive or difficult to produce.

(b) Because the enzyme is held in a matrix, the product will not be contaminated by the enzyme.

(c) The matrix protects the enzyme so that it is more stable at extremes of temperature and pH.

(d) The above properties make immobilised enzymes very suitable for continuous fermentations.

(e) Immobilised whole cells mean that several enzymes can participate in the process simultaneously.

Immobilised enzyme technology is still developing rapidly and there are likely to be many new applications for immobilised enzymes in industry, medicine and waste disposal.

8.5 Abzymes

Biotechnologists are no longer restricted to using those enzymes found in living organisms. They are now able to manufacture enzymes to catalyse a whole range of reactions for which there are no natural enzymes. Enzymes catalyse reactions because they increase the chances of molecules colliding with each other and reacting. Enzymes are large molecules which can fit closely with the substrate in a 'lock and key' fashion, making it easier for chemical bonds to be made or broken. The energy required for a chemical reaction to occur is called **activation energy**. Enzymes reduce the activation energy required for the reaction to take place; without enzymes, most metabolic reactions would otherwise need enormous levels of heat and even pressure, which would not be possible in a living system. Enzymes are highly specific, and the position on the enzyme where the substrate fits is called the **active site** (fig 8.4).

Antibody molecules, like enzymes, are large proteins. Biotechnologists are able to make antibodies which fit the substrate closely, and can therefore act in a similar way to enzymes. Firstly, substrate molecules are injected into a mouse. The mouse mounts an immune response,

Fig 8.4
The induced-fit model of enzyme action

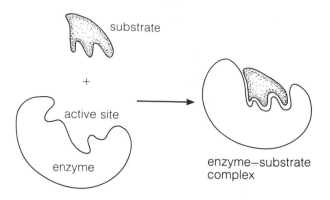

producing antibodies specific to that substrate (see section 11.7.1). Using monoclonal antibody cloning techniques (see section 4.1.4), large amounts of these so-called **abzymes** can be manufactured to order.

At present, more than 20 functional abzymes have been made, but research is only in its infancy. Abzymes are likely to be useful as medical drugs, for example for dissolving blood clots, attacking cancerous growths, removing scar tissue or destroying viruses. Industrially, they could be used to produce a range of pharmaceuticals and chemicals under normal conditions, considerably reducing energy costs in industry. Conventional industrial catalysts, by contrast, usually require high temperatures and pressures.

Questions

1 Why are microorganisms particularly suitable as a source material for enzyme production?

2 Construct a table, using the headings below, including as many examples as possible.

   Substrate
   Microorganism
   Enzyme
   Use

3 Outline the main steps in the industrial preparation of a *named* enzyme.

4 What advantages are there in using immobilised enzymes? Give two examples of their use.

5 Increasingly, immobilised *whole* microbial cells are being used as biocatalysts. Why is this an important production process?

6 Construct a flow chart to summarise the production of abzymes. What potential uses for them can you foresee?

9 Microbial degradation

9.1 Biodegradation and biodeterioration

Microorganisms are so diverse that most substrates can be used as a carbon or energy source by at least one species. The recycling of materials by microorganisms is a natural process occurring in ecosystems, whereby dead plants, animals and their wastes are broken down. Humans have exploited this in the treatment of waste material, such as the production of methane from municipal waste in landfill sites (see section 6.4). Microorganisms are also used in the treatment of contaminated water. The use of microorganisms to break down substances is usually called **biodegradation**. However, microorganisms often break down substances in a way that is not beneficial to humans, for example in causing food spoilage. This activity is generally called **biodeterioration.**

9.2 Sewage

Sewage is composed of the following

(a) **Human waste** made up of human excreta mixed with waste household water. This contains many microorganisms including potential pathogens. A major pollutant from waste household water is detergent, which causes persistent foam and has high levels of phosphates.

(b) **Industrial wastes** which are variable in nature, depending on the industry. Some can be very toxic to microorganisms and must undergo pretreatment so that they do not kill or inhibit the microorganisms which degrade the sewage. Many industries are required to treat their own sewage, either wholly or partially.

(c) **Road drainage** consists of rain water together with grit and other debris which enters the sewers from roadside gutters.

9.3 Sewage treatment

Sewage is treated in two or three stages as follows.

Primary treatment. Materials which will settle out are removed. The sedimented solids pass on to a digester for further treatment, while the liquid (effluent) continues into the secondary treatment stage (fig 9.1).

Secondary treatment. Aerobic microorganisms are used to break

133

down most of the organic matter in the effluent. Any sludge produced in this process is passed on to anaerobic digesters.

Tertiary treatment This involves chemical and biological treatment which renders the sewage effluent fit for drinking. However, this is a very expensive treatment, so it is only carried out when absolutely necessary.

There are two main reasons for treating sewage. Firstly, sewage can contain pathogens which cause diseases, such as *Salmonella typhi* (typhoid), pathogenic *Escherichia coli* (gastroenteritis) and *Ascaris lumbricoides* (roundworm). Secondly, by treating sewage, pollution of the environment can be avoided.

9.4   Primary treatment

Sewage is passed through a series of screens to remove large objects, such as boxes and rags, then through a finer screen to remove grit, which could otherwise harm the machinery. The sewage then passes

Fig 9.1
A conventional sewage treatment works

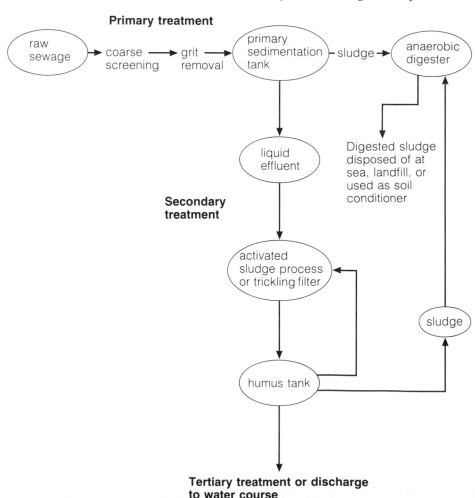

into **sedimentation tanks**. The flow-rate is greatly reduced here, so large organic particles sediment out to form a sludge. The sludge is taken off for anaerobic digestion. The supernatant liquid, or effluent, passes on to the next stage for secondary treatment.

9.5 Secondary treatment

The modern method, used in large sewage works, is the **activated sludge process**. The organic matter in the sewage is used as a nutrient medium for the growth of a great variety of aerobic microorganisms in large tanks (fig 9.2). Oxygen levels are kept at a very high level by constantly aerating the sewage, either by bubbling air through or by rapidly rotating paddles.

The activated sludge tanks contain a complex mixture of microorganisms. Bacteria and fungi tend to break down the sewage into simpler substances. There are many other organisms, such as ciliated protozoa, nematode worms and rotifers present in the sludge. These feed off the organic matter in the sludge and digest it to simpler compounds. Among the bacteria found in the activated sludge process are *Brevibacterium*, *Caulobacter*, *Cytophaga*, *Flavobacterium*, *Hyphomicrobium* and *Sphaerotilus*.

Fig 9.2
Sewage treatment: the activated sludge process

Organic compounds containing sulphur are broken down by organisms, such as *Proteus*, to form hydrogen sulphide, which *Thiobacillus* converts to sulphates. *Bacillus* releases ammonia from organic nitrogen sources, such as proteins, which is converted to nitrites (NO_2^-(III)) by *Nitrosomonas* and thence to nitrates (NO_3^-(V)) by *Nitrobacter*. *Thiobacillus* converts organic phosphorus sources to phosphates. Organisms such as *Aeromonas*, *Alcaligenes* and *Pseudomonas* release carbon dioxide and water from a variety of organic substances in the sewage.

At the end of this process, much of the organic matter has been removed, but a sludge consisting of surplus microorganisms is produced. Some of this sludge is recycled to act as an inoculum for the next batch of effluent, while the rest is anaerobically digested.

An older method for secondary treatment, still used in smaller sewage works, is the **trickling filter** or **sprinkler bed** (fig 9.3). The filter is made of a layer of porous clinker or plastic piping, about 2 m deep. A film of slime-forming bacteria and fungi grows over the surface of the filter bed, together with small invertebrates such as worms, insect larvae and rotifers.

Fig 9.3
A simplified diagram of a section through a trickling filter

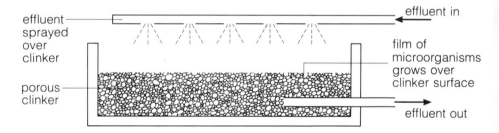

The breakdown of organic matter occurs in a similar manner to that described for activated sludge. The slime-forming bacteria and fungi carry out most of the initial degradation, with ciliated protozoa feeding off them. This is vital as over-growth of the film can block the filter and reduce oxygen levels. Invertebrates such as worms and rotifers feed off the protozoa.

After passing through the activated sludge process or the trickling filter, the effluent passes into a humus tank which removes small organic particles which may still remain, together with microbial biomass which has not settled out. Floc-forming bacteria such as *Zoogloea ramigera* secrete a polysaccharide which helps to bind these particles into a larger floc. This is then passed to the anaerobic digesters. The effluent from the humus tank is usually discharged into the water course. However, in highly populated areas where the water course is used to supply drinking water, tertiary treatment may be necessary.

9.6 Anaerobic digestion

Methane is only produced in strictly anaerobic conditions. The pH must be kept between 6 and 8 and the temperature must not fall below 15 °C. The methane gas produced is used to heat up the digester. Sometimes it is used to generate electricity which can be used to power the sewage plant or be fed into the National Grid.

Digested sludge can be dried. Often it is dumped at sea, or used as landfill to produce methane as a cheap fuel for housing estates (section 6.4). Sludge may be applied to agricultural land as a 'soil conditioner'. It improves the water-retaining quality of the soil and supplies certain mineral salts, such as phosphates and nitrates.

9.7 Other methods of sewage treatment

Septic tanks and pit latrines   These are small, local ways of dealing with sewage. The microorganisms naturally present in the sewage are used to break down the organic matter. In the case of pit latrines, the environment is able to cope with the comparatively small amount of effluent. In septic tanks, the volume and strength of the sewage is greatly reduced by microbial action. Remaining sludge is emptied by a tanker at intervals.

Sewage lagoons   This method is used in the Mediterranean and tropics. A series of lagoon lakes is constructed with sewage entering at one end and effluent coming out at the other end. Photosynthetic algae aerate the sewage, with anaerobic digestion occurring in the muddy substrate.

A variation on this idea is the **stabilisation pond**. A range of large green plants flourish in the organic matter, while microorganisms grow on their roots. These systems give an effluent with lower numbers of microorganisms and fewer pathogens; this is highly desirable in warm countries. It is also seasonal. Summer temperatures increase the rate of sewage breakdown, thereby coping with the increased sewage volume in the summer as a result of tourism.

9.8 Tests of effluent quality

There are three main criteria for judging effluent quality.

(1) **Suspended solids (SS)**
   This measures the suspended particles which are retained by a glass fibre filter. Units used are mg solid/dm³ dry mass. This gives an indication of light penetration. If the river water is clear, green plants will be able to photosynthesise and release oxygen. Suspended solids will prevent light reaching the plants.

137

(2) **Faecal coliforms (FCs)**

This is determined by means of the **presumptive coliform test**. This gives an indication of the bacteriological quality of the effluent. Coliforms are motile, Gram negative bacteria, present in large numbers in excreta. They should die during the sewage treatment process. Coliforms are relatively safe but, as they have come from the same source as potential pathogens, they are considered to be good indicator organisms to show the likelihood of pathogens being present. In good quality effluent, FCs should be below 100 per cm^3.

(3) **Biochemical oxygen demand (BOD)**

This is determined by means of the **five-day BOD test**. Samples of effluent are collected and diluted with well-oxygenated water. The proportion of volume of effluent to total volume used in the test is chosen by experience, but the aim is to use up not more than 50% of the dissolved oxygen in the container after five days. The initial concentration of dissolved oxygen is measured in each sample. The samples are then stored at 20 °C in dark containers to prevent photosynthesis from producing any oxygen. After five days, the oxygen is again measured and the difference between the two readings indicates the demand that effluent would have on the dissolved oxygen of a river or lake. Weak sewage will have a BOD below 200 mg dm^{-3}, whereas very strong sewage will have a BOD value above 500 mg dm^{-3}.

Other tests of water quality may also be carried out.

Questions

1 What is the nature of domestic sewage? What might be found in industrial wastes?

2 What toxins may be present in industrial waste? How might these affect sewage treatment?

3 How do you think modern 'convenience products', such as prepared foods, detergents and insecticides, may have affected the problems of waste treatment?

4 Suppose you own 20 ha of seaside land that you want to develop into holiday chalets. The property is in a conservation area, so you are required to provide safe and effective sewerage. Furthermore, the site is one of outstanding natural beauty, so you must take this into consideration. What are the advantages and disadvantages of each of the following:

(a) individual septic tanks for each building;
(b) trickling filter;
(c) sewage lagoon system.

Would your answers be different if the seaside development was on the Mediterranean coast?

5 Plan a system for sewage disposal that could be used in a space station.

6 Fig 9.4 shows the effect on a river of discharging sewage effluent into it.

Fig 9.4
The effect of discharging sewage effluent into a river

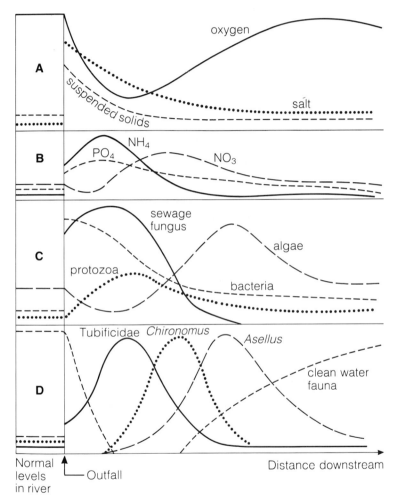

(a) Looking at graph A, explain the increase in suspended solids following the addition of sewage effluent and the fall in oxygen levels.

(b) Looking at graph C, why are there fewer algae in the water after the effluent has been added?

(c) There is an increase in phosphates after the effluent has been added. Where do you think these phosphates have come from?

(d) Graph B shows a peak in ammonium levels after the outfall, followed by a peak in nitrate levels. What can you deduce from this about the chemical conversions taking place. What are the sources of ammonium and nitrates?

(e) Graph D shows the populations of 'sensitive small animals'. To what, do you think, are these animals sensitive?

(f) Looking at all the graphs together and from what you have read of effluent laboratory tests, discuss the advantages and disadvantages of using biological methods of testing water quality.

7 Construct a table to show some of the microorganisms involved in sewage treatment and their precise role.

9.9 Water supply

There are four main sources for drinking water: underground sources, such as wells and boreholes, springs, rivers and rainwater which has run off hills and mountains and is stored in reservoirs. Underground water from a **deep well** is usually comparatively clean as it has been filtered by layers of underground rock. Shallow wells are often polluted by sewage or field drainage, so are not suitable for drinking water supply. **Spring water** is usually unpolluted and does not need treatment, although it may be chlorinated as a safeguard. Pure water does not contain enough nutrients to support the growth of many microorganisms. Reservoir water is often quite pure, but it does contain some plant material, such as microscopic algae. **Reservoirs** are ideal for the storage of drinking water supplies. Their large surface area allows the Sun's ultraviolet rays to penetrate, reducing bacterial numbers. Photosynthetic plants aerate the water and fish consume microorganisms. Recreation is strictly controlled to prevent pollution. **Rivers**, likewise, contain organic material, but are suitable sources of drinking water provided they do not receive field drainage or sewage.

9.9.1 Water treatment

Fig 9.5 shows the treatment of drinking water at a typical treatment works.

Huntington Water Treatment Works at Chester has an interesting biological screening process for its incoming water supply. Water from the River Dee is passed through tanks containing trout, which can only tolerate very clean river water. Sensors linked to a computer monitor the trouts' gill movements. Should a pollutant be present in the water, the fish will react by increasing their gill movements. The computer will then alert personnel and the water supply can be cut off until the pollutant is no longer present. This comparatively simple system is much more successful than chemical analysis, since the fish will react to a much wider range of chemicals than standard laboratory tests.

Fig 9.5
Summary of treatment of
water at typical water
treatment works

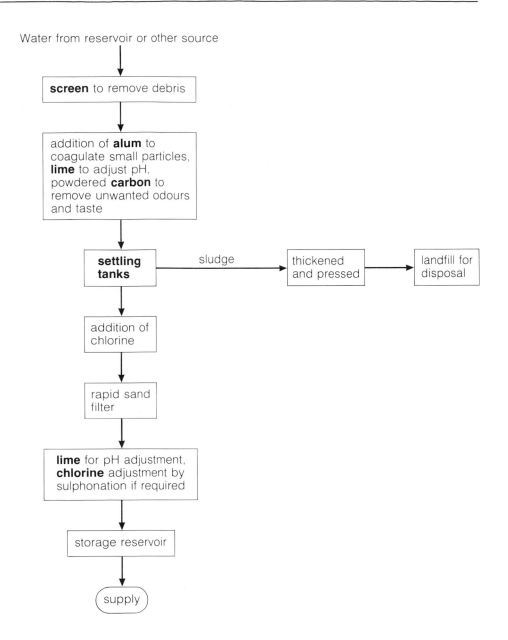

The incoming water passes through screens to remove debris, such as plastic bottles, leaves and twigs. **Activated carbon** may be added in controlled amounts to remove any unpleasant smell or taste, and **lime** is used to adjust the pH to slightly alkaline. This prevents excessive corrosion in pipes and lead being dissolved out of lead pipes in older plumbing systems. **Aluminium sulphate** (alum) is added which flocculates small particles. The water is run into settling tanks, where these flocculated particles settle out to form a sludge. The sludge is thickened and pressed into cakes, which are sent to landfill sites for disposal.

The water is now led out of the settling tanks, and is usually chlorinated at this stage. **Chlorine** gas or chlorine dioxide is added to the water in carefully controlled amounts. This kills bacteria in the water.

The water then enters **rapid sand filters** which are beds of sand built over a layer of pebbles and grit. The water filters through the sand and small particles are filtered out. The filter is cleaned periodically by back-washing. An older method is the slow sand filter. Here, the filter has the same construction, except that a film of protozoa and other microorganisms forms on the sand, which feed on bacteria present in the water.

After passing through the sand filters, the chlorine levels are adjusted. It may be necessary to add more chlorine, or remove any excess by reacting it with sulphur dioxide, a process called **sulphonation**. A final pH adjustment may also be necessary. The water is then stored in large storage reservoirs before being pumped into the supply system.

Questions

1   Compare the different sources of drinking water. Which sources are best, and why?

2   Aluminium sulphate, lime, carbon and chlorine are all added to drinking water. Explain the role of each.

3   Water from lakes and rivers is not always unsafe for drinking. Under what circumstances would you consider such water fit to drink?

4   'The treatment of sewage is primarily a biological process, whereas the treatment of drinking water is essentially chemical.' How far would you agree with this statement? Why are the two processes different?

5   Explain the advantages of a biological monitoring system for water supply, such as that used at Chester. Suppose the fish alarm was activated, what steps could be taken to trace and identify the pollutant as quickly as possible?

9.10   The microbial breakdown of oil and petroleum products

There are microorganisms which can utilise virtually any carbon source, and oil and petroleum are no exception. The microorganisms involved require water and oxygen, so this degradation occurs at the oil/water interface. Basically, the hydrocarbons are degraded to alcohols, then aldehydes and finally fatty acids. There are at least 20 different kinds of bacteria involved in this process, since oil is a complex mixture of different substrates.

It has been found that leaving oil spills to be degraded by these bacteria generally causes less environmental damage than dispersing the oil with detergents. However, rather than relying on a mixture of bacteria, it is now possible to use genetically engineered 'superbugs'. Various genes coding for oil-splitting enzymes can be inserted into plasmids, which are then introduced into the bacterium *Pseudomonas*. These bacteria have been used successfully to clean up small oil spills but they are still too slow-acting to deal with large oil spills such as are found after major accidents involving oil supertankers.

Oil-degrading bacteria can become a nuisance under some circumstances. *Desulphovibrio* sp. convert sulphates in jet engine fuel to soluble sulphides, which are corrosive. Hydrogen sulphide is also produced, which is explosive. *Cladosporium resinae* is a fungus that uses the water which condenses out in the fuel tank to degrade the fuel. The fungus binds dirt and debris to form a sludge which can block filters and pipes.

Questions

1 It has been stated that at least 20 different kinds of bacteria can degrade oil, yet natural oil deposits have not degraded, despite being several million years old. Why?

2 Explain why allowing minor oil spills to be degraded by microorganisms is considered to be less damaging to the environment than using detergents.

3 Suggest ways in which airlines could reduce the chance of microbial degradation of jet engine fuel.

9.11 Food spoilage

Shops and supermarkets today provide a tremendous range of fresh and preserved foods. In recent times, many developments in food processing and packaging have taken place. Air and sea freight ensure a worldwide range of foods. However, the industry faces constant problems in avoiding spoilage of these products. There is a constant battle against microorganisms which are the major cause of food spoilage. Despite major efforts to ensure high standards, the incidence of food poisoning in Britain is increasing. Recent outbreaks of salmonellosis, listeriosis and botulism have heightened the consumer's awareness of the need for food hygiene.

Food spoilage ranges from an obvious growth of mould or pigmented bacteria, or a slight change in colour, texture or smell, to hardly noticeable changes, such as food poisoning due to bacterial toxins.

Most spoilage involves the breakdown of proteins, fats and carbohydrates. Proteins are hydrolysed to amino acids, amines, ammonia and hydrogen sulphide. Fats are hydrolysed to fatty acids and glycerol, while carbohydrates are fermented into acids, alcohols and gases.

It can be seen that food spoilage is more likely when the food is rich in nutrients, oxygen and water are present and temperature and pH conditions are suitable. These factors are taken into account when preserving food.

Microorganisms cause the deterioration of food because they produce enzymes, mostly extracellularly. These degrade the food rapidly, given the right conditions.

9.11.1 Fruit and vegetables

It is difficult for microorganisms to enter undamaged fruit and vegetables but, when the surface is damaged, spoilage organisms can quickly become established. **Bacterial soft rot** is caused by *Pseudomonas*. These secrete pectinases which soften the tissues of vegetables such as carrots, celery, and potatoes. Various **moulds** affect fruit and vegetables too; for example, grey mould rot on soft fruit such as strawberries, caused by the fungus *Botrytis*; blue mould rot on oranges caused by the fungus *Penicillium*; and citrus soft rot on citrus fruits caused by *Alternaria*.

Spoilage may be prevented by avoiding injury to the fruit when it is handled or transported, washing in chlorinated water, spraying with antimicrobial substances and storing at low temperatures or in anaerobic conditions.

9.11.2 Cereals

Unless grain is stored in a dry atmosphere, moulds such as *Penicillium* and *Aspergillus* may grow. In very damp conditions, yeasts, coliform and lactic acid bacteria grow. A further danger is that some fungi can produce **mycotoxins** which can poison the person who ingests them. Some species of *Aspergillus* and *Penicillium* can grow on damp nuts and grain, producing aflatoxin, and the toxin is not destroyed by cooking.

9.11.3 Bread

Baking destroys any microorganisms present in the dough, but spores may survive. Slicing and wrapping also provide an opportunity for spoilage organisms to enter. Bread can be spoiled by moulds, such as *Penicillium* and *Aspergillus*. 'Ropiness' is a condition where the dough becomes sticky because of the polysaccharide capsules of *Bacillus subtilis* or *B. licheniformis*. Bakeries aim to prevent spoilage by filtering the air to remove spores, ultraviolet irradiation of the atmosphere, cooling loaves rapidly to avoid condensation, sterilising slicing equipment and adding fungal inhibitors to the dough.

9.11.4 Meat

Surface slime can be caused by *Pseudomonas*, *Achromobacter*, *Streptococcus* and *Bacillus*. Meat can become discoloured through the action of bacteria such as *Serratia marcescens* which causes red spots, or *Flavobacterium* which produces a yellow colour. Anaerobic bacteria such as *Clostridium* sp. bring about putrefaction, in which evil-smelling compounds are produced. Fish is more susceptible to spoilage, because of contamination from gut microorganisms. For example, *Pseudomonas*, *Achromobacter* and *Flavobacterium* produce offensive odours.

Spoilage of meat and fish can be avoided by deep freezing or refrigeration, gutting fish as soon as possible after catching, and strict hygiene such as sterilising knives and chopping boards in abbatoirs and shops.

9.11.5 Tinned foods

The canning process involves high temperatures and sealed containers, so canned food should be sterile. However, spoilage does occur when the canning process is faulty in some way, though this is quite rare. There was an outbreak of botulism in Birmingham in the 1970s, when tinned salmon had been cooled in contaminated water and *Clostridium botulinum* entered the tins through a faulty seal. This organism grows in anaerobic conditions and produces a powerful toxin which does not alter the taste of the food. In 1989, this organism contaminated tins of hazelnut puree which were used to flavour yogurt. This resulted in one death and several people were seriously ill.

9.11.6 Milk and dairy products

Although fresh milk from healthy cows is usually sterile, it can easily become contaminated with microorganisms from the cow, such as *Escherichia coli*, *Streptococcus lactis* and *Lactobacillus*. Streptococci and lactobacilli ferment milk sugars into acids, which coagulate the milk producing curds. This process is the basis of cheese and yogurt production.

Pseudomonas, *Proteus* and *Bacillus* can turn butter rancid, by producing lipases which break down butter fat.

Spoilage of dairy products can be prevented by washing cows' udders before milking, and sterilising milking equipment. Bulk milk tanks on the farm ensure rapid cooling. Pasteurisation kills many bacteria in milk, and refrigeration slows down the growth of the remaining bacteria.

Questions

1 You are the Provisions Buyer for a large chain of supermarkets. Write guidelines for issue to each department in the store, to ensure that food reaches the customer in excellent condition.

2 Explain the following observations.

   (*a*) Fungi tend to cause surface spoilage of food.
   (*b*) Milk, meat and fish are very easily spoiled by microorganisms.
   (*c*) Fungi are the main spoilage organisms of fruit and vegetables, whereas bacteria are the main spoilage organisms of meat, fish and milk.
   (*d*) Spore-forming bacteria are more of a problem in food preservation than non-spore-formers.

3 You know that fungi produce extracellular enzymes and are mostly aerobic organisms. Relate this to the kinds of food spoilage they cause.

4 Why do bacteria rarely cause spoilage of undamaged fruit and vegetables?

5 Food spoilage can be very noticeable or it may be completely unapparent. Give examples of **named** organisms to illustrate these extremes.

9.12 Food preservation

Table 9.1 shows a number of methods used to preserve food.

Table 9.1 Methods of food preservation

Method	How it works
Deep freezing	Food is stored at approximately $-18\,°C$. At this temperature microorganisms are unable to grow. However, they are still present, so food should be consumed soon after it is thawed. It is also important that food, once thawed, is not re-frozen.
Refrigeration	Food is stored at about $4\,°C$. At this temperature the growth of most microorganisms is slowed down, so the food will last longer.
Curing	Food is hung over charcoal fires. The methanal (formaldehyde) in the smoke kills most bacteria.
Vacuum packing	Food is placed in a container, then all the air is sucked out using a vacuum pump. The container is then sealed completely. Most microorganisms are unable to survive without oxygen so the food will last much longer.
Sterilisation	Food is exposed to very high temperatures (boiling point or above) which kill microorganisms. Provided that the food is sealed to exclude any further contamination, it will last for a considerable time. Milk is often sterilised, and the UHT (ultra-heat treatment) method is generally preferred. In this method, the milk is heated to a temperature above boiling point for a brief time, since this has a lesser effect on taste than conventional sterilisation.

Table 9.1 *(Cont.)*

Method	How it works
Pasteurisation	This is a process which kills pathogenic bacteria, and is widely used for dairy products such as milk. There are two processes. The high temperature, short time (HTST) method involves heating the food to 72 °C for 15 seconds then rapidly cooling to about 10 °C. The second method involves heating the food to 63–6 °C for 30 minutes, followed by rapid cooling to 10 °C. As this treatment will only kill some bacteria, mainly any pathogens, the food still needs careful storage.
Bottling	Food is sealed in airtight jars and then boiled. The high temperature and pressure kills any microorganisms present.
Canning	The food is heated strongly to expel air from the can, then the can is sealed. This method is similar to bottling; microorganisms are killed by the high temperature and pressure.
Pickling	The food is soaked in a strong salt solution, then placed in vinegar. The acid conditions provided by the vinegar prevent the growth of most microorganisms.
Lowering the solute potential of food	The usual method is salting, for meat and fish products, or adding large quantities of sugar, as in candied fruits or jam. If the food has a lower (i.e. more negative) water potential than the microorganisms' cells, then the microorganisms in the food will lose water by osmosis and be unable to grow.
Drying	Water is removed from the food and, without it, microorganisms are unable to grow. The food will remain preserved as long as it stays dry. However, bacteria may still be present, and will start to grow if the food becomes damp. Freeze-drying is a variant of this; water is removed from the food in a dessicator at a very low temperature.
Irradiation	This is a method of food preservation which is likely to become increasingly important. It can be used to increase the shelf-life of fruit and vegetables, particularly soft fruit like strawberries. Short-wave ionising radiation from electrons, X- or gamma-rays is administered to the food in strict doses. Different doses are needed for different purposes; parasites are destroyed by very low levels of radiation, whereas higher doses are needed to destroy bacteria and fungi.

Questions

1 Find examples of food preserved by each of the methods given in table 9.1.

2 Looking at table 9.1, make a list of the methods which destroy microorganisms in food, and then make a separate list of those methods which do not destroy the microorganisms but simply inhibit their growth.

3 What are the advantages and disadvantages of each method? Why are so many different ways of preserving food necessary?

4 Why is it considered dangerous to thaw frozen meat and then refreeze it?

147

5   You are the quality assurance manager for a firm importing bananas into Britain. You are asked to prepare a report, advising on precautions which should be taken at each stage to ensure that as little fruit as possible is damaged. Outline the main recommendations of your report.

6   *Essay* (you will need to use information from other chapters).
    Write an account of the role of microorganisms in the treatment of domestic and industrial waste. You may wish to include reference to sewage treatment, microbial metal leaching of low-level mine waste and degradation of plastics and oils.

                                                                    20 marks

JMB Option C June 1989

10 Some human diseases

10.1 Rabies

Rabies is the most lethal of all virus diseases, with the possible exception of the human immunodeficiency virus (HIV) (section 10.3). Until very recently there were hardly any recorded examples of recovery from rabies once the clinical symptoms appeared. The name originates from the Latin *rabidus* for madness and the disease turns normally quiet animals into vicious biting beasts. Rabies is usually transmitted to humans by the bite of a rabid cat or dog. There is a long incubation period as the virus spreads along nerves from the site of the wound to the central nervous system (CNS).

10.1.1 *The organism*

The virus particle is a bullet-shaped cylinder with one rounded and one flat end (fig 10.1). It is protected by an outer envelope bearing short knob-like spikes of **glycoprotein**. These are **haemagglutinin** and help the virus to attach to specific receptors in the host cell membranes. Beneath the envelope is an inner layer of matrix protein which encloses the helical nucleocapsid of single-stranded RNA. The virus also carries the enzyme RNA polymerase which is required during replication.

    The infectivity of the rabies virus is destroyed by lipid solvents which damage the envelope. The virus also deteriorates on drying. This fact was first used by Pasteur, who developed an attenuated (weakened) strain, for use as a vaccine to protect against rabies infection.

Fig 10.1
The structure of the rabies virus (based on electron micrographs)

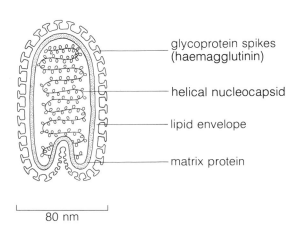

glycoprotein spikes (haemagglutinin)

helical nucleocapsid

lipid envelope

matrix protein

80 nm

10.1.2 *Epidemiology and transmission*

Rabies is a **zoonosis**, a disease of warm-blooded animals, and all mammals are therefore susceptible. Infection is via the bite of a rabid animal and the virus is in the saliva. The main source of human infection is domestic animals. The disease is rare in Europe, the USA and Australia because of control measures over domestic pets. Vaccination can prevent the disease from developing after infection.

The World Health Organisation records about 1000 human rabies fatalities every year. In the United Kingdom there have been only eight cases of human rabies since 1946, all fatal and all acquired abroad. In the USA, cattle are most commonly affected. Islands such as Britain, Australia and New Zealand have strict quarantine laws. Britain, for example, has a compulsory six months quarantine on all imported cats and dogs and compulsory vaccination of imported animals. Coupled with heavy fines for anyone caught evading the quarantine laws, the spread of rabies to Britain has so far been avoided. Rabies is endemic in wild carnivores in the rest of Europe and there is concern about the disease spreading to Britain once the Channel Tunnel is completed. At present, rabies is reaching epidemic proportions in France, and has spread to many of the channel ports. There is an extensive campaign to help control the disease by dropping food pellets baited with the rabies vaccine in an attempt to vaccinate wild hosts such as foxes and feral cats.

In the USA, coyotes, skunks, foxes, raccoons and wolves are common sources of infection for domestic animals. In South America, vampire bats are an important source. The virus seems to be persistent and apparently does not affect the bats. They suck the blood of cattle causing widespread fatal infection. In South America, there have been several recorded cases of humans becoming infected with rabies, by droplet infection from bats, in poorly ventilated caves.

10.1.3 *The disease*

Following a bite by an infected animal, the virus is deposited in the wound and here it multiplies for a few days. It then migrates along the axons of the nerves to the CNS. It travels at a rate of 42 mm per day and this accounts for the long incubation period. Bites on the head and face are the shortest distance from the brain and it may be as little as 10 days before the disease symptoms start to appear. The average incubation period in humans is 40 days, but it has been known to be as long as two years. This means that artificial immunisation can take place after infection and that the quarantine period for imported animals must be several months.

Once the virus reaches the brain, the neurons are destroyed. This is known as **encephalitis**. The symptoms of rabies are, at first, a general feeling of being unwell, with headaches and restlessness. These are followed by a high fever, convulsions and delirium (uncontrolled nervousness). The most characteristic symptom is where the muscles around the throat go into spasms whenever swallowing is attempted. This is known as **hydrophobia** and it becomes impossible to drink. Even the sight of water is enough to cause the contractions. The virus is now present in the saliva and extreme caution must be taken by medical staff to avoid becoming infected themselves.

Once the clinical symptoms have developed, death is usually inevitable within 3–10 days. This is due to paralysis and asphyxia. There have been some recent developments in sedation and the use of life-support systems which have allowed patients to survive this stage and show recovery; however this is very rare.

10.1.4   Treatment

Provided that treatment is started immediately after a bite by a suspected rabid animal, clinical rabies can be prevented. The wound is washed thoroughly and anti-rabies serum (antiserum) is applied to it. Next, an injection of antiserum is given. This is **passive immunisation** since the antiserum contains rabies antibodies which will give protection until the patient can produce his own antibodies. Finally, a course of vaccine is started and eventually there should be enough antibody, produced by the patient's own immune system, to prevent the virus from entering the nervous system.

10.1.5   Control and prevention

(a)   Compulsory quarantine (six months minimum) for all animals entering Britain, unless a special veterinary licence is issued.

(b)   Severe penalties for people breaking quarantine regulations and illegally importing animals.

(c)   Education of the public so that they understand the need for quarantine regulations. They should report any animal which appears sick or which is behaving strangely and not handle them.

(d)   Vigilance must be maintained at all ports and airports to watch out for any attempts to smuggle animals into the country.

(e)   Vets and other people at risk of contracting rabies should be vaccinated.

(f)   In areas where rabies is endemic, dogs and cats can be vaccinated. Strays must be eliminated and any animal which bites a human must be isolated and tested for the disease.

(g)   Should an outbreak occur, the reservoir of infection must be eliminated, all wild carnivores within a certain area must be destroyed. All dogs will have to be muzzled when in public areas.

10.1.6 Vaccination

Louis Pasteur developed a vaccine and, in 1885, succeeded in saving the life of a boy who had been bitten by a rabid dog. The vaccine was prepared by passing the virus through a series of rabbits, each time injecting a rabbit with the emulsified spinal cord of an infected rabbit. The emulsion was finally dried or mixed with phenol to inactivate it and then used as the vaccine. This method of vaccine preparation was used until about 20 years ago. The disadvantage of this was a long course of painful injections was needed and some recipients developed an allergic reaction. Since 1980, a new safer vaccine has been developed which requires only 3–5 injections over 10 days. The virus is grown in human fibroblast cells using tissue culture techniques (see chapter 4) and inactivated with beta-propiolactone which has fewer side-effects. Research is currently taking place to develop a new vaccine based on the purified haemagglutinin protein found in the rabies virus envelope.

There are several attenuated strains of the rabies virus that are used to produce vaccines for use in protecting domestic animals. These have helped to restrict rabies even in areas where it is endemic.

10.2 Influenza

Huge worldwide pandemics of influenza, as well as more localised epidemics, have taken millions of lives. In 1918, a pandemic affected over half of the population of the world and is estimated to have killed 20 million people, even more than the First World War itself.

10.2.1 The organism

The influenza virus is a myxovirus which is commonly found in the mucus lining the respiratory tract. It has an ability to bind to and attack the cell membrane glycoproteins. It is pleomorphic and when viewed with the electron microscope can be seen in a number of different forms, from being filamentous to almost spherical. The typical virus particle is a rounded ovoid with a diameter of about 100 nm (fig 10.2). It has an outer lipid envelope, derived from the cell surface membrane of the host cell, with short spikes which stick out from the surface. There are two types of spike, some made of **haemagglutinin**, which are rod-shaped, and others made of **neuraminidase**, which are mushroom-shaped. Both types are involved in the infectivity of the virus. Haemagglutinin helps the virus to bind to specific receptors on the host cell membrane and the neuraminidase is an enzyme which helps penetration of the virus through the mucus layers and the host cell membrane. The nucleocapsid consists of single-stranded RNA coiled with a protein to form a helical core. Between the envelope and the core is a layer of matrix protein. The viral RNA is not a single thread, but consists of eight separate segments, each of which is surrounded by capsid protein and each is a single gene.

Fig 10.2
The structure of the influenza virus (based on electron micrographs)

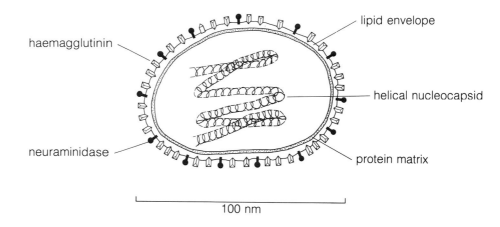

haemagglutinin

lipid envelope

helical nucleocapsid

neuraminidase

protein matrix

100 nm

10.2.2   Epidemiology and transmission

The epidemiology of influenza is still not completely understood. Epidemics occur every 2–4 years during the winter, with smaller outbreaks during the intervening years. Every 10–20 years, a pandemic of influenza spreads throughout the world, usually from the East. During his lifetime, a person may have influenza several times, an individual who contracts the disease during one epidemic is not protected during the next. This is because the influenza virus shows genetic variation and each epidemic is caused by a strain slightly different to the one before. The surface antigens are changing constantly. These small changes have been called **antigenic drift**. When pandemics occur, it seems that a more radical change to the surface haemagglutinin (and sometimes to the neuraminidase too) has taken place. This has been called **antigenic shift**. In the 50 years since the virus was discovered, there have been four recorded antigenic shifts. Drift produces a new viral strain, whereas shift produces a new subtype (species).

10.2.3   The disease

Influenza is the most important respiratory disease of humans. The infection is usually localised in the respiratory tract. It is spread by droplets of infected respiratory secretions, or by personal contact. It settles on the mucous membrane which lines the nose, pharynx, trachea and bronchi. The neuraminidase enzyme on the surface of the viruses helps them to penetrate the mucoproteins (glycoproteins) in the mucus layer. The viruses then attach to the epithelial cells of the respiratory tract and replicate within them. The incubation period is 24–48 hours and the epithelial cells are destroyed, leading to inflammation, causing the symptoms of influenza to appear. These are fever, sore throat, headache and generalised muscular aches and pains. There is an excessive discharge of mucus from the nose and respiratory tract causing sneezing and coughing, both of which ensure the transmission of the virus to others. As the cells break down, the products are distributed by the bloodstream which leads to the more general symptoms. Usually the fever and other acute symptoms subside within 48 hours. However, in some cases, the infection may spread to the lower part of the respiratory tract. This is much more serious and may lead to viral pneumonia which can be fatal. The lungs may fill with fluid and damage to the epithelium causes haemorrhage. Often in such cases, secondary bacterial infections may occur. Before the advent of antibiotics, this was often fatal and accounted for many of the 20 million deaths in 1918. Today, antibiotics can help to reduce the chances of secondary infection, although the very young or very old are still at risk.

10.2.4 Treatment

For most people who develop influenza, there is no treatment other than bed rest and perhaps aspirin or paracetamol to alleviate some of the symptoms, such as headache and fever. A vaccination is available for people who are particularly at risk from influenza, such as the elderly, and there is an antiviral drug, amantidine, which can be administered to people seriously at risk. The drug tends to be preventive rather than curative.

10.2.5 Control and prevention

Because of the research into the epidemiology of influenza, it is becoming possible to predict when an epidemic or pandemic is likely to occur and to take steps to immunise susceptible people. Since there are a limited number of influenza subtypes which infect humans, it is possible to prepare vaccines in advance of an expected epidemic. Also, there is the drug amantadine which can help to prevent people at special risk from becoming infected. The drug seems to inhibit replication of the virus in the respiratory epithelium.

10.2.6 Vaccination

Because the influenza virus is constantly changing, it is very difficult to produce an effective vaccine. Only partial protection is given by immunisation. New strains are constantly being monitored by the

World Health Organisation. Inactivated virus vaccines are the most widely used since they can be produced more rapidly than trying to produce an attenuated form. The viruses are cultured in the allantoic fluid of fertilised, embryonated hens' eggs. The virus is separated by centrifugation at high speed and inactivated with methanal (formaldehyde). The vaccine is usually a concentrated mixture of the current strains and is given by intramuscular injection.

The disadvantages of this type of vaccination are:

(a) it is only 70% effective at best;
(b) immunity only lasts a few months, so annual boosters are required;
(c) there may be side-effects, such as hypersensitivity to egg proteins, a high body temperature (particularly in children) or, very rarely, some brain damage may occur.

A new vaccine has recently been produced consisting of haemagglutinin and neuraminidase proteins. This is having more success and the toxic side-effects are minimised.

Research is also taking place into producing and testing avirulent strains and subtypes quickly enough to avoid an epidemic. Genetic engineering is being used to make hybrid viruses which may have the desired combination of properties. It is hoped that soon a nasal spray vaccine will be available for more rapid and convenient immunisation against influenza.

10.3 Acquired immune deficiency syndrome (AIDS)

Until 10 years ago it was widely believed that infectious disease was no longer a major threat to public health in the developed world. However, in the early 1980s, the devastating new disease AIDS was identified, caused by a retrovirus that had never before been found to affect humans. Between the epidemic first being noted in 1982 to the middle of 1984, progress made by scientists was rapid. The **human immunodeficiency virus** (**HIV**) was isolated and shown to cause the disease. A blood test for the presence of HIV was developed and the target cells in the body were identified. Since then, progress has been slow, no cure or vaccine is yet available and the epidemic continues to spread.

10.3.1 *The organism*

The virus is spherical and measures 0.1 μm in diameter (fig 10.3). It has a glycoprotein envelope, with protein knobs on the envelope surface. The core is cone-shaped and contains RNA which carries the viral genetic information. There is also an enzyme called **reverse transcriptase**. This enzyme enables the virus to make DNA which corresponds to the viral RNA. The DNA inserts itself into the host cell's chromosomes and can remain latent until it is activated to make new virus particles. This rare type of virus is called a **retrovirus**.

Fig 10.3
Diagram of the structure
of the HIV virus

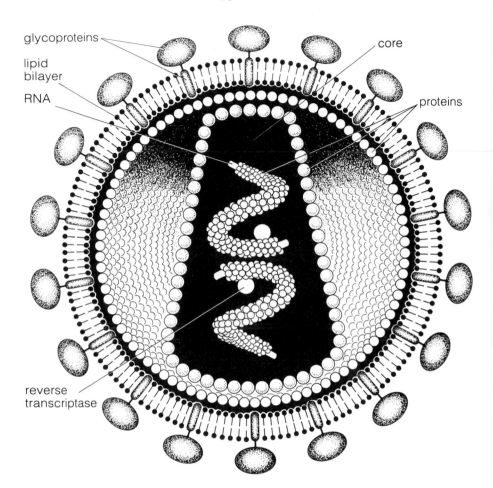

glycoproteins

lipid
bilayer

RNA

core

proteins

reverse
transcriptase

10.3.2 Epidemiology and transmission

HIV is transmitted primarily through sexual contact or by exposure to infected blood and blood products. It is also transmitted from mother to child either via the placenta or during breastfeeding.

In the USA and Britain, most sexual transmission has been among homosexual men. Indeed, the disease was first recognised among homosexuals in California and New York. The risk of infection increases with the number of sexual partners. In central Africa, the disease has been found to be primarily transmitted among the heterosexual population.

There is also a variability in the infection rate. People with AIDS, or showing HIV symptoms, are more likely to transmit the disease than those who are at an earlier stage of infection.

Transfusion of a single unit of infected blood is very likely to result in infection. A large number of people have unfortunately been infected in this way, particularly before the disease had been formally recognised. This includes many haemophiliacs who require regular injections of the blood clotting factor 8 which may be prepared from donated blood. Today, all donated blood and blood products must be screened for the presence of HIV antibodies. A new process using genetic engineering has been developed to produce factor 8 safely. Today, high-risk people such as drug users and homosexuals are actively discouraged from donating blood. There is still a major problem in less-developed countries.

Many injecting drug users tend to share needles. This may result in infected blood being injected into the body. In the USA, intravenous drug abuse is now the major source of HIV transmission among heterosexual men and women. It is also the major source of perinatal transmission. In Britain too, there has been a disturbing rise in the number of AIDS and HIV positive cases among the heterosexual population and their children. This is a problem in cities such as Edinburgh where prostitutes are injecting drug abusers.

Doctors, dentists, nurses and other health workers may become infected if they accidentally puncture their own skin with needles or instruments contaminated with the blood of HIV patients. Extreme caution must be taken when dealing with infected blood and the safe disposal of syringes is essential. Most cities now have specialist units where AIDS patients may be treated in isolation.

HIV has been shown to be transmitted from an infected mother to her unborn child probably across the placenta or during birth. It has also been found in breast milk and is known to have been transmitted by breast feeding. This has forced the closure of some human milk banks.

There is no evidence to suggest that casual contact with an HIV infected person transmits the virus. HIV has been recovered from the saliva of an infected person, but the concentration of viruses is very low. In many families studied so far, there has been no evidence to suggest that there is any form of 'household transmission'. The risk of transmission at work or at school is even lower and so HIV infected people, particularly children, are encouraged to lead a normal life.

Studies, particularly in Africa, are currently investigating the possibility of blood-sucking insects being capable of transmitting the disease. So far there has been no evidence for this. HIV does not grow in insects fed on infected blood.

10.3.3 The disease

Once HIV enters the bloodstream, its primary targets are macrophages and a particular kind of T-helper cell, the T_4 cells. Macrophages can survive HIV infection and may act as 'shuttles' that carry HIV to infect more T_4 cells. The viruses have a powerful affinity for the T_4 surface protein, called CD4, to which they bind. A complex process of protein interaction then takes place and the T_4 cell membrane is made to form a vesicle, which traps the viruses within the cell. This means that the HIV surface antigens are no longer present on the cell surface. Without surface antigens, the cell-mediated part of the immune system can no longer detect the infection and will not attack the HIV. The HIV then attacks more T_4 lymphocytes in the same way. These cells are responsible for the immune response to infection (see chapter 11). The result is a profound depression of the immune response and an increased liability to infection.

HIV may be passed from cell to cell in an individual, or may even be transmitted in body fluids to another person while still remaining hidden. The virus can later infect a variety of tissues in the body. It may hide in the cells of the central nervous system, where it causes damage and is protected from drugs by the blood–brain barrier.

A condition referred to as 'full-blown AIDS' is when the infections become unmanageable, as the immunosuppression becomes worse, with fatal results. Treatment with antibiotics can help to prolong life by fighting secondary infection. However, previously rare 'opportunistic' infections often set in, such as a type of pneumonia caused by the protozoan *Pneumocystis carinii*. Sometimes a type of cancer called Kaposi's sarcoma and other malignancies are found. However, infection with HIV does not always lead immediately to full-blown AIDS. Some develop antibodies to the virus with no illness, while others get a mild illness with a temperature and swollen lymph glands. Others show a more prolonged illness with lymph gland enlargement. These conditions are referred to as AIDS-related complex (ARC). We do not yet know how many of these infected cases will end up with full-blown AIDS.

10.3.4   Treatment

One drug, azidothymidine (AZT) is already in clinical use as an AIDS treatment. It has been shown in trials to prolong the survival period and quality of life in certain AIDS patients. AZT was already in use as a cancer treatment but was tested and found to stop HIV replication in the test tube. However, it is not a final answer since it can have toxic side-effects and patients often develop anaemia (decrease in red blood cells).

Research is taking place into developing a variety of agents to attack HIV at different stages in the life cycle.

10.3.5   Prevention and control

(a)   People must be educated and counselled about how to avoid behaviour that results in the transmission of HIV. They must be encouraged to use condoms and reduce their number of sexual partners.

(b) People found to be HIV positive must be counselled and educated to avoid transmitting the disease.

(c) There must be treatment and prevention of injecting drug use. There must be a reduction in the sharing of HIV contaminated needles. In some areas, needle exchange schemes are available for drug users.

10.3.6   Vaccination?

The development of a vaccine is a top priority of AIDS research and offers the best hope of stemming the AIDS crisis. However, the production of an effective AIDS vaccine is a tremendous challenge, since the virus infects the very cells that the vaccine needs to activate.

Some of the problems to be overcome are listed below.

(a) HIV is a retrovirus which inserts its own genes into the cell it is infecting, thus establishing a permanent infection. Even if a cell is not actively producing viruses, it may still harbour dormant retroviral genes. Because no viral antigens are on the cell surface, it remains invisible to the immune system.

(b) Retroviral genes have been found to disrupt the normal growth of a cell. In other words, retrogenes cause cancer. So if a vaccine is made from attenuated whole viruses it could cause cancer.

(c) HIV is constantly mutating and changing its envelope protein by altering the sequence of amino acids.

(d) The virus has a great affinity for CD4, the T_4 cell surface protein to which it binds. Attempts have been made to produce antibodies to the part of the virus that binds to CD4, to try to prevent binding. This has proved more difficult than at first thought, because it seems that a second round of antibodies is produced against the first. These attack the CD4 and destroy the T_4 cells themselves. These are the very cells that are under attack from the virus.

Researchers are still trying to find a 'weak spot' by which to attack HIV and most studies have been of the envelope protein. This is a glycoprotein, where the protein component is like string wrapped around the matrix and covered on the outside by a 'cloud' of sugar molecules. These sugars are made by the host cell and are not antigenic. Scientists are trying to develop a vaccine which will expose the protein beneath the sugars, particularly the CD4 binding sites. This should then promote an immune response.

Several types of vaccine are currently under development, shown in table 10.1, and some have been tested in humans.

**Table 10.1
AIDS vaccine research**

Type of vaccine	Type of immunogen	Immunogens tested in people
killed virus	whole or disrupted HIV with genetic material removed	whole inactivated HIV in already infected people
HIV subunit	HIV envelope, pieces of envelope proteins or other antigens made by genetically engineered cells or synthesised in the laboratory	glycoprotein (GP) 120, GP 160, synthetic fragments of protein e.g. P17
HIV subunit in a virus vector	gene for HIV envelope is inserted into vaccinia virus or adenovirus, or cells infected with HIV/vaccinia recombinant	vaccinia/HIV recombinant; cells infected with recombinant
antibody (anti-idiotype)	antibody against CD4	antibody against CD4

This is only a partial list, the field is growing rapidly; medical researchers worldwide are in the race to develop an AIDS vaccine.

One major problem for researchers, is that there is no good animal 'model' for the disease on which to test or produce a vaccine. Most animals do not get AIDS from HIV. Chimpanzees can be infected with HIV but none so far have developed AIDS. Macaque monkeys have been infected with HIV-2 which is a variant found in West Africa, and have developed AIDS. However there has been no success with the more pathogenic and common HIV-1.

There is also a shortage of human volunteers willing to try the many new vaccines being developed. Each one requires up to 100 high-risk volunteers for the first phase of trials and later, thousands of people would be needed for testing. Yet, despite all these difficulties, scientists all over the world are working towards defeating HIV.

10.4 Salmonella

This is a large genus of bacteria, which consists of nearly 2000 serotypes (species). They are **enteric** organisms, being found in the intestines and most are able to invade the cells of the gut causing disease. The most serious infections are enteric fevers such as **typhoid fever,** caused by *Salmonella typhi,* or *S. paratyphi* causing **paratyphoid.** Typhoid causes a widespread septicaemia which may last for several weeks and may be fatal. **Salmonellosis** food poisoning is becoming more frequent in Europe and the USA and is often due to *S. typhimurium* or *S. enteriditis.* This is usually less severe than typhoid fever but does cause vomiting, diarrhoea and abdominal pain. It is usually limited to the digestive system, but it may be fatal in those who are weak, very young or very old.

10.4.1 The organism

Salmonellae are flagellated, motile, Gram negative, rod-shaped bacteria (fig 10.4). They are not able to ferment lactose, so this is used as an indicator in their identification. All salmonellae are able to withstand high concentrations of bile salts. *S. typhi* often infects the gall bladder. This is why some selective growth media (such as MacConkey agar) for enteric organisms, contain bile salts. Most are sensitive to acid and may be destroyed by stomach acid. Most species of *Salmonella* infect many animal species as well as humans; however, *S. typhi* only infects humans.

Fig 10.4
Transmission electron micrograph of *Salmonella typhimurium* (× 20000)

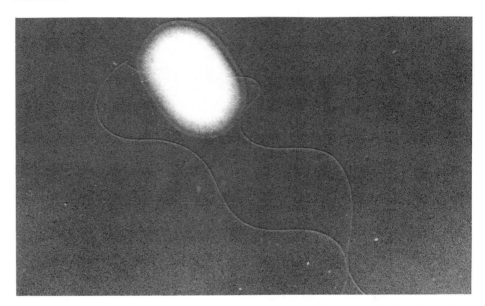

Salmonellae are invasive pathogens. When taken into the body with contaminated food or drink, they stick to the surface of the epithelial cells of the intestine and are taken into the cells by phagocytosis. The cells are damaged when the bacteria multiply and produce an **endotoxin**, which causes fever and inflammation of the tissue. Cells lyse and the bacteria are released to damage further cells. *S. typhi* and *S. paratyphi* are very invasive and spread to the lymph nodes and are carried by the bloodstream to other internal organs causing widespread damage. The less virulent salmonellae usually remain in the intestinal mucosa and cause gastroenteritis. They produce an enterotoxin which causes diarrhoea.

10.4.2 Typhoid fever

Outbreaks of typhoid fever are quite rare in countries which have good standards of public health, with adequate water treatment and sewage disposal. Fig 10.5 summarises the effects of typhoid fever.

Fig 10.5
A summary diagram of
typhoid fever

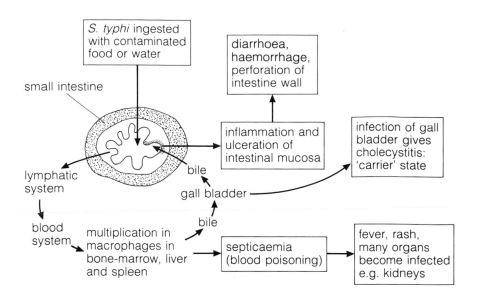

10.4.3   *Epidemiology and transmission*

Typhoid organisms are carried in infected water contaminated with human faeces. Paratyphoid tends to be carried mainly in infected milk or dairy products such as ice-cream. Both organisms must be acquired ultimately from patients or carriers via faeces to mouth. In the days before purification and chlorination of water supplies, there were about 9000 deaths per year reported in Britain. During the decade 1971–80 there were only 26 deaths. Milk is a major source of infection in countries where it is not pasteurised. In tropical areas, flies may carry the organisms from latrines on to food. Some people who recover from typhoid fever continue to excrete the organism in their urine and faeces but show no further symptoms. These people are called chronic carriers of typhoid and are a particular problem when employed in food handling industries, water works or in dairies. One notorious example is that of Mary Mallon who was employed as a cook in New York between 1901 and 1914. She earned the name 'Typhoid Mary' when she caused over 1300 outbreaks of typhoid fever.

In 1964, a large can of imported corned beef caused a serious outbreak in Aberdeen. Joints in the can had not been effectively sealed and unchlorinated river water containing the typhoid pathogen had entered. Since then there have been sporadic outbreaks in the UK, but most people have been infected whilst abroad. In the summer of 1989 several Britons were infected with typhoid fever while on holiday in the resort of Salou in Spain. The source of the outbreak has not been identified, but bathing in sewage-contaminated sea water seems to be a common factor.

10.4.4 Treatment

The antibiotic **chloramphenicol** usually produces rapid recovery. It has little effect on carriers, who often must have their gall-bladder removed or sometimes respond to treatment with **ampicillin**.

10.4.5 Control and prevention

(a) Pasteurisation of milk.
(b) Purification of drinking water.
(c) Isolation of patients.
(d) Banning chronic carriers from food handling.
(e) Good hygiene practices to be encouraged (washing hands after using toilet and before handling food).

10.4.6 Vaccination

A killed vaccine is available and is given to protect individuals exposed during an epidemic.

10.4.7 Food poisoning (gastroenteritis)

Bacterial food poisoning may be caused by several organisms, including *Salmonella, Clostridium perfringens* and *Staphylococcus aureus*.

10.4.8 Epidemiology and transmission

Salmonella infections are **zoonoses** and are usually transmitted from animals to humans. The number of animals which can harbour the infection is enormous. Usually humans become infected by eating contaminated poultry and meat which have not been cooked thoroughly or refrigerated adequately. The largest single source in the USA and the UK is contaminated poultry (chicken, ducks, turkey) and poultry products, such as eggs and egg products like frozen egg whites. All these are used in huge quantities by the catering trade. In abbatoirs, healthy carcasses may become infected by cross-contamination from diseased ones.

Animal feeds made from contaminated offal products may transmit *Salmonella* to livestock and poultry. Rats and mice may also transmit the disease. There must be a major effort to improve conditions on farms and in abbatoirs. In Denmark all animal feeds are heat-treated to kill salmonellae before distribution. This has significantly reduced infection.

Salmonella food poisoning does not simply require that food is contaminated with the organism. It must be given the right conditions for growth; warm, damp conditions are ideal. Thorough cooking of food will destroy the organism. Food which is frozen, partially thawed or chilled will take longer to cook thoroughly. Microwaves may not penetrate far enough into the food to kill any salmonellae present. Precautions must be taken to ensure that raw food, which may be contaminated, should never have contact with cooked food. This often tends to happen in overloaded domestic refrigerators.

10.4.9   *The disease*

Fig 10.6 summarises the effects of salmonella food poisoning.

Fig 10.6
A summary diagram of
salmonella food poisoning

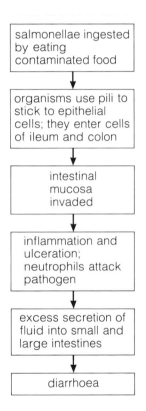

Several species of *Salmonella* are able to produce food poisoning; however, a high dose of the organisms must be ingested to cause infection, so the organism must have been allowed to multiply for several hours in the food.

All species invade the epithelial cells of the intestine and damage the cells lining the ileum and caecum. Sometimes ulcers form and the infection leads to diarrhoea, pain in the abdomen, vomiting and fever. These symptoms may start about 12–24 hours after the contaminated food was ingested and may last for 2–5 days. The faeces produced are very watery, containing mucus and sometimes blood. Dehydration can be a serious complication, particularly in the young or the elderly.

10.5 Listeriosis

Bacteria such as *Listeria monocytogenes* have been associated with food poisoning in recent years. *Listeria* is widely distributed in the environment, but is able to multiply at temperatures down to 4 °C. It is causing increasing concern, particularly with coleslaw, chilled prepared salads, milk and dairy products.

Listeriosis is unlike other forms of food poisoning in that it gives a mild influenza-like illness in most people. However, the symptoms can be much worse, especially in the very young, the elderly or immune-suppressed, where meningitis and septicaemia may develop. Listeriosis is a particular hazard for pregnant women, where it can destroy the placenta and lead to miscarriage.

10.5.1 *Control*

(a) Supermarkets and kitchens should observe instructions on food carefully, particularly 'use by' dates.

(b) Ensure refrigerators are at correct working temperature, that is 1–4 °C.

(c) Reheat cook/chill products thoroughly if they are to be eaten hot and take particular care to observe the recommended 'standing times' when using a microwave oven for reheating.

(d) Do not reheat cook/chill food more than once.

(e) Do not consume dairy products which have not been pasteurised, since pasteurisation kills the *Listeria* bacterium.

10.6 Sexually transmitted diseases (STDs)

STDs are spread by sexual contact. Of these, gonorrhoea and syphilis are the most important. While AIDS can also be considered to be an STD, it is dealt with separately (section 10.3), since it can also be spread non-sexually.

There are several social and medical reasons for the spread of STDs:

(a) more women use the pill or IUD for contraception rather than condoms which give protection;

(b) antibiotic treatment is available so there is less fear about the consequences of STDs;

(c) rapid air travel means that infected people can spread the disease worldwide;

(d) there is insufficient sex education;

(e) infected women and passive male homosexuals may show no symptoms;

(f) the diseases are highly infective;

(g) the incubation period is very short;

(h) some strains, particularly of *Neisseria gonorrhoeae*, are resistant to antibiotics.

10.6.1 Gonorrhoea

Gonorrhoea is probably the commonest communicable disease in the world today. It has existed in the human population since ancient times and has reached epidemic proportions in some countries. In the USA there are over one million cases reported annually. In the UK there has been a steady decline with around 60 000 cases annually in the late 1970s. There has been an even sharper decline in the 1980s, due to education and concern about AIDS. There is some indication that there is a changing attitude towards casual sex, with an increased use of protective condoms.

10.6.2 The organism

Neisseria gonorrhoeae, commonly called *Gonococcus*, are Gram negative, aerobic, non-motile cocci, usually found in pairs. They are fastidious and difficult to culture, requiring a complex medium. They are invasive and interact with neutrophils in the tissues causing acute inflammation. Gonococci have many pili (fimbriae) on their surface (fig 10.7), which help them to stick onto the surface of the cells they are invading. They are therefore not washed away with the flow of urine. Their cell walls contain a lipopolysaccharide endotoxin. It is this which damages the host cells.

Fig 10.7
(*a*) The structure of *Neisseria gonorrhoeae* (based on electron micrographs). (*b*) Detail of the outer structure of *N. gonorrhoeae* (generalised) to show the pili (fimbriae)

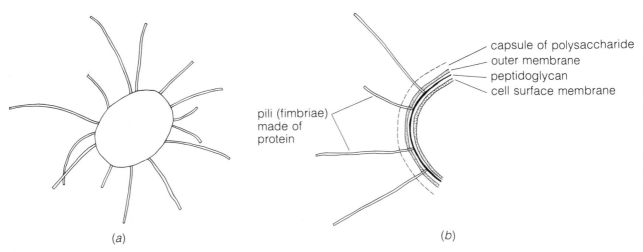

(a)   (b)

10.6.3 Epidemiology and transmission

Gonococci are very sensitive to heat, drying and soap and water, so intimate contact is needed to transmit the disease, which is usually during sexual intercourse. It has been transmitted by hand to eye contact which can lead to blindness. Also the infection of the eyes of a newborn baby, as it passes through the infected vagina, has been found to occur.

10.6.4 The disease

In males, the symptoms usually develop about 2–10 days after infection. The cells lining the urethra are damaged by the gonococci and a greenish-yellow pus is formed. This is known as acute urethritis. Urination becomes very frequent and painful and pus is discharged through the urethra. If the disease is not treated, the bacteria may spread to surrounding tissues and glands, causing abscesses and eventually it may lead to sterility.

Females are usually infected during intercourse from the male discharge. The gonococci invade the cervix and surrounding glands. The symptoms may appear after 2–10 days, but in many cases, none are noticed. Infected 'asymptomatic' women may carry the disease for several months. If the disease remains untreated, the gonococci may spread via the uterus and oviducts into the peritoneal cavity. This causes peritonitis with severe pain in the abdomen and a high fever. Damage to the oviducts may lead to sterility. Further complications can include inflammation of the joints, similar to that caused by arthritis and, if the eyes are infected, may lead to blindness.

10.6.5 Treatment

Immunity to gonorrhoea is unknown and vaccines are not available. It does respond to treatment with antibiotics, usually penicillin. Recently, penicillin-resistant strains have developed due to the presence of R-plasmids carrying the gene for penicillinase. These strains are completely resistant to penicillin and ampicillin and have serious implications for the eventual control of gonorrhoea. There have been recent outbreaks of resistant strains in Liverpool and in the USA and most seem to originate in the Far East.

10.6.6 Control and prevention

Control of gonorrhoea is based on tracing and treating the contacts of patients. Asymptomatic women are still a problem as they may spread the disease without knowing it. The use of condoms does give protection and it is most effective if the number of sexual partners are restricted.

10.6.7 Syphilis

Historical records show that the venereal disease syphilis is quite 'new', having been around for less than 500 years. It first reached Europe in 1493 and it is popularly believed to have been brought here by sailors returning from a voyage to the West Indies with Columbus. Syphilis is a serious disease which if untreated can lead to mental disease and death. It is a much less common sexually transmitted disease than gonorrhoea, with around 50 million cases a year reported worldwide. Since the advent of antibiotics, and penicillin in particular, there has been a decline in the incidence of the disease.

10.6.8 The organism

The disease is caused by a spirochaete called *Treponema pallidum*. The cells are slender, flexible, and helical, up to 15 mm long but very thin, being around 0.1 mm wide (fig 10.8). They are not flagellated but are actively motile, rotating around the long axis like a corkscrew. They are very difficult to stain and are best viewed using dark-ground microscopy when they appear as bright spirals against a dark background. *T. pallidum* is microaerophilic and survives best at an oxygen tension of around 1–5%. The organism is proving impossible to culture and has to be propagated in the testes of animals such as the rabbit.

**Fig 10.8
The structure of
*Treponema pallida***

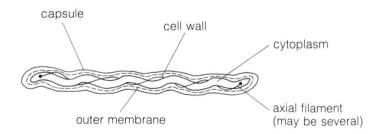

10.6.9 Epidemiology and transmission

T. pallidum is rapidly killed by drying, heat and cold, exposure to the air and to disinfectants. Therefore, it must be transmitted by direct personal contact, usually during sexual intercourse, but occasionally by kissing or other close personal contact. It may pass from mother to unborn baby via the placenta. It has been known for syphilis to be transmitted by blood transfusion with fresh blood. Most blood is stored at 5 °C for 72 hours which destroys the organism.

10.6.10 The disease

After an incubation period of 3–4 weeks, a primary lesion or chancre appears on the external genitals, usually at the site of infection. This is a small, hard, painless red nodule which forms an ulcer about 1 cm in diameter. Lymph glands in the area become inflamed. This chancre is highly infective and contains many living treponemes. Some organisms are spread around the body by the bloodstream. The chancre eventually heals with slight scarring and then the symptoms disappear for 2–24 weeks.

In the secondary stage, a rash appears with lesions in the skin and mucous membranes. These are very infective and widespread; they may occur in the meninges around the brain, or in bones, the eyes or the liver. They cause great damage to vital organs if the disease is not treated. The host does have an immune response to the infection and, in most cases, the lesions heal but may recur. The host by now is immune and enters a latent phase which may last for several years. The organisms remain in the body, usually in the spleen and lymph nodes.

After this time the treponemes emerge and give rise to tertiary syphilis. There are three forms of tertiary syphilis recognised.

(1) **Benign**, where large growths called **gummas** develop in organs such as the liver, testis or bone. They cause severe damage to these organs but contain few organisms and are not infective.
(2) **Cardiovascular**, which affects the aorta and aortic valves. This form may take up to 40 years to appear and leads to heart failure and death.
(3) **Neurosyphilis**, which at any stage may affect the meninges around the brain and spinal cord. The brain itself may be affected and eventually leads to insanity.

Congenital syphilis   This occurs when the mother's disease is not diagnosed and treated during pregnancy. In most cases, routine antenatal tests detect the disease and thus is quite rare. Treponemes present in the bloodstream of a pregnant woman cross the placenta during the later stages of pregnancy. The baby may be stillborn or will show the secondary stage of syphilis, with widespread lesions in the skin, mucous membranes and bones. Congenital syphilis may be treated with antibiotics but later in life, the adult teeth may be deformed, as may the long bones.

10.6.11   Treatment

Syphilis can be cured by penicillin and resistant strains have not yet emerged. If treatment is given during the primary stage, no immunity develops. If treatment is given later, usually immunity is permanent.

10.6.12   Control and prevention

All the sexual contacts of an infected person must be contacted and treated with penicillin. In women, the primary lesion may be in the vagina and go unnoticed. If she is promiscuous, she may transmit the disease to several partners. There is no vaccination yet available against syphilis. Control measures are as for gonorrhoea.

10.7 Oral thrush

Oral thrush is a common disease in babies and infants. It infects the epithelial tissue lining the mouth. Thrush is caused by a yeast-like fungus, *Candida albicans* or occasionally *C. parapsilosis*.

10.7.1 *The organism*

Candida is a common, harmless commensal of humans and may be found in the mouth and faeces of most normal individuals. It is a deuteromycete fungus (imperfect fungus) and is 2–4 mm in diameter (fig 10.9). Oral thrush is an opportunistic infection and takes advantage of any situation where the normal resistance is reduced, for example, after taking antibiotics.

Fig 10.9
Candida albicans

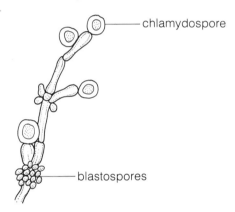

chlamydospore

blastospores

10.7.2 *The disease*

The disease is known as candidiasis. Babies are thought to become infected from the infected vagina of their mother during birth. *Candida* readily infects babies as they are born without any commensal flora. Most babies' dummies can be shown to carry the organism. The mouth of an infected baby has fluffy white patches on the surface (fig 10.10). If they are lifted, they are red beneath where the hyphae are penetrating the surface epithelium. This speckled appearance of the mouth gives the disease the name 'thrush'. The infection causes irritation and may give rise to secondary bacterial infections such as abscesses.

10.7.3 *Other forms of thrush*

In adults, *Candida* infects the gut, lungs, vagina, fingernails and occasionally becomes disseminated over the whole body. It can be fatal

Fig 10.10
Close-up photograph of the mouth of a person suffering from AIDS, showing severe oral thrush (white patches)

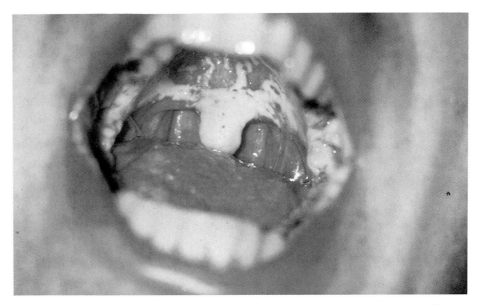

in immune-suppressed patients, such as those on drug treatment after an organ transplant. Vaginal thrush is the most common, especially in women who are taking the contraceptive pill, or during pregnancy. In these cases, the pH and sugar content of the vaginal secretions are affected by the hormone oestrogen. *Candida* does not usually infect healthy individuals because of competition from other commensal flora. Following the use of broad-spectrum antibiotics, the normal balance is upset and thrush may develop. This may also occur with the long-term use of anti-inflammatory drugs, such as corticosteroids used in the treatment of conditions such as eczema. Space scientists have found that during long space flights, *Candida* increases in the bodies of astronauts. This may be due to stress, or also because it survives and competes with other commensals in space conditions.

10.7.4   Treatment

(a)   There may be an underlying cause which predisposes the patient to the disease. If this cause is dealt with, the disease may disappear on its own.

(b)   Gentian violet or magenta paint can be applied to the inflamed areas. This old-fashioned remedy is still very effective, though the colours produced are unsightly.

(c)   The antibiotic nystatin is effective and safe against *Candida*. It cannot be taken orally as it is broken down in the gut but is effective as a lotion or cream which is applied to the surface.

(d)   Natural yogurt is used as an effective treatment for vaginal thrush by many women. It has an acid pH which inhibits the growth of *Candida* and a large population of harmless live bacteria which compete with the *Candida*.

10.8 Malaria

Malaria is a disease affecting humans, apes, monkeys, birds and reptiles. It is one of the earliest recorded diseases of humans, having been recorded as early as the fifth century BC. It is a worldwide disease, but is more prevalent in the tropics and is one of the most important fatal diseases of humans.

10.8.1 *The organism*

Plasmodium species are the protozoan parasites responsible for producing the disease **malaria** in humans. The disease is transmitted to humans by the female *Anopheles* mosquito which feeds on blood prior to laying eggs. The male mosquito feeds on fruit juice instead.

The cycle starts when a female mosquito bites a human suffering from malaria. The mosquito picks up **gametocytes** with the infected blood (fig 10.11). These escape digestion in the mosquito's stomach and develop into *male* and *female sex cells*. The nucleus of the male gametocyte divides into several fractions, each of which moves into a long thin portion of cytoplasm on the surface of the male gametocyte. Each of these then breaks away to fertilise a female gametocyte. The fertilised female gametocyte becomes a **motile ookinete**. The ookinete swims through the digesting food and through the stomach wall. It forms an **oocyst** in the stomach wall, within which it undergoes multiple fission to produce numerous **sporozoites**. Later, the cyst breaks open, releasing the sporozoites into the body cavity. The sporozoites migrate towards the mosquito's salivary glands.

When this mosquito bites a human, an anticoagulant is injected from the salivary glands to prevent the blood clotting in the insect's mouthparts. Sporozoites are injected into the human bloodstream along with the anticoagulant. They migrate around the body, but primarily towards the liver. The sporozoite continues to grow, and develops into a **schizont**. Within the liver, the schizont undergoes multiple fission to produce enormous numbers of **merozoites**. The merozoites are released from the liver and invade red blood cells, feeding on the cell contents. When fully grown, the merozoite becomes amoeba-like and almost fills the red blood cell. Each amoeba undergoes further multiple fission, to form sixteen merozoites. The merozoites are released into the blood, along with the remaining cell contents and waste products, causing the periodic high fevers typical of malaria. Each of the newly released merozoites then enters another red blood cell and the cycle continues until enormous numbers of the parasites are present in the blood.

Some of the merozoites do not continue in this way however. Instead, they develop into male and female **gametocytes**, and remain in the blood until they are sucked up by a feeding female mosquito and the cycle begins again.

Fig 10.11
Summary of the life cycle
of *Plasmodium vivax*

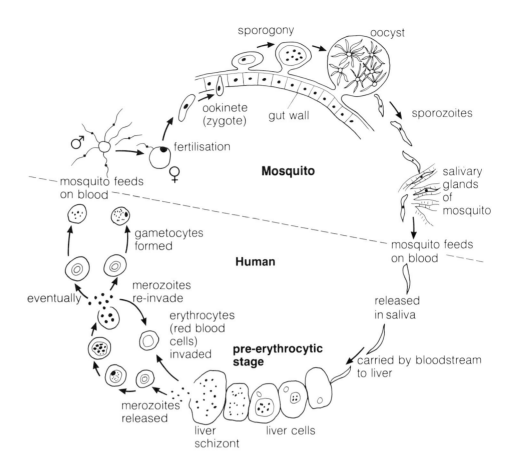

10.8.2 *Epidemiology and transmission*

Malaria is only transmitted to humans by female anopheline mosquitoes. The female only is a bloodsucker, whereas the male feeds on fruit juice. Malaria is not found north of latitude 60 °N or south of latitude 30 °S, because a certain minimum temperature is required for the sexual reproduction of *Plasmodium* within the mosquito. The most efficient transmitter of malaria is *Anopheles gambiae*, which is the main vector of the disease in tropical Africa, where most adult humans suffer from malaria to varying extents. Outside tropical Africa, malaria is transmitted by much less efficient vectors, shorter-lived mosquitoes which are not specific human-feeders. In these places, malaria tends to be a seasonal epidemic illness. During the dry season, the breeding of mosquitoes declines and the human population seems to lose part of its immunity. When mosquitoes breed more freely during the wet season, epidemics of malaria frequently occur.

Malaria was once common in south-east England where marshy land provided ideal breeding grounds for mosquitoes. With lower ambient temperatures today and drainage of the fenlands, malaria has died out in this area.

It can be seen that the availability of suitable vectors is a major factor in determining the distribution of the disease. It is a great killer of infants and children, although those who do survive develop considerable immunity to the disease. When anopheline mosquitoes are accidentally transferred to another part of the world, dreadful epidemics can occur. One example was Brazil in the 1930s, when *A. gambiae* was accidentally introduced, probably by aeroplane. Thousands of lives were lost before the mosquito population was eradicated using insecticides.

10.8.3   The disease

Ten to 14 days after infection, the first attack occurs. It may be preceded by tiredness, aching and vomiting. There are three stages (fig 10.12).

Cold stage. Shivering, with chattering teeth, lasts for 1–2 hours. This is caused by the release of merozoites from the red blood cells. These quickly invade the new red blood cells and the disease quickly progresses to the next stage.

Hot stage. The body temperature rises to 40 °C or higher, maybe as high as 41.5 °C, with increased pulse and breathing rates. The patient has headache, nausea and general discomfort, lasting 3–4 hours.

Sweating stage. Heavy sweating occurs bringing the temperature back down to normal, or just below. This lasts 2–4 hours. The patient, although exhausted from the fever, feels recovered, and is frequently able to continue with normal activity until the next bout of fever.

Fig 10.12
Temperature chart of a patient suffering from malaria (*P. vivax* infection)

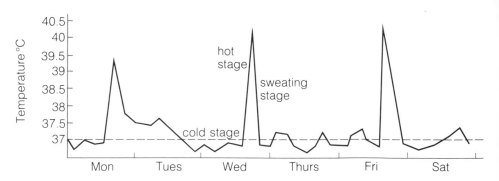

Fever occurs at different intervals, depending on the species of *Plasmodium*. *P. vivax* has a 48-hour cycle, *P. malariae* a 72-hour cycle, *P. ovale* a 3-day cycle, while *P. falciparum* is very irregular. Sometimes people have mixed infections, resulting from different mosquito bites on different occasions, so the pattern of fever can be irregular or even continuous.

Malignant malaria is caused by *P. falciparum*. It produces very severe symptoms, including a high fever and very heavily parasitised blood cells. The red blood cells become sticky and stick to the walls of the blood vessels of the brain, lungs, kidneys and intestines. This can cause blockages of blood vessels, leading to convulsions, coma, brain damage, kidney failure and pneumonia. Unless treated, it is fatal within a few days.

10.8.4 Control and prevention

In 1955, the Eighth World Health Assembly initiated a programme to eradicate malaria. This objective is still nowhere near achievement. Many methods of fighting malaria rely on killing the vector, the mosquito. The eggs are laid in water and hatch into larvae which live and grow attached by a breathing tube to the surface film of water. Ultimately they transform into pupae in which the adult flies develop.

Control measures centre upon destruction of either the vector or the parasite.

Eradication of the vector

(a) **Drainage of the mosquito breeding grounds**. This is expensive and difficult to achieve. It is virtually impossible to drain all small ditches and ponds where mosquitoes might breed.

(b) **A surface film of oil** may be applied to the water which will suffocate the larvae. This is of limited use since it pollutes the water and renders it unsuitable for other forms of life.

(c) **Biological control** in the form of carnivorous fish can be introduced into the water. This has limited value in controlling the disease.

(d) **Insecticides**. A major effort has been made to spray indoor surfaces of dwellings with a persistent insecticide such as pyrethrum, benzene hexachloride (BHC) or dieldrin. Adult mosquitoes entering houses tend to rest on walls during the day and thus are destroyed. These have been quite successful in the past, despite the insecticides causing considerable environmental damage. Recently, some mosquitoes have developed resistance to these insecticides and this method alone will not be successful. Insecticides are also used in certain areas of water to kill larvae and adults when egg-laying.

Eradication of the parasite

(a) **Drugs**. No single drug is available to kill all forms of the parasite. When patients are acutely ill, the aim is to stop multiple fission in the red blood cells, thus preventing the breakdown of large numbers of cells and the vast liberation of merozoites and waste products into the general circulation. The drugs used are quinine, chloroquine and quinacrine. Quinine is the oldest drug used in the treatment of malaria. It has been used for many centuries as a fever relief, but is expensive to produce and has gradually been replaced with powerful synthetic anti-malarial drugs. Many anti-malarial drugs have unpleasant side-effects and the parasite has developed resistance to many of them. The most difficult stage to treat is the exo-erythrocytic stage in the liver.

Another recent problem is that many western tourists have used anti-malarial drugs as a preventative while travelling in malaria areas and there was widespread use of these drugs during the Vietnam war. This over-use has lead to the resistance of *Plasmodium* to all the drugs currently available and there are now areas of the world where there is no effective anti-malarial drug available.

(b) **Vaccines.** Recently a vaccine has been developed, but its use has so far been confined to western travellers going to malaria-endemic areas as a preventive measure. The development of the vaccine faced many difficulties as the parasite has so many different stages and several strains with different antigens.

10.9   Bovine spongiform encephalopathy (BSE)

Bovine spongiform encephalopathy (BSE), commonly called 'mad cow disease', was first recognised in November 1986. At present the disease is confined to Britain, where 0.01% of cattle have become infected. The infectious agent is described as a **prion** (proteinaceous infective particle). Other diseases caused by prions include scrapie, a disease of sheep and goats, as well as Kuru and Creutzfeldt–Jacob disease in humans. All these diseases which are, or are suspected of being, caused by prions have similar features: loss of co-ordination, difficulty in walking, dementia, lack of response by the immune system, impaired nerve impulses, and vacuoles appearing in the brain giving it a spongy appearance.

Prions seems to vary in size, from being nearly as large as bacteria to being smaller than the smallest viruses. It has been suggested that they are, in fact, aggregations of tiny particles, each in the order of one hundred times smaller than the smallest virus. They seem to have little or no nucleic acid. The bulk of the protein in prions is a glycoprotein designated PrP for 'prion protein'. Treatments such as ionising radiation, which disrupts nucleic acid, have very little effect on prions, but treatments which destroy or disrupt enzymes greatly decrease their infectivity. If these particles lack nucleic acid, scientists must explain the fact that prions can replicate themselves. It could be that they are normal viruses, using the host cell to replicate themselves. Alternatively

PrP itself might bring about a 'reverse translation' of protein to DNA or RNA, which could then be used to synthesise more PrP. A third suggestion is that the DNA code for PrP is already present in the mammalian genome, and is triggered by the invading prion.

Scrapie has been known for over 200 years, although an infectious agent was not demonstrated until 1935. Usually, the infection passes from ewe to lamb, but sometimes from sheep to sheep as well. The disease has a long incubation period, lasting years, between the time of infection and the appearance of symptoms. In the 1960s, scrapie-infected sheep carcases or abbatoir waste was fed to ranch-reared mink. This led to an outbreak of transmissible mink encephalopathy (TME). However, unlike scrapie, this was not transmissible from mink to mink and quickly died out.

BSE is clearly another member of the scrapie family. The source of infection was abbatoir waste that had been converted to meat-and-bone meal as a protein supplement to cattle food. The adding of such meal to cattle feed was banned by the Government in July 1988.

An area of great current concern is the question of whether BSE can be passed to humans. The possibility that Creutzfeldt–Jacob disease, a rare disease causing only about 30 cases annually in the UK, might be linked to scrapie has been extensively researched for 20 years and no causal link found. The Department of Health argue that this is extremely convincing evidence that BSE cannot infect humans. As further precaution, infected cattle are destroyed. The central nervous system and parts of the lymphoreticular system, such as the spleen, thymus and tonsils, have been banned for use as human food. Other scientists are less certain: all meat contains some nervous tissue where the agent might be present, and argue that a mutant organism which does not behave like scrapie could be causing BSE. They are also concerned that infected animals are being slaughtered for food, since there is a long incubation period when the agent is present but no symptoms have developed. There is still a great deal to be learned, both about prions in general, and diseases like BSE in particular.

Questions

1 Copy and complete table 10.2 to form a summary chart for the human diseases covered in this chapter.

2 Name two diseases caused by organisms that enter the body via the respiratory tract, two which are sexually transmitted and two where the organisms are ingested.

3 Name (*a*) a fungus, (*b*) a protozoan, (*c*) a virus, (*d*) a bacterium which cause disease in humans.

4 There has been an outbreak of food poisoning in students who all had lunch in the college canteen. You have been called in as an expert to

Table 10.2
**Summary chart of some
human diseases**

Disease	Rabies	Influenza	AIDS	Typhoid	Salmonellosis	Listeriosis	Thrush	Malaria
Organism								
Host/s								
How transmitted								
Incubation period								
Symptoms/ clinical features								
Importance								
Treatment								
Prevention								
Control								

investigate the source of the outbreak and to advise on the actions to be taken to avoid a further outbreak.

(a) What tests would you carry out?

(b) What advice would you give to the canteen supervisor?

11 Fighting disease

11.1 How disease-causing organisms enter the body

Of all human pathogens, bacteria cause the greatest number of human diseases, closely followed by viruses. Fungi can also cause disease in humans. Furthermore, there are many commensal bacteria on and in the human body but these can become pathogens if circumstances change. There are several ways in which pathogens enter the body, and these are summarised in fig 11.1.

Fig 11.1
How pathogens enter the body

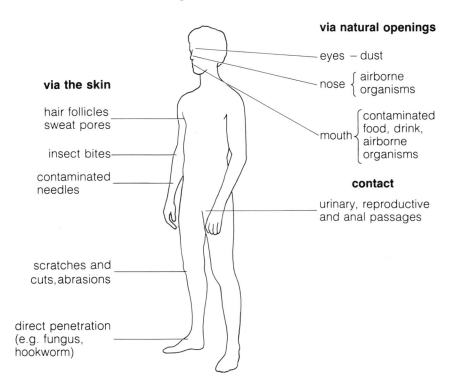

via natural openings

eyes – dust

nose { airborne organisms

mouth { contaminated food, drink, airborne organisms

via the skin

hair follicles
sweat pores

insect bites

contaminated needles

scratches and cuts, abrasions

direct penetration (e.g. fungus, hookworm)

contact

urinary, reproductive and anal passages

Through natural openings   Examples include the nose, mouth, urethra, anus and vagina. Each of these openings is lined with a moist, mucous membrane, providing ideal conditions for microbial growth. From these areas, microorganisms can infect other organs.

Wounds and breaks in the skin   Undamaged human skin is a good barrier against pathogenic microorganisms. Staphylococci, which cause boils and pimples, invade hair follicles setting up local infections. Damage to the skin allows bacteria to enter, which may make wounds become septic, or fungi may enter causing diseases such as athlete's foot and ringworm. Deep wounds allow pathogens to infect muscles and

179

joints, which are normally sterile, causing the rapid development of disease. Bites, mostly by insects, are an important source of infection. Blood-sucking mosquitoes may inject malarial parasites through the skin, directly into the bloodstream. The bite of a rabid dog injects the virus present in its saliva into the victim.

11.2 How disease-causing organisms are spread

Fig 11.2
How diseases can be spread. (a) 'Coughs and sneezes spread diseases'. (b) **How the housefly spreads disease**

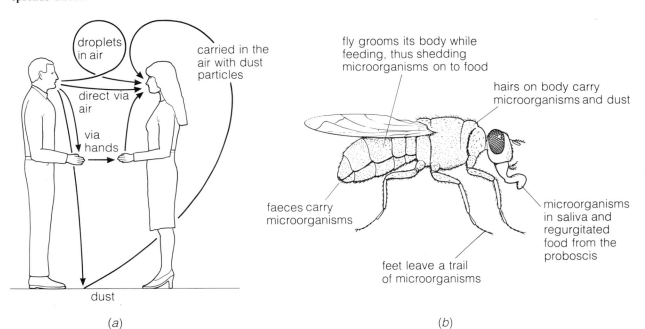

(a)

(b)

Water Many gastrointestinal infections, such as cholera and typhoid fever, are spread by contaminated water. The faeces of an infected individual will contain pathogens, so poor sanitation or sanitary habits will increase the spread of the pathogen.

Food Pathogens multiply rapidly in food, given the right conditions. Many of the organisms which are spread by water can also be spread in food. If food is not hygienically prepared, it can be contaminated from unwashed hands, dirty water, flies carrying pathogenic microorganisms, or septic wounds. Some bacteria, such as *Salmonella*, causing typhoid, paratyphoid and food poisoning, or *Clostridium*, causing botulism, an often fatal food poisoning, are able to multiply in protein-rich food such as meat, milk and eggs.

Droplet infection   Small droplets of moisture are produced whenever breathing or talking, but many more are released by coughing or sneezing (fig 11.2a). If bacteria or viruses are present in the droplets, these may be inhaled and cause respiratory infections.

Contagious diseases   Some diseases are spread by direct contact, such as AIDS and other kinds of sexually transmitted disease. AIDS is only spread by direct contact, since the HIV virus cannot survive outside the body. Fungal diseases, such as ringworm and athlete's foot, can be spread by contact, though it is usually spread by contact with skin fragments bearing the fungus that have been rubbed on to a towel or a floor surface from an infected person.

Infection by insects   Insects transmit disease-causing organisms both on the outside of their bodies and inside their guts or salivary glands. Houseflies are particularly important vectors of many intestinal diseases (fig 11.2b). Flies are attracted by smell to faeces and also to food destined for humans. When they feed, they place their proboscis, a kind of feeding tube, on the food and release saliva. This digests the food which is then sucked up. The proboscis picks up any microorganisms present and should these include pathogens, these will be spread to any food the fly settles on.

Cockroaches are vectors of many diseases, mostly intestinal. They hide in places where dirt can accumulate and they feed on human food which they contaminate with pathogens.

Some insects are bloodsuckers and enable pathogens to evade the skin barrier. These have been discussed above.

Other animal vectors   Rats, mice and other mammals may also spread diseases. Such animals as rats and mice are attracted to places where food is stored and may contaminate food with pathogens carried on their fur and feet. Some also carry *Salmonella*, causing typhoid, paratyphoid and food poisoning, in their urine and faeces. Rats carry *Leptospirosis*, causing Weil's disease, a severe form of jaundice which can be fatal. Rats also act as reservoirs of infection for many other diseases, including bubonic plague which caused the Black Death of Europe in the Middle Ages, the Great Plague of London in 1665, and many other outbreaks.

11.3   Disease transmission: some definitions

Some diseases are said to be **infectious** which means that they are caused by a pathogen that interferes with normal body function. Examples of these diseases include leprosy, rabies, mumps, typhoid and syphilis. Other diseases are said to be **non-infectious**, such as cancer, birth defects, diabetes, and vitamin deficiencies.

Epidemiology is the study of the distributions and causes of disease found mostly in humans. Scientists study epidemiology because it may help them to understand factors which predispose individuals to disease. For example, there is a high incidence of coronary heart disease among people who smoke, and in countries where fat is a major dietary component.

Other terms are used to describe the distribution of a disease in a population. A disease may be described as **endemic**, which means the disease is constantly present in a population but involves relatively few persons. Examples of such diseases include leprosy and tuberculosis. An **epidemic** is an unusual occurrence of a disease involving a sizeable proportion of a population for a limited period of time. Diseases such as influenza and poliomyelitis often reach epidemic proportions and AIDS is now reaching epidemic proportions in many Western countries. A **pandemic** is a series of epidemics affecting several countries, or even the major portions of the world. The influenza pandemic of 1918–19 was worldwide. **Sporadic** diseases are uncommon, occur irregularly and affect only a relatively few persons. Infections such as diphtheria and scarlet fever occur sporadically. These, and other infectious diseases, may ordinarily be sporadic or endemic, but, depending upon factors such as the lack of immunity in the population, poor sanitation, or the occurrence of natural disasters, they can sometimes become epidemic.

When an outbreak of a disease occurs, findings are commonly expressed in terms of **morbidity** and **mortality** rates. Morbidity is generally defined as the number of individuals having the disease per unit of the population within a given time period. Usually, 100 000 is taken as the unit of population for such calculations. The mortality rate is the number of deaths caused by a particular disease per unit of the population (usually 1000) within a given time period. Sometimes, a disease particularly affects one portion of a population. Consequently, morbidity and mortality rates may be calculated for that portion alone, for example infant mortality rate. There are certain infectious diseases which are **notifiable**. This means that a doctor must report the case to the local health authority, such as diphtheria and salmonella food poisoning.

11.4 The body's reaction to infection

The human body is constantly aiming to keep itself free of pathogens. Its mechanisms for doing this fall into two basic categories: passive defences and active immunity.

11.4.1 *Passive defences*

Passive defences are all mechanical or chemical means of protecting the body against infection, but they are non-specific. Examples of these are:

(a) the intact skin which provides a sound mechanical barrier to infection;
(b) mucus and cilia which line the respiratory and digestive tracts;
(c) the acid pH of the stomach and vagina which kills many microorganisms;
(d) lysozyme, an enzyme found in tears, sweat and nasal secretions, which brings about lysis of bacteria

11.4.2 *Antimicrobial substances*

Interferon   Interferon is a protein made by cells which are infected with a virus. Interferon then binds to surface receptors on neighbouring cells and causes them to make another antiviral protein which inhibits viral replication.

Complement   Complement is a group of eleven proteins found in blood serum. Antibodies (which will be discussed shortly) bind to antigens and activate complement. Antigen–antibody complexes also fix complement to the surface of the invading pathogen. Activated complement destroys microbes in four different ways.

(a) It creates holes in the pathogen's cell membrane, leading to cell lysis.
(b) Some complement proteins bind to receptors on phagocytes, encouraging phagocytosis. This is called **opsonisation**.
(c) Some complement proteins encourage inflammation by causing the release of histamine from certain blood components. Histamine increases the permeability of blood capillaries.
(d) Some complement proteins are chemotaxic, causing large numbers of leucocytes to be drawn to the area.

11.5 Phagocytosis

This is another non-specific mechanism, whereby pathogens that have entered the human body can be destroyed. The pathogen adheres to the phagocyte, a process which may be aided by opsonins (fig 11.3). The phagocyte produces pseudopodia, engulfing the pathogen. A phagocytic vesicle is formed, which collides with lysosomes, bringing about digestion.

11.6 Inflammation

When cells are damaged, an inflammatory response follows. The symptoms are redness, pain, heat, swelling and sometimes loss of function. The stages of inflammation are as follows.

Fig 11.3
Phagocytosis

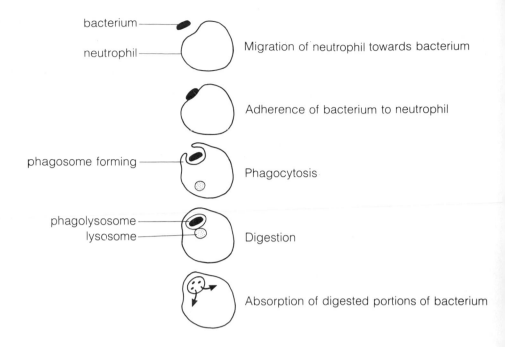

bacterium
neutrophil
Migration of neutrophil towards bacterium

Adherence of bacterium to neutrophil

phagosome forming
Phagocytosis

phagolysosome
lysosome
Digestion

Absorption of digested portions of bacterium

(a) Vasodilation occurs and the blood vessels become more permeable. This allows certain blood cells and components to reach the injured site more easily.

(b) Phagocytes migrate to the affected area. Neutrophils migrate through the wall of the blood vessel by diapedesis, a process which resembles amoeboid movement.

11.7 Immunity (specific resistance to disease)

Immunity is the production of a specific type of cell or molecule (antibody) to destroy a particular antigen. An **antigen** is a foreign chemical substance, usually of high molar mass, usually a protein, conjugated protein, or polysaccharide. The antigen triggers the production of the antibody.

An **antibody** is a special kind of protein, called an **immunoglobulin**, produced by the body in response to an antigen. It will combine specifically with that antigen. Most antibodies are made up of two, long, identical polypeptide chains called heavy chains. In addition, there are two, shorter, identical chains called light chains. At the top of the Y-shaped molecule are the variable regions, which contain the antigen binding site (fig 11.4). The variable region is different for each type of antibody and it is this region which allows the antibody to recognise and bind with a specific antigen. Antigens are bound between the light and heavy chains of the variable regions.

Fig 11.4
An immunoglobulin
antibody molecule

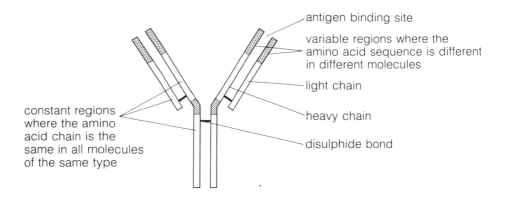

antigen binding site

variable regions where the
amino acid sequence is different
in different molecules

light chain

constant regions
where the amino
acid chain is the
same in all molecules
of the same type

heavy chain

disulphide bond

11.7.1 Cellular and humoral immunity

Cellular, or cell-mediated, immunity is particularly effective against
fungi, parasites, intracellular viruses, cancer cells and tissues
transplanted from a donor. It consists of specially sensitised
lymphocytes which attach to the foreign agent and destroy it.

Humoral (antibody-mediated) immunity is particularly effective
against bacteria and viruses. It consists of antibodies which circulate
and destroy the pathogen.

Both types of immunity derive from lymphocytes. T-lymphocytes are
responsible for cellular immunity and B-cells for humoral immunity.
Both B- and T-cells derive from stem cells in the bone marrow of the
embryo, but T-cells mature in the thymus gland, and B-cells mature in
the bone marrow, before settling in the lymphoid tissue.

Cellular immunity   Macrophages engulf the antigen by phagocytosis,
but the antigen remains on the surface of the macrophage, which
presents it to a T-cell (fig 11.5). This T-cell is now said to be sensitised.
It grows, differentiates and divides to produce a clone of identical
T-cells. These cells then differentiate into several types of T-cell.

(a) **Killer T-cells** migrate from the lymphoid tissue to the site of
infection. They attach to the pathogen and secrete lymphotoxins
which destroy it directly. Lymphotoxins also bring about lysis of
the pathogen. The T-cells also secrete lymphokines which assist
destruction of the pathogen indirectly, by such means as
attracting macrophages.

(b) **Helper T-cells** induce antibody formation by descendants of
B-cells and secrete interleukin-2, which causes the proliferation
of killer T-cells. The macrophage which presented the antigen to
the sensitised T-cell secretes interleukin-1, which stimulates the
formation of helper T-cells.

(c) **Suppressor T-cells** inhibit killer T-cells and antibody production
by plasma cells several weeks after the pathogen activated them.

(d) **Memory T-cells** recognise the original antigen. Should the same

185

Fig 11.5
Summary of immunity: the
cellular and humoral
response to a pathogen

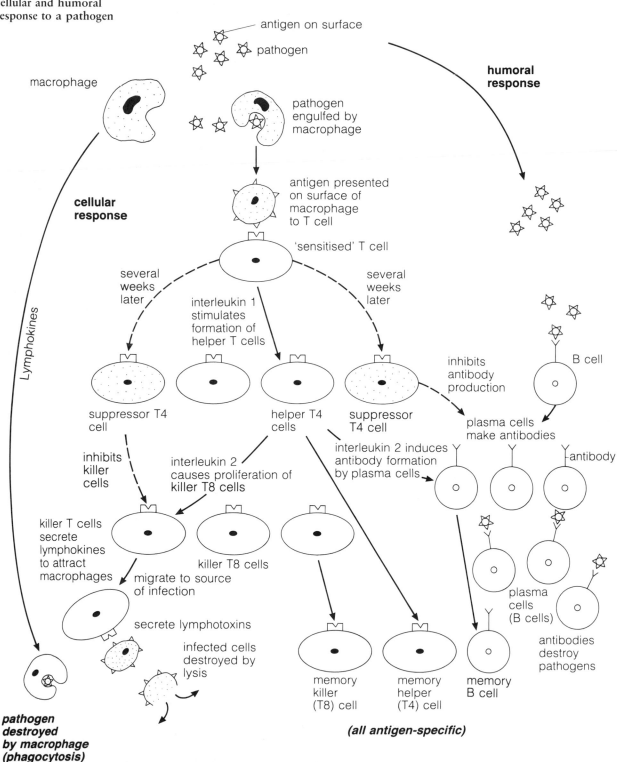

pathogen infect the body at a later date, the memory cells can bring about a much faster reaction than the first, often destroying the pathogen before any symptoms are noticeable.

(e) **Natural killer cells** are lymphocytes which are able to kill certain cells without interacting with lymphocytes or antigens, by bringing about cell lysis. They can also produce interferon which inhibits viral replication and enhances their own killing action.

Humoral immunity The macrophage presents the antigen to a B-cell in the lymphoid tissue. This cell is now activated, so it enlarges and divides to form two different kinds of B-cells. Interleukin-1, secreted by the macrophage, stimulates this process. One clone consists of **plasma cells**. These secrete specific antibodies into the circulation. The other clone consists of **memory B-cells** which recognise the original antigen (fig 11.5).

When an antigen/antibody complex is formed, the antibody activates complement enzymes which attach to the surface of the antigen and assist in the destruction of the pathogen.

Vaccines work by stimulating the generation of memory cells without posing any threat of disease.

11.8 Primary and secondary response to infection

When the body contacts an antigen for the first time, there is a delay before any antibodies appear. This is because it takes a few days for the B-cells to become sensitised and committed to producing the appropriate antibody. After this, antibody levels rise to combat the antigen but, as the body recovers, antibody levels drop again. This is called the **primary response** (fig 11.6). However, memory B-cells remain in the lymphoid tissue so, if the same antigen is contacted again, there will be no delay in producing antibodies. This **secondary response** is quicker, produces higher antibody levels and lasts longer than the primary response (fig 11.6).

Fig 11.6
Primary and secondary responses to the injection of an antigen

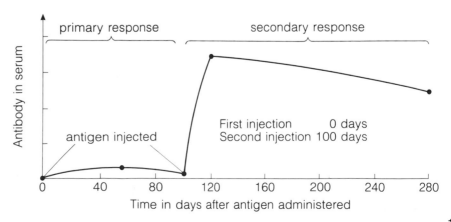

187

This principle is used to provide **immunisation** against disease. A controlled dose of a specific antigen, for example inactivated polio virus, is given to sensitise a person. The person will then produce antibodies to the pathogen and a clone of memory B-cells. Should this person become infected with the pathogen at a later date, there will be a rapid secondary response to the infection and the pathogen will be destroyed, usually without the person even developing any symptoms.

11.9 Chemotherapy

Chemotherapy is the treatment of a disease with antimicrobial agents. Chemotherapeutic agents include antifungal, antibacterial and antiviral agents.

In choosing a suitable chemotherapeutic agent to treat a patient, there are many factors which a doctor needs to consider, as shown in fig 11.7.

Fig 11.7
Choosing the best
chemotherapeutic agent

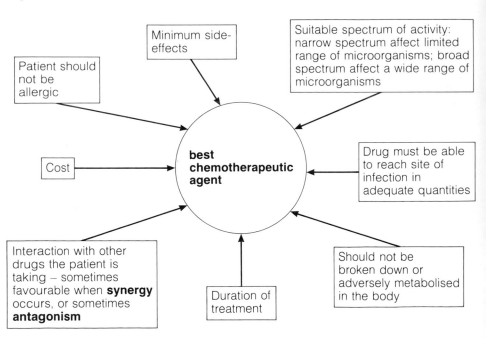

11.9.1 Antibiotics and antimicrobials

Antibiotics are substances produced by microorganisms which, in low concentrations, kill or inhibit the growth of other microorganisms; whereas **antimicrobials** are wholly synthetic molecules which work in a similar way to antibiotics, for example sulphonamides.

Antibiotics may be bactericidal or bacteriostatic. **Bactericidal** antibiotics kill the pathogen, whereas **bacteriostatic** agents simply prevent replication, leaving the host's defences to kill the existing pathogens. The difference may be seen in the graph in fig 11.8.

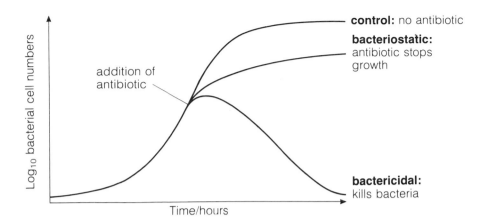

Fig 11.8
To show the effect of
antibiotics on the growth
curve of bacteria

Antibiotics work in various ways, as summarised in fig 11.9. The aim
is to exploit the differences between prokaryotic cells and eukaryotic
cells. If a drug affects a target which does not exist in eukaryotic cells,
such as the bacterial cell wall, then the toxic effects of that drug on the
patient are likely to be reduced.

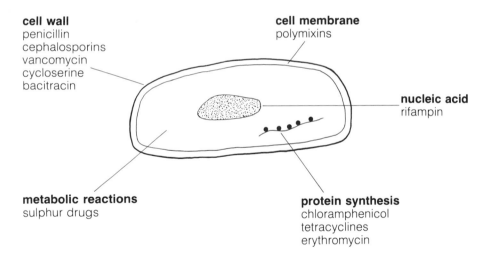

Fig 11.9
Targets in the bacterium
for various antibiotics

Cell wall disruption   These antibiotics, such as penicillin, prevent the
synthesis of mucopeptide, and are said to be bactericidal (fig 11.10).
This is because the bacteria have weakened cell walls and are easily
lysed. Gram +ve bacteria are affected more than Gram −ve, since the
outer layer of Gram −ve bacteria offers some protection against the
antibiotic. Eukaryotic cells totally lack mucopeptide, so these antibiotics
should be non-toxic. Some of these antibiotics are, in fact, toxic, but
this is because of other effects. Semi-synthetic derivatives can be made
by changing the R group.

Cell membrane disruption   These antibiotics kill cells by affecting the
permeability of the cell membrane. Some antibiotics in this category

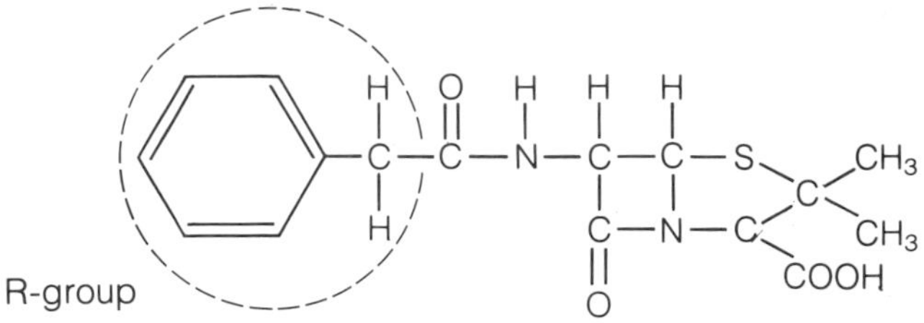

Fig 11.10
The structure of
penicillin G

react with ergosterol, a sterol found in fungal cell membranes. This
gives them selective toxicity, since human cells do not contain
ergosterol but cholesterol instead. Nevertheless, they can still harm
human cells and must be used carefully. Polymixins interact with the
phospholipids in the cell membrane, creating holes which alter its
permeability.

Protein synthesis disruption   Tetracyclines prevent the binding of
tRNA to 70S ribosomes. They do not affect 80S ribosomes, so they are
specific for prokaryotes and are also **broad-spectrum** which means that
they are effective against a wide range of microorganisms.
Erythromycin and chloramphenicol prevent peptide bond formation
during prokaryotic protein synthesis. They are bacteriostatic since they
do not damage the ribosomes.

Nucleic acid disruption   Rifampin is a very selective drug which
inactivates bacterial mRNA polymerase, thereby preventing mRNA
transcription.

Disruption of bacterial metabolism   Sulphur drugs are very similar in
structure to para-amino benzoic acid (PABA) (fig 11.11). These agents
are usually competitive inhibitors of the enzymes involved in bacterial
metabolic reactions.
   Normally PABA is enzymatically converted to folic acid, an essential
cofactor needed by bacteria to build new nucleotides. Sulphur drugs
bind reversibly with the active site of the enzyme and prevent folic acid
synthesis. They are therefore bacteriostatic agents. Human cells obtain
all their folic acid from dietary sources and are therefore not affected.

Fig 11.11
Sulphur drugs and PABA

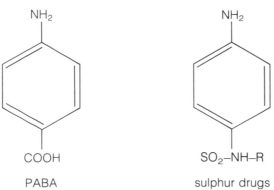

Fig 11.12
Antibiotic susceptibility tests. (*a*) **Disc diffusion method.** (*b*) **Minimum inhibitory concentration (MIC)**

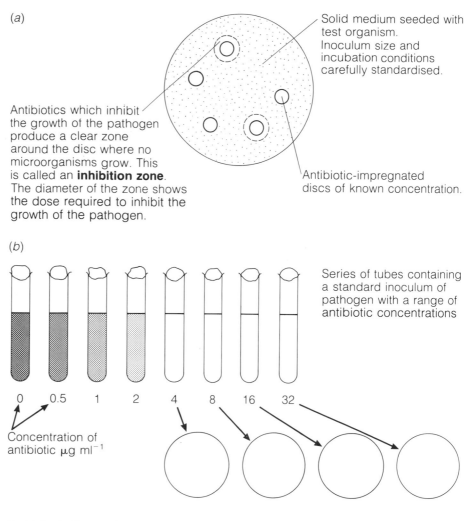

(*a*)

Antibiotics which inhibit the growth of the pathogen produce a clear zone around the disc where no microorganisms grow. This is called an **inhibition zone**. The diameter of the zone shows the dose required to inhibit the growth of the pathogen.

Solid medium seeded with test organism. Inoculum size and incubation conditions carefully standardised.

Antibiotic-impregnated discs of known concentration.

(*b*)

Series of tubes containing a standard inoculum of pathogen with a range of antibiotic concentrations

0   0.5   1   2   4   8   16   32

Concentration of antibiotic μg ml^{-1}

Turbidity indicates the growth of microorganisms; thus the MIC is the lowest concentration of antibiotic which will inhibit growth. All the non-turbid tubes are then plated out onto solid agar medium and incubated:

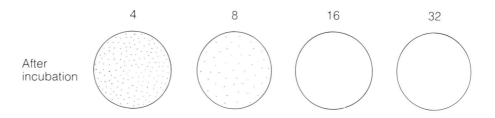

4   8   16   32

After incubation

The minimum bactericidal concentration (MBC) is the lowest concentration of antibiotic which shows no growth.

In this case, 4 μg ml^{-1} is the MIC and 16 μg ml^{-1} is the MBC.

11.9.2 Antibiotic susceptibility tests

Ideally, before an antibiotic is given, a test should be carried out to find out which drug is most suitable (fig 11.12).

The **minimum inhibitory concentration** (MIC) of a drug is the lowest dose that will inhibit the replication of the pathogen. However, this MIC must be achieved *at the site of infection* if the drug is to prove effective. Tissue levels of antibiotic are known to be much lower than serum levels, so serum antibiotic levels of 2–8 times the minimum inhibitory concentration (MIC) are aimed at. It is also important that safe dosages are not exceeded, since serious side-effects can occur with some drugs. Antibiotic concentration in fluids can be monitored using a bioassay, as shown in fig 11.13.

Fig 11.13
Monitoring antibiotic concentrations in tissue fluids using a bioassay

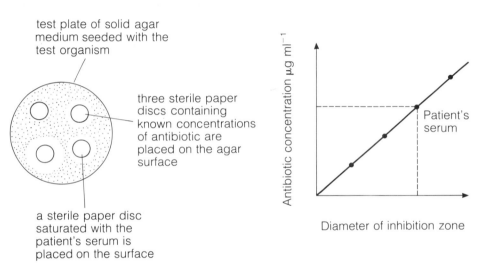

test plate of solid agar medium seeded with the test organism

three sterile paper discs containing known concentrations of antibiotic are placed on the agar surface

a sterile paper disc saturated with the patient's serum is placed on the surface

After incubation, the inhibition zones are measured and plotted on a graph.

Thus the antibiotic concentration in the patient's serum can be found.

11.9.3 Antiviral agents

There are still, despite many years of research, very few drugs available to treat viral disease. None of these agents can cure the disease.

Amantadine   This blocks the entry of influenza virus A into cells, but cannot prevent replication of the virus once it has entered cells. It is usually used to protect the elderly, and others highly at risk, during an influenza epidemic. It can also shorten the duration of symptoms once the disease has been contracted.

Acyclovir   This specifically inhibits the synthesis of herpes virus DNA. The drug is only activated in virus-infected cells, so has few side-effects. It can be applied to oral or genital herpes lesions to reduce the duration of symptoms. It does not rid the body of the virus, which is established in the nervous system and further episodes of infection can occur. It is used systemically to treat herpes infections in immuno-suppressed patients, for example after transplant operations. It will also help to reduce symptoms in *Herpes zoster* (shingles).

Idoxuridine   This inhibits DNA replication, but is highly toxic as it can affect both host and viral DNA. It is applied to herpes virus infections of the eye, since cells of the cornea are not actively dividing.

There are several other antiviral drugs currently being tested.

Human interferon   In 1957, Isaacs and Lindemann discovered that cells infected by the influenza virus produced a protein which enabled other cells to resist viral infections. They called this substance **interferon**. The discovery was exciting since it was found to protect against a wide range of viruses. It was found to be potent and, being a natural substance, it seemed likely to have low toxicity. However, it was not to be the long hoped-for 'viral penicillin'. Interferon is now known to be a large group of proteins, varying between and even within species, and can be induced by a wide range of substances. Its action is complex and largely unknown. It is secreted in minute amounts and therefore it is very hard to purify.

Interferon is not virus-specific because it does not interact with the virus but with the host cell instead (fig 11.14).

Fig 11.14
How interferon works

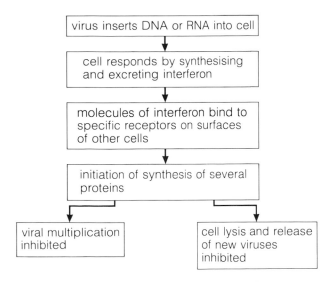

Interferon has other effects:

(*a*)   in many cases it inhibits cell proliferation;
(*b*)   it stimulates natural killer lymphocytes which destroy foreign cells, and possibly cancer cells.

These properties explain reports that interferon can cause regression of some cancerous tumours. However, progress has been restricted by the great shortage of interferon and its high cost. The work is further complicated by an inability to obtain pure samples of interferon.

Recently, gene sequences have been found for certain human interferons. The gene can be inserted into *Escherichia coli* and the recombinant bacterium used to synthesise large quantities of interferon. Monoclonal antibodies are used to purify the product.

The main side-effects of interferon are fever, chills, muscle aches and mild gastrointestinal upsets. These symptoms usually disappear with time. Interferon can also cause fatigue and lack of appetite; these symptoms increase with higher dosage and length of treatment.

Certain types of cancer do show regression; for example kidney cancer, malignant myeloma and multiple myeloma. At present, only a few types of interferon are available; it is possible that more types will be available in the future to treat other cancers.

11.10 Antimicrobial resistance

Some microorganisms are innately resistant to antimicrobial agents, while others acquire resistance.

11.10.1 Innate resistance

The antibiotic may act on a target which the microorganism does not have. An example of this is mucopeptide. This is only found in bacteria, so antibiotics, which prevent mucopeptide synthesis, will not be effective against protozoa and fungi.

11.10.2 Acquired resistance

There are many forms of acquired resistance.

(a) The microorganism may produce enzymes which inactivate the antibiotic. For example penicillinases are produced by many species of bacteria.

(b) The microorganism changes the target so that it is no longer affected by the drug. For example, some bacteria develop streptomycin resistance by producing modified ribosomes which the antibiotic cannot bind to.

(c) Antibiotics which inhibit metabolic reactions can sometimes be resisted by by-passing the critical step in the pathway. For example, some bacteria develop resistance to sulphur drugs by developing the ability to absorb folic acid.

(d) Some microorganisms develop changes in their membranes which make it more difficult for the drug to enter the cell.

The main problem associated with the use of antimicrobial drugs is that microorganisms are rapidly achieving resistance. Bacteria often develop resistance by means of 'R-factors', that is genes present on plasmids (see table 1.3), and these are rapidly spread by bacterial conjugation. Development of new antibiotics is only a partial solution as resistance to these quickly appears. Measures must be taken if existing antibiotics are to continue to be therapeutic.

In recent years, a strain of *Staphlococcus aureus* has appeared in hospitals all over the world. It is resistant to all antibiotics except vancomycin, which has highly toxic and often lethal side-effects. Very strict hygiene measures can be used to reduce the spread of this organism, but it illustrates the need to guard against the development of resistant strains.

11.10.3   *Reducing the problem of antimicrobial resistance*

As resistance to antimicrobial drugs is an increasing problem, there are many techniques in use now to try and prevent this.

(a)   Prevent the spread of the disease, thereby reducing the number of infections.

(b)   Sometimes antibiotics are used to prevent, rather than treat, infection. This is called **prophylaxis**. The use of prophylactic drugs should be strictly limited to those rare situations where it is necessary, for example after surgery on the gastrointestinal tract which releases large numbers of potential pathogens into the abdominal cavity.

(c)   Identify viral disease so that antibacterial drugs are not prescribed unnecessarily.

(d)   Use laboratory tests to find the effective antibiotic.

(e)   Some antibiotics are narrow-spectrum (effective against a small range of microorganisms) while others are broad-spectrum (effective against many different microorganisms). In the past, doctors have preferred broad-spectrum drugs as these eliminate the need for accurate laboratory tests. However, using narrow-spectrum drugs in conjunction with laboratory tests reduces the likelihood of microbial resistance developing.

(f)   If general agreement could be reached, certain antibiotics could be reserved for use only against infections that do not respond to other antibiotics. The reserve drugs would then be used so rarely that resistant microbes would be unlikely to develop.

(g)   Farm animals are often fed antibiotics and antibiotic waste as this enhances meat production. This also means that their gut bacteria are likely to develop antibiotic resistance. Similarly, there has been much over-prescribing of antibiotics for humans, both prophylactically in hospitals and because patients expect a 'wonder-drug' for all ailments, however trivial. This greatly increases the chance of resistant bacteria developing.

(*h*) People often stop taking prescribed antibiotics when they feel better. This means that some bacteria may still be present, although inhibited. On discontinuing the drug, these bacteria can proliferate and may acquire resistance. Therefore, it is important always to finish the prescribed course of antibiotics.

Questions

1 Name six factors which should be considered when choosing a therapeutic agent.

2 Distinguish between:

(*a*) antibiotics and antimicrobials;
(*b*) bactericidal and bacteriostatic agents;
(*c*) chemotherapy and chemoprophylaxis;
(*d*) minimum inhibitory concentration and minimum bactericidal concentration;
(*e*) broad-spectrum and narrow-spectrum antibiotics;
(*f*) bactericidal and bacteriostatic antibiotics.

3 Name the five target sites for antibacterial drugs and give one example of a drug in each category.

4 Why are there so few antiviral drugs? Why do these not cure the disease?

5 Fig 11.15 shows blood levels of a standard dose of an antibiotic administered in different ways. Suggest reasons for the different blood levels achieved by the different methods of administration.

Fig 11.15
The concentration of antibiotic in the blood due to a standard dose of antibiotic administered in different ways

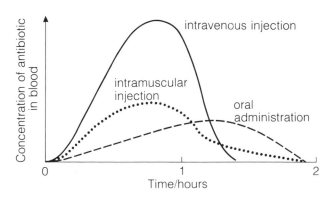

6 Explain how bacteria can develop antibiotic resistance so easily and pass on this quality so quickly.

Suggest measures which could be taken to avoid bacterial resistance developing.

7   (*a*)   Give an account of the defence mechanisms which mammals possess to counteract the invasion of the body by foreign organisms.   (10)

       (*b*)   Fig 11.16 shows the events which occur in the human body over a period of time following the administration of a vaccine such as the typhoid vaccine.

Fig 11.16

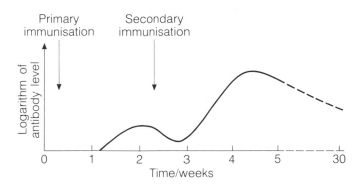

Explain the body's response to the administration of the vaccine

       (i)   between the primary and the secondary immunisation;

       (ii)   after the secondary immunisation.   (5)

       (*c*)   (i)   Explain briefly the difference in production between a dead (inactivated) and a live (attenuated) vaccine.

            (ii)   Apart from a vaccination programme, how might the spread of typhoid be limited or prevented?   (5)

                                                   Total marks = 20

JMB Option C July 1988

8   (*a*)   Define the term chemotherapeutic agent. Name **two** different types of such agents.

       (*b*)   Fig 11.17 shows an assay plate used for testing chemotherapeutic agents. Samples of the agent were placed in small wells punched in the agar and the nutrient agar seeded with a test bacterium.

            Following incubation, the plate had the appearance shown in fig 11.17.

            (i)   Explain the significance of the clear zones around some of the wells.

            (ii)   Suggest **two** factors which could affect the areas of these zones.

            (iii)   What is the value of this technique to the pharmaceutical industry?

JMB Option C June 1988 (part question)

9   (*a*)   Explain how the nutrients of an appropriate culture medium satisfy the growth requirements of a typical mould or yeast.   (5)

Fig 11.17

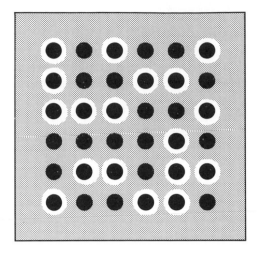

(b) Fig 11.18 shows a fermentation process in which *Penicillium chrysogenum* is being grown using the batch culture method. From 40 hours, glucose was added slowly and continuously.

Fig 11.18

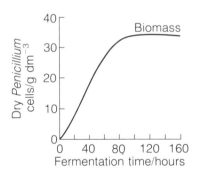 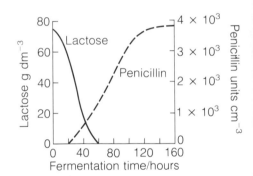

(i) What is meant by a 'batch culture'?

(ii) Explain the shape of the biomass curve.

(iii) What evidence from the graphs supports the conclusion that penicillin is a secondary metabolite?

(iv) Glucose feeding starts at 40 hours. Why is this necessary at this time?

(v) State, giving a reason, what is the most beneficial time to harvest the penicillin.

(vi) Outline the procedures that might be required to obtain crystalline penicillin. (10)

(c) Outline various techniques which could be used to improve efficiency of antibiotic production by a particular species of fungus. How might this efficiency be tested? (5)

Total = 20 marks

JMB Option C July 1989

10 Fig 11.19 shows an agar plate with three wells, **A**, **B** and **C**, cut into the agar. Well **A** contained whole mouse serum, **B** contained rabbit antibodies against whole mouse serum, and **C** contained mouse immunoglobulin G. Contents from the wells diffused outwards and after eight hours precipitations occurred in regions indicated by the lines.

Explain

  (a) the appearance of the precipitation lines between **A** and **B** and between **B** and **C**;

  (b) the absence of lines between **A** and **C**.

JMB June 1989 (part question)

Fig 11.19

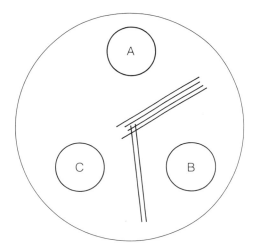

11 With reference to named examples give **three** ways in which pathogenic microorganisms gain access to the human body.

JMB option C June 1989 (part question)

12 Plant disease

12.1 The economic importance of plant disease

There is no doubt that plant disease has a serious effect on crops, and modern agriculture has come to rely on efficient fungicides and the development of disease-resistant crop plants. Late blight of potato is not only notorious for the great potato famines in Ireland, but it has even been suggested that the damage it inflicted on the German potato crop during the First World War helped to end the war itself. In Ghana, cocoa production has fallen from 118 000 tons in 1936 to 40 000 tons in 1982, because of the effects of the cocoa swollen shoot virus.

12.2 Disease

Disease is a condition in which the normal functions of the plant are disturbed. This may be caused by environmental factors, such as a lack of mineral salts in the soil, or by pathogens, genetic defects or a combination of these factors. **Injuries** can result in similar symptoms, but differ from disease in that they tend to be sudden. Disease is generally a slower process.

There are several categories of microorganisms which cause plant diseases: fungi, bacteria, mycoplasmas and viruses. Of these, fungi and viruses are the most important. This contrasts with the situation in animals where fungi are relatively unimportant. One reason for this difference is that plants provide a very different environment from animals for microbial pathogens (table 12.1).

Bacteria colonise animal hosts, because these offer a more efficient transport system. Similarly, they have difficulty penetrating the cuticle of plants, so tend to be dependent on wounds or insect vectors. Bacteria thrive in warm, alkaline conditions, such as animals offer. The

Table 12.1
A comparison of flowering plant and mammal cells as hosts

Flowering plants	Mammals
rigid cell wall present	no cell wall
no circulatory system to transport pathogen round host, although vascular tissue offers limited transport	circulatory system
acid pH	alkaline pH
structural materials are largely carbohydrates	structural tissues largely based on proteins
internal temperature is not regulated, it fluctuates	internal temperature regulated, therefore environment warmer

Fig 12.1
Plant disease. A mildew fungus on apple.

structure of animals is based on proteins, giving bacteria the high nitrogen levels they require. Another difficulty bacteria encounter when infecting plant cells is dispersal. Plants are sedentary, so a plant pathogen must have an effective dispersal strategy, such as motile spores. Bacteria which infect plants tend to rely on rain drop splashes to carry them. Or they spread through infected host tissue, for example by contact with infected tubers such as potatoes.

Fungi are more effective plant pathogens than bacteria. Some are able to produce enzymes to digest plant tissues, or they form special infection structures called **appressoria** (fig 12.3). They have less need for transport round the plant, since their hyphae spread rapidly through the plant tissue. Fungi grow better at the lower temperatures found in plants and prefer the acid pH and lower nitrogen levels which result from the carbohydrate-based structure of plants. They have special dispersal mechanisms whereby spores are released into the air. Many fungal pathogens can form dormant resting spores.

Viruses invade plant cells by following the lytic cycle (see section 1.7.3). A virus may have several plant hosts, but may not show obvious symptoms in most of their hosts. However, they can cause great damage in certain hosts, and are of major economic importance. Cucumber mosaic virus attacks a wide range of horticultural crops, but is symptomless in chickweed which acts as a reservoir of infection. Viruses encounter the same difficulties as bacteria in entering plant tissue and in dispersal. They are transmitted mainly by vegetative propagation, or in seeds, sometimes in tissues such as bulbs, and by vectors, especially sucking insects. In laboratory or horticultural situations, a few highly virulent viruses, such as tobacco mosaic virus, are spread by contact between plants, especially if the plant is slightly damaged by wounding.

12.3 How pathogens enter plants

Fig 12.2 shows some ways in which pathogens enter plants.

**Fig 12.2
How pathogens enter
plants**

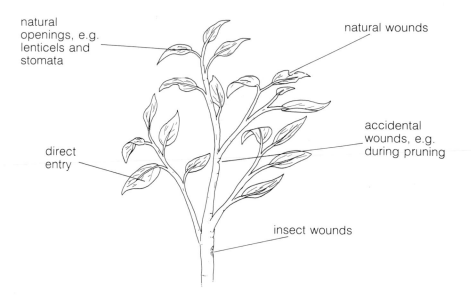

natural openings, e.g. lenticels and stomata

natural wounds

accidental wounds, e.g. during pruning

direct entry

insect wounds

12.3.1 Direct entry

It is difficult for a pathogen to enter a plant directly, because there are layers of wax, cutin, pectin, and cellulose on the outside of the plant. Generally, pathogens able to penetrate do this by using special infection structures. A fungal spore germinates forming a germ-tube. The hyphal tip swells to form an **appressorium** (fig 12.3). A thin hypha called an **infection peg** forms on the underside of the appressorium. This peg sometimes invades the plant tissue by mechanical pressure, but some species of fungi produce enzymes to assist this process.

12.3.2 Natural openings

Plants have natural openings, such as stomata and lenticels. These are particularly important for bacterial and viral pathogens. Bacteria may enter stomata in water droplets, for example *Pseudomonas citri* in citrus fruits. Rust fungi also enter leaves via stomata.

12.3.3 Wounds

Wounds result from many types of damage: severe weather, pests, insect vectors, pruning, natural abcission of leaves in the autumn or the emergence of lateral roots are some examples. Pathogens may be drawn into wounds when the water tension in the xylem is broken. Fresh wounds also lack protective layers.

Fig 12.3
Stages in the penetration of a leaf by *Peronospora parasitica*

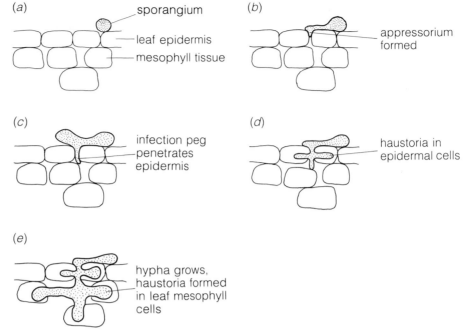

(a) sporangium — leaf epidermis — mesophyll tissue

(b) appressorium formed

(c) infection peg penetrates epidermis

(d) haustoria in epidermal cells

(e) hypha grows, haustoria formed in leaf mesophyll cells

12.4 Necrotrophs and biotrophs

Plant pathogens can be loosely divided into two groups: **necrotrophs** and **biotrophs**. Necrotrophs first kill the host tissue, then feed off the dead cells. Biotrophs feed off living host tissue. The differences between the two categories, however, are not always clear-cut. Some pathogens, such as *Phytophthora infestans* which causes late blight of potato, show characteristics of both types. It has a narrow host range and produces haustoria (biotrophic characteristics, see table 12.2) yet causes rapid death of host cells and can be grown in artificial culture (necrotrophic characteristics). Necrotrophs rarely have special adaptations for feeding, since they live off dead plant material. Biotrophs, on the other hand, need to be highly adapted to their hosts. They frequently have specialised feeding structures, called **haustoria** (fig 12.4). These are extensions of the hyphae which penetrate the host cell wall, pushing aside the host protoplast. The membrane of the haustorium lies adjacent to the host cell's surface membrane, so that the fungus is able to derive nutrients from its host. Note, however, that the haustorium is not a true intracellular structure, since it only penetrates the cell wall but leaves the living part of the cell, the protoplast, intact.

Erysiphe graminis, which causes powdery mildew in cereal crops, is an example of a biotroph. Once the host cell is infected, the germ tube grows inside the epidermal cell forming a long haustorium with a single nucleus. The haustorium has finger-like projections developing from

Fig 12.4
Haustorium of *Erysiphe pisi*, powdery mildew (based on electron micrographs)

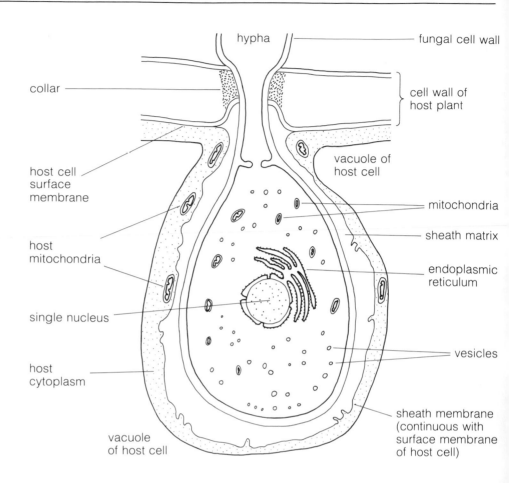

hypha

fungal cell wall

collar

cell wall of host plant

host cell surface membrane

vacuole of host cell

host mitochondria

mitochondria

sheath matrix

endoplasmic reticulum

single nucleus

host cytoplasm

vesicles

vacuole of host cell

sheath membrane (continuous with surface membrane of host cell)

opposite ends. The whole of the haustorium is enclosed in a sheath. The haustorium contains a single nucleus, mitochondria, endoplasmic reticulum and many vesicles. Below where it penetrated the host cell, the neck of the haustorium is surrounded by a collar formed of material deposited on the host cell wall. Outside the wall of the haustorium is a wide **sheath matrix**. This is bounded by a **sheath membrane** which is continuous with the surface membrane of the host cell. This sheath membrane is where materials are exchanged between the host cell and the pathogen.

12.4.1 Dutch elm disease

This is a necrotrophic disease caused by a fungus called *Ceratocystis ulmi*, which is spread by an insect vector, the bark beetle *Scolytus scolytus* (fig 12.5). The bark beetles create a maze of tunnels in the cambium tissue of the tree, and carry the spores of *Ceratocystis ulmi* on their bodies. The fungus readily establishes itself in the xylem vessels of the tree.

	Necrotrophs	Biotrophs
Table 12.2 **The main features of** **necrotrophs and biotrophs**	must kill host cells in order to feed	need to keep the host cells alive
	host cells quickly killed	host cells killed more slowly
	toxins and cell-destroying enzymes produced	few or no toxins and cell-destroying enzymes produced
	do not form specialised feeding structures	generally form specialised parasitic structures for feeding, e.g. haustoria
	entry to host usually via wounds or natural openings	entry to host usually by direct penetration or natural openings
	wide range of hosts	narrow range of hosts
	able to grow as saprophytes when not in host, for example in soil	rarely survive as saprophytes away from host; need to survive as resting structures, e.g. spores
	can generally be grown in a pure culture away from the host	generally cannot be grown artificially away from host
	attack immature, wounded or old parts of plants	able to attack healthy plants at various stages in their life cycles

Fig 12.5
Dutch elm disease,
Ceratocystis ulmi

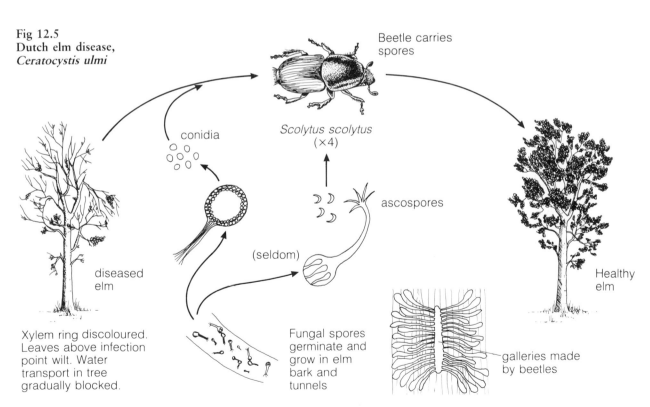

Beetle carries spores

conidia

Scolytus scolytus
(×4)

ascospores

(seldom)

diseased elm

Xylem ring discoloured. Leaves above infection point wilt. Water transport in tree gradually blocked.

Fungal spores germinate and grow in elm bark and tunnels

galleries made by beetles

Healthy elm

Ceratocystis ulmi is an example of a **vascular wilt** disease. These tend to show similar symptoms:

    (a)   the respiratory rate of the plant increases;

    (b)   the leaves turn yellow (chlorosis) and wilt;

(c)   the fungal hyphae grow into the xylem vessels of the host and secrete a toxin. This creates a gel in the xylem and impedes water flow.

(d)   in response to the infection, the host xylem forms **tyloses**, which are outgrowths from the neighbouring parenchyma which block the xylem completely (fig 12.6).

(e)   water stress leads to the petioles bending downwards. The stomata close and the plant wilts.

Most vascular wilt fungi enter the roots of the plant via the soil, such as *Fusarium* sp. and *Verticillium* sp. Dutch elm disease is unlike most vascular wilts in being spread by a vector.

Fig 12.6
Dutch elm disease:
symptoms and tyloses

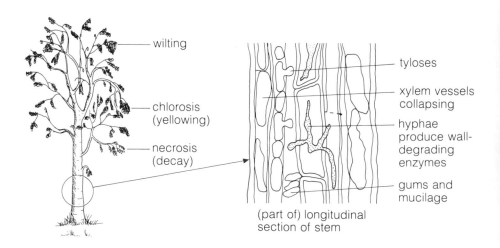

Control

(a)   Sanitary measures, such as felling dead elms and burning the wood to destroy the beetle's habitat.

(b)   Control of the beetle using insecticides and of the fungus by using systemic fungicides.

(c)   Growing species of elm which are more resistant to the disease, such as American Elm, *Ulmus americana*.

(d)   Using biological control. There is a type of wasp which parasitises the beetle and a species of *Pseudomonas* which attacks the fungus.

12.4.2   Late blight of potato

Potato blight is caused by *Phytophthora infestans*. The disease is particularly virulent in warm, wet conditions, since these conditions encourage the formation of motile zoospores, which are more effective in transmitting the disease than sporangia. It produced numerous famines in Ireland, most notably that of 1845–7, when it caused over one million deaths from starvation. It led to mass emigration from Ireland to the United States, and within a few years halved the population of Ireland.

Phytophthora infestans overwinters in potato tubers from the previous year. A mycelium develops from these, producing enormous numbers of asexual spores called **sporangia** (fig 12.7). These spread by means of air currents to healthy plants. In cool conditions (below 18 °C) they germinate immediately, but above this temperature they produce flagellated **zoospores**. These are potentially more efficient at spreading the disease, since they are motile. The germ tube which is produced by the germinating spore is capable of penetrating the epidermis directly, or it may enter via stomata. The mycelium inside the leaf produces sporangiophores which hang from the stomata on the underside of the leaf, releasing numerous **sporangia**. The fungus relies mainly on asexual reproduction as described, but sometimes a female **oogonium** develops, which is fertilised by the male **antheridium**. A resistant **oospore** is produced, which can survive long periods in the soil, before germinating into motile zoospores which are capable of reinfecting other plants.

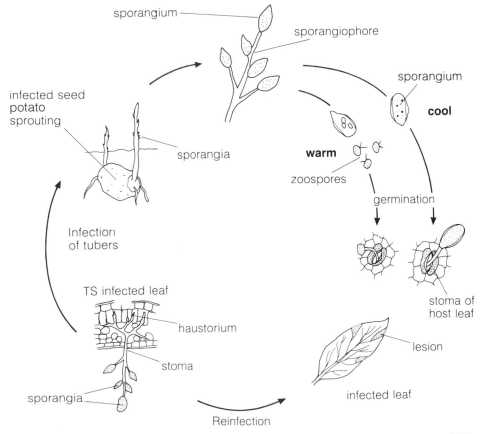

Fig 12.7
Potato blight: the life cycle of *Phytophthora infestans* (sexual stage omitted)

The first sign of potato blight is the appearance of small watery spots at the leaf margin. These become blackened and necrotic, spreading down the leaves to the petioles. Photosynthesis is impaired due to loss of leaf area and spores from the infected leaves invade the tubers.

Control

(a) Effective sanitary measures are required. The use of a defoliant to destroy the surface plant before harvesting potatoes, to avoid the fungus infecting tubers, can be effective.

(b) Use only certified disease-free stock as seed potatoes.

(c) 'Earthing-up' of potatoes as they grow, to decrease the likelihood of spores washed off leaves reaching the tubers.

(d) Use of fungicides, such as Bordeaux mixture, based on copper salts.

12.4.3 Damping-off

Pythium sp. is a necrotroph which grows saprotrophically in the soil. It can however, parasitise newly germinated seedlings, especially in damp conditions (fig 12.8). Within about five days of infection the host plant collapses at about soil level. *Pythium* secretes pectic enzymes to digest the middle lamella between host cells, making it easier for the fungal hyphae to penetrate.

**Fig 12.8
Damping-off fungus
(*Pythium debaryanum*)**

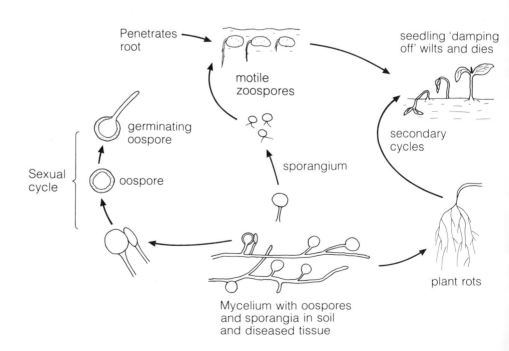

Control *Pythium* is hard to control because it can grow saprotrophically in the soil, and has many hosts. It can be avoided to some extent by:

(a) growing crops in well-drained soil and avoiding overcrowding of seedlings;

(b) in greenhouses, sterilisation by steam or chemicals can reduce its incidence.

12.4.4 *Loose smut of oats*

Ustilago avenae is a biotroph which generally infects the plant at the base of the ovary, but can also infect the germinating seedling. Flower development is affected and so crop yield is reduced, as is the growth rate.

It overwinters as a **teleutospore** or as mycelium in the grain. When the infected seed germinates, the mycelium grows through the tissues of the seedling towards the flower. It destroys the flower and replaces the grain with masses of smut spores. Flowers may also become infected with the prolific asexual spores, conidia.

Control

(a) Dusting seeds with fungicide to prevent any spores present on the seed surface infecting the germinating seedling and using systemic fungicides on crop.

(b) Careful selection of non-infected plants to provide seed for next year's crop.

(c) Breeding completely smut-resistant plants has proved difficult, but varieties of cereals which have flowers that do not open are less likely to become infected.

12.4.5 *'Take-all' of wheat*

Gaeumannomyces graminis is a necrotrophic fungus which infects wheat roots, causing the death of infected seedlings. If older plants are infected, they produce small seed-heads which ripen prematurely, causing substantial loss of yield. Infected roots become blackened and die, but the plant often manages to survive by producing adventitious roots faster than the fungus can kill them. The fungus grows on the outside of the root, extending small feeding hyphae into the root cortex and eventually into the vascular tissue. The feeding hyphae kill the host cells, but the fungus spreads rapidly along the root, quickly infecting the whole root system.

Control

(*a*)   In the case of this disease, there are no resistant varieties.

(*b*)   Fungicides are not very effective, since they are not downwardly translocated.

(*c*)   At present, the best means of control is by careful horticultural practice, particularly crop rotation, since this pathogen cannot survive very long as a saprotroph in the soil.

12.4.6   *Black stem rust of wheat*

This is caused by *Puccinia graminis*, which is one of about 7000 species of rusts. It is a biotroph which has a complicated life cycle. It can live indefinitely on wheat, but is only capable of asexual reproduction within that host. For sexual reproduction to occur, it must spend part of its time on the barberry.

Basidiospores of *Puccinia graminis* infect the barberry in the spring (fig 12.9). They are of separate + and − strains and develop into **spermagonia** on the upper surface of the leaves. Each spermagonium produces both **receptive hyphae** and chains of small cells called **spermatia**. If a + receptive hypha from one spermagonium contacts a − spermatium of another spermagonium, or vice versa, they fuse to form dikaryotic hyphae. These produce aecial primordia which grow downwards from the spermagonium, producing **aecia** on the lower surface of the leaf. The aecia produce chains of dikaryotic aeciospores which infect the wheat.

The aeciospores germinate on the wheat producing rust-coloured streaks on the leaves. This is called the **red stage** and the streaks are uredinia containing uredospores. These uredospores are produced throughout the summer and reinfect the wheat. Later in the summer and autumn, the mycelium darkens, and the uredinia develop into **telia** containing two-celled **teleutospores**. This stage is called the **dark stage**. The teleutospores do not infect either the wheat or the barberry, but remain overwinter in the soil. In early spring, the two haploid nuclei in the two-celled teleutospore fuse to give a single diploid nucleus. The spore starts to germinate and meiosis occurs, producing basidiospores. These infect the barberry and the life cycle is completed.

Control   The main method used to combat black stem rust is to breed resistant varieties. However, the rust fungus is able to mutate quickly and form new genetic combinations, making resistance short-lived.

12.4.7   *Powdery mildew* (Erysiphe)

Erysiphe graminis causes **powdery mildew** which is a classic case of a biotrophic disease in grasses and cereal crops. There are a number of

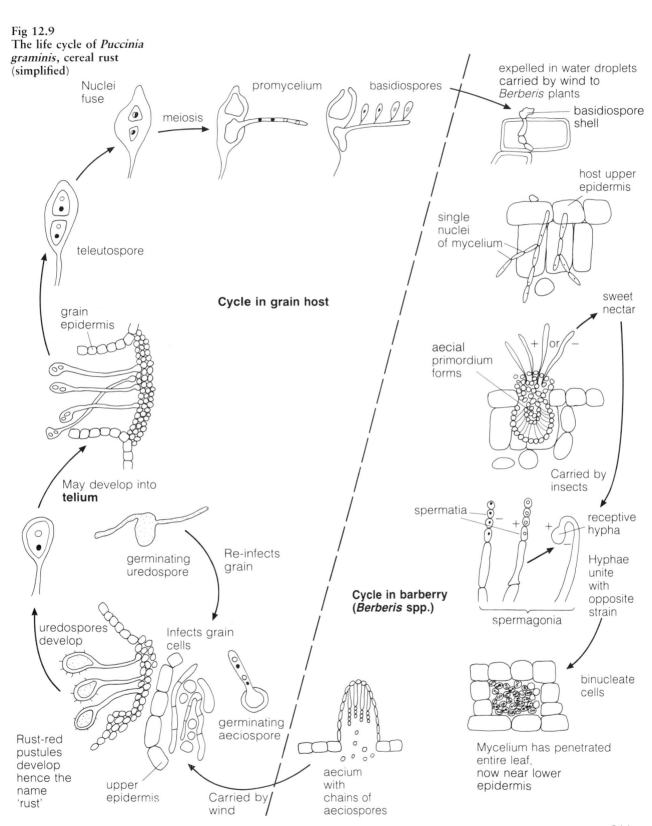

Fig 12.9
The life cycle of *Puccinia graminis*, cereal rust (simplified)

Nuclei fuse

meiosis

promycelium

basidiospores

expelled in water droplets carried by wind to *Berberis* plants

basidiospore shell

teleutospore

Cycle in grain host

host upper epidermis

single nuclei of mycelium

sweet nectar

grain epidermis

aecial primordium forms

+ or −

Carried by insects

May develop into **telium**

germinating uredospore

Re-infects grain

Cycle in barberry (*Berberis* spp.)

spermatia

− + +

receptive hypha

Hyphae unite with opposite strain

spermagonia

uredospores develop

Infects grain cells

Rust-red pustules develop hence the name 'rust'

germinating aeciospore

binucleate cells

upper epidermis

Carried by wind

aecium with chains of aeciospores

Mycelium has penetrated entire leaf, now near lower epidermis

host-specific forms: *E. graminis tritici* infects wheat and *E. graminis hordei* infects barley. Both diseases may seriously reduce crop yields. The disease first appears as white to pale brown pustules (small raised spots) containing conidia on the leaves of cereal crops in the late summer and autumn. The conidia germinate within 1–2 days to form short germ tubes, which attach to the epidermis by a pad or **appressorium**. Beneath this pad, a fine **infection tube** grows out and penetrates thc host cell wall by secreting enzymes (fig 12.10*c*). Some species of cereal are resistant to infection by *Erysiphe* and it is thought that they are able to repress the cell wall degrading enzymes.

Once the host cell is infected, the germ tube grows inside the epidermal cell forming a long haustorium.

In a susceptible host, the infected cell remains alive and the mycelium develops branches with further appressoria and haustoria spreading through the leaf. Within 7–10 days, conidia begin to develop. If the host is not susceptible to *Erysiphe*, then the host cell undergoes rapid necrosis and the cells around may also die (hypersensitivity). This restricts the further development of the pathogen.

The conidia develop from a flask-shaped mother cell by mitosis (fig 12.10*e*). Each conidium has a single nucleus. They become swollen and barrel-shaped and are blown away by the wind to infect more susceptible hosts. The conidia of *Erysiphe* are able to germinate even in dry conditions, which is unusual. They have a very high water content (70%) and a large lipid reserve which also releases water when respired. Powdery mildews are abundant in hot, dry seasons.

Erysiphe may also form **ascospores**. These develop inside asci which are surrounded by a **perithecium** (fig 12.10*f*). The perithecia of *E. graminis* are dark brown globules which grow on the basal leaves and leaf sheaths of cereals. The wall of the perithecium is several cells thick. The contents swell and crack open the perithecium and the asci discharge their spores. Ascospores of *E. graminis* formed in one season may germinate immediately but they have been known to survive for up to 13 years.

An infection with *E. graminis* results in increased respiration of the host and a decrease in photosynthesis. This means that an infected leaf is unable to export carbohydrate. In fact, areas of a healthy leaf near to the mildew pustule produce carbohydrate which is translocated towards the pustule. This means that in a crop plant, the growth rate of shoots and roots is reduced and the ultimate yield of ears of grain is seriously reduced.

Control   Chemical control is by dusting or spraying with a fungicide containing sulphur. Some systemic fungicides may be used, such as ethirimol, which give protection against powdery mildew throughout the growing season. Increases in yield of barley up to 100% have been

Fig 12.10
Erysiphe graminis.
(*a*) Conidium on a leaf
surface. (*b*) Development
of the appressorium.
(*c*) Penetration of the
epidermal cell by an
infection tube. (*d*) Section
of an epidermal cell
showing the penetration
point and a haustorium.
(*e*) Mycelium and
conidiophores on the leaf
surface. (*f*) Section of a
perithecium showing
several asci. (*g*) An ascus
containing eight ascospores

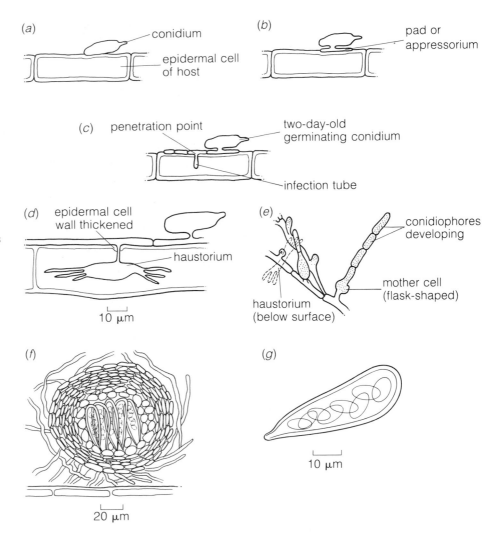

obtained using systemic fungicides. The quality of the grain is also
improved. Control can also be achieved by selecting and breeding
resistant host varieties (see chapter 13).

12.4.8 Crown gall disease

Unlike most bacterial pathogens of plants, *Agrobacterium tumefaciens*
is a biotroph, affecting over 1000 different species of plants. It usually
enters through wounds in the stem and interferes with the plant's
growth regulators, causing a large growth or tumour to be formed on
the stem close to ground level. The bacterium causes this disease
because it carries the **tumour inducing (Ti) plasmid**, which becomes
incorporated into the host cell's genome. It is therefore a disease of
great interest to genetic engineers.

Fig 12.11
Crown gall disease caused by *Agrobacterium tumefaciens*

Control

    (*a*)   Sanitary methods: destruction of all infected tissue.

    (*b*)   Crop rotation.

    (*c*)   Avoidance of wounding.

    (*d*)   Antibiotic treatment, such as terramycin or aureomycin, although this is expensive.

    (*e*)   A related species, *A. radiobacter*, produces an extracellular toxin which destroys *A. tumefaciens*. This can be exploited as a form of biological control.

12.4.9   *Fireblight*

Fireblight is caused by *Erwinia* sp. Like most bacterial pathogens of plants, it is a necrotroph, which enters plants via wounds. One example is fireblight of pear blossom, *E. amylovora*, which also affects apples. Alternative hosts are hawthorn and *Cotoneaster*.

It can be transferred by bees from plant to plant, or by rain-splash from one part of a plant to another. It multiplies in the nectaries of flowers, and in suitable wet, moist weather a bacterial exudate forms (fig 12.12). The bacteria may move along the stem, from where it can spread to infect the fruit, kill flowers and fruit, or spread along the whole branch, causing an extensive canker. It may even enter the root system. Affected trees look as if they have been scorched by fire. The bacterium overwinters in stem cankers (which are slowly decaying bark and wood). They surface as a bacterial exudate and are carried to new hosts in spring by bees or rain-splash.

Another species, *E. carotovora*, causes post-harvest soft-rot of carrots and other root vegetables. It produces pectolytic enzymes which digest the middle lamella between cells, causing the cells to separate. This creates soft spots in the plant tissue.

Fig 12.12
The life cycle of *Erwinia amylovora*, fire blight of apples and pears (alternative hosts are hawthorn and *Cotoneaster*)

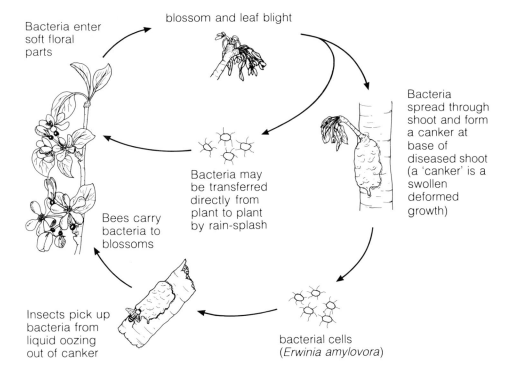

Bacteria enter soft floral parts

blossom and leaf blight

Bacteria spread through shoot and form a canker at base of diseased shoot (a 'canker' is a swollen deformed growth)

Bacteria may be transferred directly from plant to plant by rain-splash

Bees carry bacteria to blossoms

Insects pick up bacteria from liquid oozing out of canker

bacterial cells (*Erwinia amylovora*)

Control

   (*a*) Fireblight of pear is a notifiable disease and must be reported to the local authorities. There is no chemical cure for the disease and affected trees must be cut down and destroyed.

   (*b*) Soft rot of carrots and root crops can be avoided by careful handling of crops during harvest, transport and storage, since the pathogen cannot enter an undamaged surface. Adding antibacterial substances to the water in which vegetables are washed may help.

12.4.10   *Beet yellows virus*

Beet yellows, like other viral infections of plants, is a biotroph. It infects sugar-beet, spinach and mangolds, as well as common weeds such as groundsel, shepherd's purse and chickweed. The upper, older leaves become yellow, brittle and thickened. Yellowing (chlorosis) begins at the tip of the leaf and gradually spreads downwards between the veins, killing the leaves. The sugar content of the phloem falls and starch accumulates, which can lead to a 50% drop in value of the crop. The disease is spread by aphids, which feed by inserting their mouthparts into plant cells and sucking up cell sap. When the insect's proboscis, or feeding tube, reaches the phloem sieve tube, the sap is forced, under pressure, into the insect's food canal. If the plant is infected with beet yellows, the sap will probably contain viruses. The beet yellows virus migrates from the stomach, across the body cavity to the insect's salivary glands. The aphid is then able to infect plants, and usually remains infective for the rest of its life cycle.

Control

(a) Systemic aphicides can be used to protect plants against the disease. Spraying plants at two-weekly intervals is necessary to keep plants free of aphids all summer. Sugar factories employ fieldmen to warn of aphid swarms so that farmers can spray at the appropriate time.

(b) Sugar-beet and mangolds stored overwinter for cattle fodder can carry the virus. They should be used before April, when aphids begin to emerge.

(c) Farmers should not grow sugar-beet near other crops which can carry the virus, such as brassicas and potatoes.

(d) Plant breeders are trying to develop varieties resistant to the disease or the aphid.

12.4.11 Tobacco mosaic virus

Tobacco mosaic virus (TMV) was the first virus to be discovered when, in 1892, Iwanowsky filtered the sap from tobacco plants infected with mosaic disease through a bacterial filter. He found the filtered sap still caused subsequent infections of healthy plants, and so a whole new class of pathogenic entities, much smaller than bacteria, were discovered.

TMV is a highly virulent pathogen of both tobacco and tomatoes. The symptoms of the disease are characteristic bright yellow blotches on the leaves, with alternate areas of dark and light green. It is spread by infected tissue, so plants with the symptoms of TMV should be destroyed. This particular virus has even been found to spread by contact from one plant to another, usually where there is wounding. In a greenhouse, gardeners can pass the virus from infected to healthy plants on their hands.

Control

(a) Sanitary measures, such as destroying all infected plants.
(b) Crop rotation.

Questions

1 With reference to *named* examples, write a brief account of the importance of insect vectors in plant disease.

2 Using the examples in the text, copy and complete table 12.3.

3 Draw a diagram to summarise the life cycle of the beet yellows virus.

Table 12.3
Plant disease summary

	Loose smut	Damping-off	Beet yellows	Dutch elm	Potato blight
Disease-causing agent					
How disease is dispersed					
How disease enters plant					
Does it have more than one host? Name the host/s					
How pathogen survives outside host					
Effect of pathogen on host					

4 Select one example of a fungal disease, a bacterial disease and a viral disease of plants. Make notes on how the selected plant disease may be controlled.

12.5 The effects of pathogens on their hosts

The effects of pathogens are varied, but the effects may be summarised as in table 12.4.

12.5.1 The effects of necrotrophs on the host

Necrotrophic pathogens, as the name implies, bring about necrosis or blackening of tissues caused by cell death. Examples include *Phytophthora infestans* or *Botrytis* sp. Necrotrophs frequently cause **wilting** by secreting enzymes and/or toxins. For example, *Erwinia* sp. secrete pectolytic enzymes which digest the middle lamella between cell walls. Other necrotrophs produce toxins, for example the wilt fungus *Fusarium* which causes early blight of potatoes. Some necrotrophs invade the vascular tissue of the host and bring about wilting, such as *Ceratocystis ulmi* or *Fusarium*. These wilt fungi also produce gums or

217

Table 12.4
The effects of pathogens
on plants

Photosynthesis e.g. rusts, mildews, potato blight Rusts produce localised pustules where photosynthesis has been destroyed and prevent photosynthetic products leaving the leaf, giving lower crop yields.	**Food stores** e.g. seedling blights, damping-off fungi (*Pythium* spp.) *Pythium* affects germinating seedlings and feeds off food stores in seeds so that the plant is destroyed.
Water conduction e.g. vascular wilts, *Ceratocystis ulmi*, *Fusarium* sp., *Verticillium* sp. Pathogen is present in xylem vessels, causing plant to wilt.	**Water/mineral absorption** e.g. root rots These enter plant via roots and prevent adequate water absorption, leading to a smaller, weaker plant which eventually dies.
Reproduction e.g. smuts These destroy the inflorescence of the flower.	**Translocation** e.g. beet yellows These viruses infect the phloem.
Shoot tips e.g. die-back These destroy the shoot tip and prevent growth.	**Growth regulators** e.g. galls, club root Pathogen interferes with growth regulators and causes increase in tissue volume or increased cell division.

gels which block the xylem vessels. Other necrotrophs, such as *Pythium* sp. or *Rhizoctinia* sp., rot the roots directly and cause wilting by preventing water absorption.

Necrotrophs may **reduce photosynthesis** of the host plant. Often, this is because of destruction of chlorophyll and chloroplasts, such as is caused by *Phytophthora*.

Another effect of necrotrophs is to **increase the respiration rate** of the host, mainly due to the increased activity of the pentose phosphate pathway and the uncoupling of oxidation and phosphorylation (see section 12.7). Most necrotrophs stimulate host respiration, such as *Phytophthora*, *Botrytis* and *Gaeumannomyces*.

Some necrotrophs cause **chlorosis** or yellowing of the host tissues. Examples include the wilt fungi, *Ceratocystis*, *Verticillium* and *Fusarium*. The host plant's **food stores** may be utilised by the pathogen. An example of this is *Pythium*.

12.5.2   *The effect of biotrophic pathogens on the host*

Biotrophs, like necrotrophs, can **reduce photosynthesis** in the host. Usually, this is because the growth of the pathogen obscures light, such as *Puccinia* or *Ustilago*. *Puccinia* alters chloroplast structure when the disease has become established. It forms pustules on the leaf and prevents photosynthetic products leaving the leaf, lowering crop yield. In the early stages of infection, however, biotrophs may actually stimulate photosynthesis of the host. Fungi such as *Puccinia* or *Erysiphe* cause an increase in photosynthesis in the area immediately around the site of infection, by stimulating host kinins. This is called the 'green island' effect and is probably a means of the pathogen turning the host's physiology to its own advantage. Viruses, such as beet yellows, impair photosynthesis by causing chlorosis (yellowing of tissue).

Biotrophs also **stimulate host respiration** and affect the permeability of the host cell membrane so that more nutrients are able to pass through. Biotrophs often affect **translocation** in the host, changing the host's metabolic products into other, less useful, substances. One example is the conversion of sucrose to starch by the beet yellows virus.

Plant growth regulators can be altered by biotrophs. An example of this is the galls produced by *Agrobacterium tumefaciens*. *Puccinia* and *Erysiphe* stimulate host kinins to produce the 'green island' effect, noted earlier.

While viruses are biotrophs and have many of the same effects as other biotrophs, they have some additional symptoms of their own. For example, some viruses produce symptoms which are similar to those of senescence or nutrient deficiencies and these symptoms can often be alleviated by feeding the plant with a fertiliser rich in nitrogen, phosphorus and potassium. Other viruses may appear symptomless. An example of this is potato paracrinkle virus. It used to be thought that this virus was symptomless in the King Edward variety of potato. However, when virus-free King Edward potatoes were obtained from meristem-tip cultures it was found that these plants gave much higher yields than the parent potatoes. The virus had only appeared symptomless because the virus had spread through the entire stock of King Edward potatoes.

12.6   Mechanisms of host resistance

Plants have several ways of resisting pathogens and their strategies can be summarised as in fig 12.13.

Passive resistance refers to mechanisms that are present in the host to *prevent* the establishment of a pathogen. Mechanical barriers to infection include the leaf cuticle, bark and epidermal cells. Some plants have extra thick cuticles. Certain cell types, such as endodermis, have thicker cell walls which are harder for pathogens to penetrate.

The natural microflora present on leaves and roots may help to combat pathogens, by competing with them. Chemical inhibitors, such as phenols, alkaloids, glucosides, tannins and resins, often add to their effect. Resins help conifers to resist wood-rotting fungi. Phenolic compounds are important inhibitors. For example, tannins are found in bark and catechol helps potatoes to resist the scab fungus, *Streptomyces scabies*. Other plants produce chemical exudates from the leaf or root which contain toxins. The inhibitors mentioned so far are present at any time in a plant. Other plants use inhibitors differently. Tulips, for example, have tuliposides, and apples contain phloridzin. Both these

Fig 12.13
Mechanisms of host
resistance

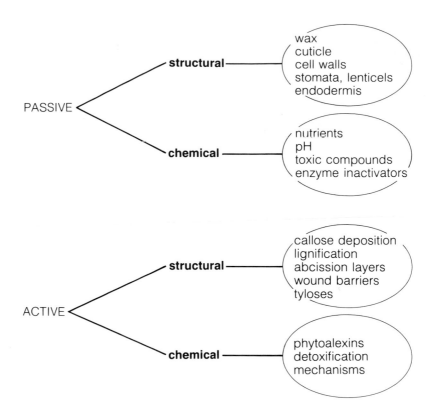

compounds are non-toxic. However, when fungi infect the host, their enzymes remove glucose from the compounds and convert them to toxins (fig 12.14).

Some hosts have cell walls which contain inhibitors of pectolytic enzymes, enabling them to resist necrotrophic pathogens. The roots of flax plants secrete prussic acid (HCN) to protect them against wilt disease caused by *Fusarium oxysporum*. Many pathogens rely on natural openings in the plant to gain entry so, at times, when stomata are closed, infection is less likely.

By contrast, **active** methods of resistance are stimulated by the presence of a pathogen. These changes affect the host cells in such a way that they inhibit the growth of a pathogen.

Changes may occur in host cell walls. If a non-pathogenic fungus attempts to invade a cereal leaf, a **wall apposition** forms, which is a plug of material immediately below the penetration site. Wall appositions may be made of oxidised phenols, such as melanins, callose, suberin, calcium, silicon or lignin. They may make the cell wall more resistant to enzyme attack, withstand fungal penetration, alter the permeability of the cell wall or be toxic to some microorganisms. (For example, lignin is toxic to many microbial pathogens.) Another strategy is the **hypersensitive approach**. This is when a few cells around the point of invasion rapidly die. It is an effective way of counteracting the

Fig 12.14
Some examples of
chemicals occurring in
plants which give some
protection from attack by
microorganisms

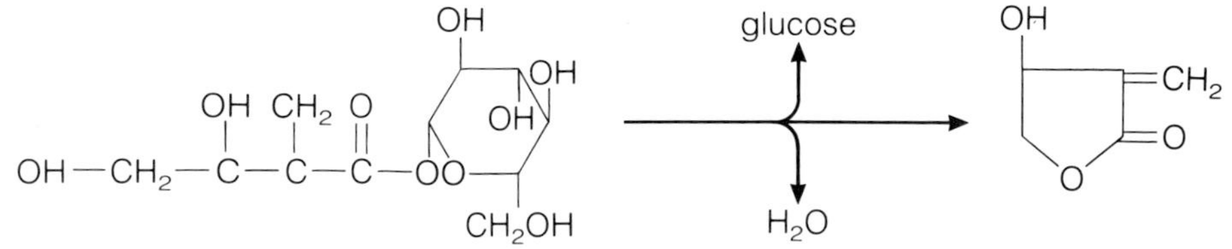

Tulips contain tuliposide B which is
non-toxic until fungal enzymes
remove glucose and/or hydrolyse it.
Then it becomes toxic to the invading
fungal pathogen.

lactone: toxic

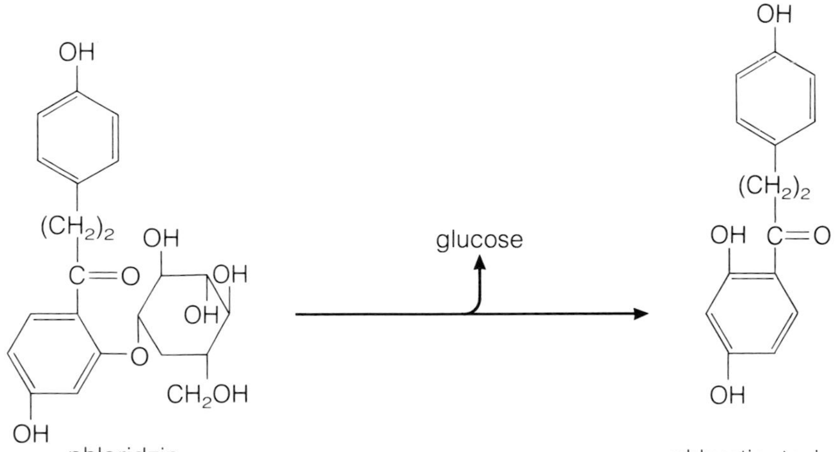

phloridzin
(non-toxic)

phloretin: toxic

Phloridzin, a non-toxic
flavenoid found in apples,
becomes the toxic phloretin
when fungal enzymes
remove glucose

pathogen, since it isolates the pathogen in dead tissue, leaving the
pathogen with no food supply.

Host metabolism is affected by pathogens. One of the first symptoms
is an increase in respiration rate, but this is mainly due to a stimulation
of the pentose phosphate pathway. Other pathways which are
stimulated are the formation of various by-products from acetyl CoA
and the citric acid cycle (fig 12.15).

Later in the infection, oxidation and phosphorylation become
uncoupled so that ATP is no longer produced. The first products of all
this increased activity are messenger RNA and proteins, to provide the
enzymes for the stimulated metabolic pathways. Next, phenols,
flavenoids, lignins, terpenoids and isoprenoids accumulate. Many of
these are antifungal agents (and some are antibacterial); they are called
phytoalexins (fig 12.16). Important phytoalexins include **wyerone** in the
bean and **rishitin** in potatoes.

Fig 12.15
The formation of by-products: a simplified outline of some of the biochemical pathways involved in the host response to pathogens

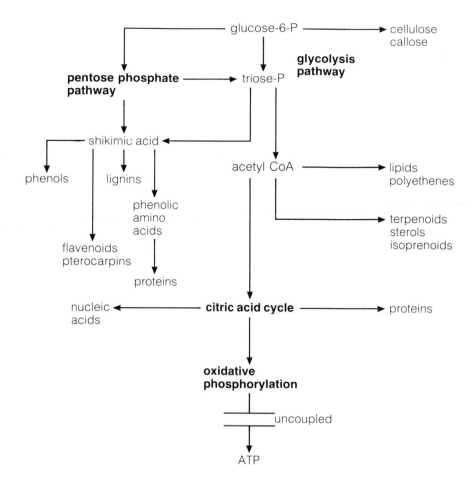

Fig 12.16 shows the results of a bioassay of phytoalexins produced by broad bean leaves in response to inoculation with the fungus *Botrytis cinerea*. Extracts from various masses of tissue were collected three days after inoculation and separated using thin-layer chromatography. Antifungal compounds were then located by spraying the plate with a spore suspension of a dark-coloured fungus, *Cladosporium herbarum*.

12.7 Assessing plant disease

Commercial growers are particularly concerned about the economic effects of a plant disease, so disease-monitoring systems have been devised. Farmers need information about the spread of a disease to protect their crops as efficiently as possible. Methods used to monitor diseases include:

(*a*) systematic surveys, usually by Government pathologists;

(*b*) aerial photography, using infrared film to show up patches of disease;

(*c*) encouraging farmers to inspect their crops regularly;

**Fig 12.16
Phytoalexins produced by
broad bean leaves**

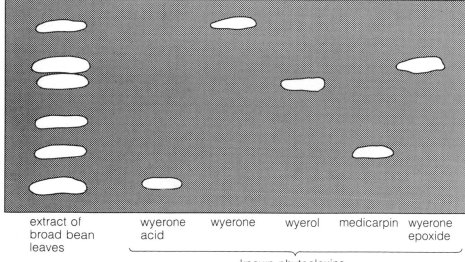

| extract of broad bean leaves | wyerone acid | wyerone | wyerol | medicarpin | wyerone epoxide |

known phytoalexins

(d) planting trap nurseries, that is widely spaced sites are chosen and planted with different cultivars, which are then closely monitored for disease susceptibility

Computers are now widely used to collate information and analyse the results.

The spread of a particular disease depends on:

(a) the susceptibility of the host;
(b) the virulence of the pathogen;
(c) the rate of reproduction of the pathogen;
(d) the dispersal mechanism of the pathogen;
(e) the effects of the environment on all these factors;
(f) the stage in the life cycle reached by the host when infection occurs.

12.8 Disease assessment methods

Disease assessment keys have been devised for many diseases, for example the key for assessment of potato blight is shown in table 12.5. However, more recent keys have also taken account of climatic effects, by comparing the yield losses in diseased plants with others sprayed regularly to keep them healthy. These keys are now standardised so that comparisons may be made between diseases.

12.9 Disease forecasting

This is more than disease assessment, since it also attempts to predict the incidence of disease. Many diseases are greatly affected by climate, so weather forecasting is important. Other factors important in disease

Table 12.5
Key for the assessment of late blight of potato (1947)

Description of crop	Percentage crop affected
Not seen on field	0
Only a few plants affected here and there; <1 or 2 spots in 12 m radius	0.1
Up to 10 spots per plant, or general light spotting	1
About 50 spots per plant or up to one leaflet in 10 attacked	5
Nearly every leaflet with lesions, plants still retaining normal form; field may smell of blight, but looks green although every plant affected	25
Every plant affected and about one-half of leaf area destroyed by blight; field looks green flecked with brown	50
About three-quarters of leaf area affected by blight; field looks neither predominantly brown or green. In some varieties the youngest leaves escape infection so that green is more conspicuous than in varieties like King Edward, which commonly shows severe shoot infection	75
Only a few leaves left green, but stems green	95
All leaves dead, stems dead or dying	100

forecasting include the history of diseases in that area, the use of resistant cultivars, whether there are alternative host plants in the area, checking of seed for disease contamination, soil type, and local environmental factors, such as proximity of hedges and woods or the topography of the land.

12.10 Disease epidemics

Epidemics of plant disease are rare in natural communities. They are much commoner in domesticated crop plants because of the extensive use of monoculture. Plant pathogens find it much easier to colonise plants rapidly when faced with a large area of genetically similar plants.
  Epidemics occur when:

(a) a large number of host plants at a suitable stage of development is available;
(b) there is a source of pathogens;
(c) environmental conditions are favourable for the development of the pathogen.

Plant diseases fall into two categories, depending on the way in which they spread.

Polycyclic diseases These are diseases such as *Phytophthora infestans* or beet yellows virus which undergo several cycles in one growing season. If the amount of disease present in a crop is plotted on a graph against time, a typical growth curve is obtained, as shown in fig 12.17.

Fig 12.17
The spread of a polycyclic pathogen in a crop

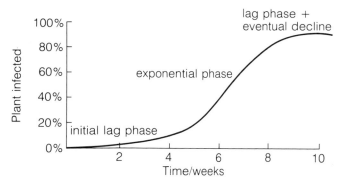

(A) *Initial lag phase*

Only a few pathogens are present, therefore there are very few infected host plants. During this time the organism establishes itself within the host and multiplies, producing spores or other means of infection.

(B) *Exponential increase*

The number of pathogens is now much greater and there are plenty of new hosts to infect, so the rate of increase of the disease is logarithmic.

(C) *Final decline*

The rate of increase of the disease falls, and the epidemic declines, because very few uninfected hosts are left. In addition, environmental conditions may become unfavourable.

Fig 12.18
The spread of a monocyclic pathogen in a crop

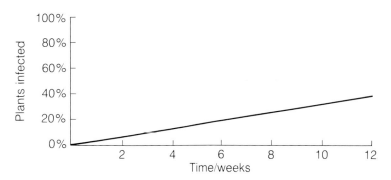

Monocyclic diseases These are diseases such as take-all of wheat, *Gaeumannomyces graminis*. These diseases only undergo one cycle in a growing season, since the inoculum for the disease is last year's crop. A graph of disease incidence against time shows a more gradual spread.

Questions

1 Explain the following terms: phytoalexin, hypersensitive approach, wall apposition.

2 Compare and contrast the effects of necrotrophs and biotrophs on the host plant, using named examples.

3   Imagine you are a plant pathologist, working for a potato crisp manufacturer, and you have several farms growing potatoes for your company. You have been asked by your manager to write a report advising the company about the best way to avoid late blight of potato, which has caused serious financial losses recently. Think about the disease from all aspects and make as many suggestions as possible in your report.

4   Compare the defences of plants against pathogens with those of animals.

5   Explain how a **named** vascular wilt fungus may affect the growth and yield of its plant host.

6   (a)   Describe the transmission of
        (i)   a **named** virus pathogenic to plants,
        (ii) a **named** fungus pathogenic to plants.   (4)
    (b)   Describe the changes in host plant structure and physiology that may be induced by infection with
        (i)   necrotrophic and
        (ii) biotrophic fungi.   (12)
    (c)   Give **four** ways by which plants may resist invasion by pathogenic microorganisms.   (4)

                                                        Total marks = 20

JMB option C June 1989

13 Controlling plant disease

13.1 How plant pathogens survive

It is important that pathogens that are able to survive the winter and other adverse conditions when they transfer from host to host. Some are able to overwinter in storage organs, such as beet yellows virus or *Phytophthora infestans*. *Ustilago* can survive in grain seed. Others survive in dead host tissue, such as *P. infestans* (which causes late blight) or *Venturia* (which causes apple scab). Some survive as saprotrophs in the soil, such as *Pythium* or *Rhizoctonia*. Most fungi produce asexual spores and these are able to survive for a few months in favourable conditions, but some are able to overwinter as dormant structures in the soil. Examples are the resistant **teliospores** of *Puccinia graminis*, resistant thick-walled **chlamydospores** of *Fusarium*, **oospores** of the downy mildew family, and **perithecia** of *Erysiphe*.

Botrytis cinerea and *Claviceps purpurea* form special structures called **sclerotia** which are tightly packed hyphae protected by an outer layer of thick-walled cells. The honey fungus, *Armillaria mellea*, forms **rhizomorphs**, which are rope-like strands of hyphae. These grow away from a place where the fungus is established, such as the stump of a felled tree and grow very rapidly towards healthy trees.

Many disease-causing bacteria are able to form resistant **endospores**, for example *Agrobacterium* and *Bacillus*.

Fig 13.1
Aerial view of agricultural fields in the USA

13.2   Plant disease control

There are several ways of controlling disease in plants:

(a)   pesticides;
(b)   breeding resistant plants;
(c)   horticultural practice;
(d)   biological control;
(e)   legislation.

13.3   Pesticides

There are very few pesticides available to combat bacterial disease, and none which are effective against viruses, so discussion here will be limited to **fungicides**. There are many factors to be considered in attempting to find an ideal fungicide. Fig 13.2 lists many desirable features of an ideal fungicide, but it is not straightforward to develop a fungicide to meet all these criteria. For example, fungicides used to kill pathogens in the soil are rarely specific enough to kill just the target pathogen and will harm other soil-dwelling microorganisms. Some fungicides must be persistent if they are to destroy the pathogen; this is particularly important in destroying post-harvest diseases in many types of fruit.

Fig 13.2
The features of an ideal fungicide

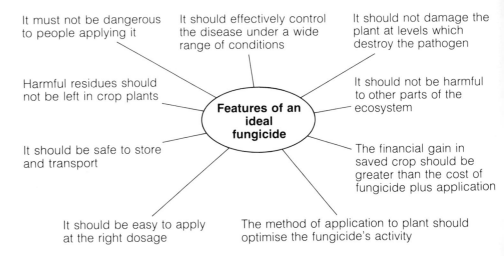

Most of the older fungicides (those discovered before 1960) are used as **protectants**, since they are present on the surface of the plant to protect against infection. They must be present *before* the pathogen attacks the plant, since they are preventive rather than curative. They need further applications as the plant grows and to counteract the effects of environmental factors, such as rainfall and temperature. Examples of such fungicides are Bordeaux mixture (a copper sulphate and lime mixture) and the organic dithiocarbamates. Most of the early

Table 13.1
Comparison of systemic and protectant fungicides

	Systemic	Protectant
Action	therapeutic	prophylactic
Mode of action	few metabolic systems affected	many metabolic systems affected
Toxicity to host	rare	common, especially if applied to wrong tissue or an inappropriate host.
Pathogens affected	variable; some extremely specific, others effective against a broad spectrum	numerous
Pathogen resistance	common	rare
Movement	translocated, usually in apoplast (xylem, cell walls)	stays on surface

fungicides were **multisite** in action, which means that they affected the fungus in several ways. Bordeaux mixture is multisite because the element copper is a potent inhibitor of many enzymes.

Systemic fungicides were developed more recently. The first one to be made was called **benomyl**, but many more have been developed since. These enter the host plant, so are much longer-lasting. They are present inside the plant and they enhance the host's natural responses. These can also be used to treat an established infection. However, they tend to be much more specific, with a single target for their action, so they are **single-site** fungicides. This means that resistance is more likely to develop (section 13.3.1).

Table 13.1 compares the features of protectant and systemic fungicides.

Insecticides are sometimes used to control plant diseases indirectly. For example, systemic aphicides are used to control the aphid which carries beet yellows virus.

13.3.1 Fungicide resistance

Protectant compounds rarely produce resistant plants but, with the advent of systemic fungicides, many plants have acquired resistance. One of the main reasons for this is that protectants interfere with many metabolic processes in the pathogen, for example by inhibiting ATP formation. Therefore, it is difficult for the pathogen to overcome the fungicide's action. Systemic compounds, on the other hand, often inhibit only one metabolic pathway in the cell. This property is useful in some respects, since it makes systemic fungicides much more specific and less harmful to the environment. However, it does make it easier for the pathogen to avoid the toxic effects of the fungicide by developing a new bypass mechanism or by increased activity in some other existing biochemical pathway.

There are various ways in which farmers and horticulturists can attempt to avoid fungicide resistance developing.

(a) Avoid using the same fungicide repeatedly, or use other fungicides with the same mode of action.

(b) When several sprays need to be applied during one season:
  (i) whenever possible use a manufacturer's formulation using at least two fungicides;
  (ii) use multisite fungicides in the spraying programme;
  (iii) minimise the number of applications by disease assessment, epidemiological and forecasting information.

(c) Do not rely on fungicides for disease control. Sprays should be used as part of a strategy incorporating the use of disease-resistant strains and cultivation methods which minimise the spread of pathogens.

13.3.2 Ways of applying pesticides to crops

Each method has its advantages and disadvantages. The choice of method depends on:

(a) the best means of getting the fungicide to the precise site of infection;
(b) reducing any hazard to human workers;
(c) minimising the effect on the environment (e.g. avoiding spraying other crops);
(d) what stage in its life cycle the crop has reached;
(e) cost of application of pesticide compared to value of crop that will be saved;
(f) ease of application.

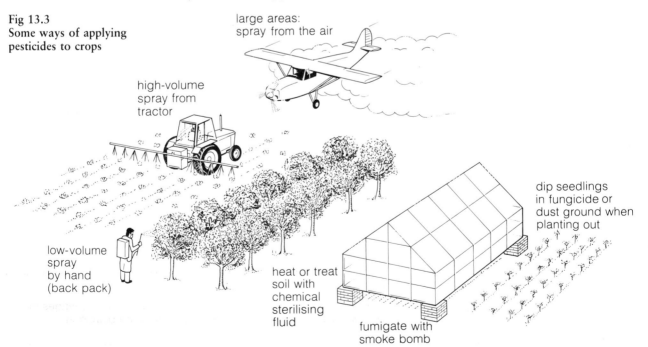

Fig 13.3
Some ways of applying pesticides to crops

large areas: spray from the air

high-volume spray from tractor

low-volume spray by hand (back pack)

heat or treat soil with chemical sterilising fluid

fumigate with smoke bomb

dip seedlings in fungicide or dust ground when planting out

To establish whether a fungicide is cost-effective means that the value of the crop saved must be greater than the cost of spraying. To calculate the value of the crop that has been saved is not easy, since it depends on accurate disease forecasting. It has been calculated that, if pesticides were banned in the USA, agricultural output would fall by 30%.

13.4 Breeding resistant plants

Up to the end of the nineteenth century, plant breeding was a slow process of selection. Farmers selected their better crops for next year's seeds and in doing so, selected for disease resistance to a small extent. However, it was not until the twentieth century that this process became more scientific. In 1912, Biffen found that resistance to yellow stipe rust in a particular type of wheat was conferred by a single recessive gene. Unfortunately, the pathogen quickly developed a means of overcoming the host's resistance. Attempts to breed disease-resistant plants have recurrently met this difficulty: a single resistance gene is found, the pathogen develops resistance, a new resistance gene is found, but the pathogen develops resistance to this also, and so on.

Some factors encourage the development of pathogens able to overcome the host's genetic resistance. For example, where crops are grown in intensive monoculture over many acres, it is much easier for resistant pathogens to survive and spread. This is because farmers tend to use the same pesticides on the same cultivar over a large area. If a resistant pathogen develops, it is able to spread rapidly throughout the entire crop.

More recently, plant breeders have tried to develop polygenic systems of plant resistance, making it much harder for the pathogen to overcome the host's defences (table 13.2).

Table 13.2
Comparison of single gene
and polygene resistance

Single gene	Polygene
one or few genes involved	many genes involved
sometimes confers resistance throughout life of plant, but sometimes may not be expressed until the plant is mature	seedlings generally less resistant than mature plants, but resistance increases as plants mature
resistance is usually conferred by hypersensitive host reaction	resistance results from a reduced rate and extent of infection, caused by slowed rate of reproduction and/or development of pathogen
resistance often limited to one or few races of pathogen	resistance usually affects all races of the pathogen
resistance likely to break down due to the development of new races of the pathogen	less likely to be affected by changes in virulence genes of the pathogen

Some plants which have developed genetic resistance have been able to retain this for many years. Such plants are said to have **durable** resistance. For example, certain oat cultivars have flowers which do not open so that their stigmata are not exposed to infection by the loose smut fungus, *Ustilago avenae*.

Traditional plant breeding programmes are limited in what they can achieve. For example, wild forms of potato are resistant to late blight of potato, *Phytophthora infestans*. Unfortunately, attempts to cross the wild species with the crop potato have failed. Using techniques of plant cell culture, the protoplasts of these two species can be fused and a hybrid plant regenerated. Alternatively, if the necessary genes in the wild potato could be isolated, these could be inserted in the crop potato's genome using a vector such as *Agrobacterium tumefaciens*. This technique has not yet been tried because the genes are not yet isolated but, even if it could be done, it is not known whether the genes would actually be expressed in the crop potato plant.

Resistance genes offer a great deal of promise in agriculture and horticulture but, if they are to be effective against pathogens for prolonged periods of time, they must be used carefully.

Plant breeders should:

(a) develop multigene cultivars, so each cultivar carries more than one resistance gene;

(b) insert different resistance genes into identical cultivars, so that farmers can grow a field of otherwise identical plants which differ only in the genetic basis of their resistance.

Seed merchants should:

market mixtures of cultivars, each with a different genetic basis for their resistance.

Pathologists and farmers should:

(a) encourage the restricted use of resistance genes, for example by using them only in certain geographical areas or in only one of a number of overlapping crops, such as either winter or spring sown cereals.

(b) grow a different cultivar in each of their fields. These would be selected from groups of cultivars known to have a different genetic basis for disease resistance.

Genetic engineers are now able to insert the gene for a viral coat protein into the host plant, thereby preventing infection. An example is Monsanto mosaic virus in tomatoes.

13.5 Biological control

When plant pathogens are in the free-living part of their life cycle, they may be attacked by other organisms. Plant pathologists can exploit this, and the process is called **biological control**. The first use of this method was in 1888 when the cotton-cushion scale insect, accidentally imported from Australia, became a pest in citrus groves in California. Two natural predators of the insect were found, a ladybird and a fly, and they were released into the citrus groves. Within a few months, the problem had been solved.

This simple method of control has not been without its failures, but there are many success stories. Recently, biological control involving microorganisms has been studied, although very few successful schemes have yet been found. One successful scheme is in controlling *Heterobasidium annosum*, which causes heart rot of pines. The fungus invades the cut stump of newly felled pines, then spreads to nearby trees through their root systems. Chemical control measures have proved ineffective. It was discovered that the disease could be controlled by painting cut stumps with a spore suspension of *Peniophora*, a wood-rotting parasite/saprotroph which competes with *Heterobasidium*. Another example is the control of crown gall disease, caused by *Agrobacterium tumefaciens*. A closely related species, *A. radiobacter*, can be used. This species produces an extracellular toxin, known as a **bacteriocin**, which inactivates *A. tumefaciens*.

13.6 Good horticultural practice

Crop rotation can be important. 'Take-all of wheat', *Gaeumannomyces*, can be controlled by using a two- to three-year crop rotation, since it is a poor saprotroph and because *Phialophora radicicola*, a fungus which competes successfully against *Gaeumannomyces*, is common on the surfaces of grass roots. Sometimes a long crop rotation, of perhaps five years, may be necessary, as some plant diseases are spread by nematode worms, which are very long-lived.

Controlling nutrient levels can control pathogens. Apple scab is a pathogen which overwinters as ascospores in infected leaves and fruits lying on the soil in an orchard. By adding nitrogen, in the form of urea, to fallen leaf litter, the natural decomposition by saprobionts is increased, reducing the number of ascospores present by the following spring.

Controlling pH reduces the incidence of some diseases. For example, *Plasmodiophora brassicae* which causes club root of cabbage can be controlled by liming the soil, since its spores will not germinate in alkaline soils.

Sowing crops at a carefully planned time is another way of avoiding disease. Some diseases are spread by means of 'green bridges', which means that host plants for the pathogen may be present in the soil all year round. Farmers can avoid 'green bridges' by sowing spring and winter crops in different areas or by allowing a short time interval between crops. **Removing weeds**, which may be alternative hosts for the pathogen, can be very effective. Chickweed and groundsel are alternative hosts for beet yellows virus. Woody hosts cause particular difficulty, since these can harbour pathogens over winter.

Strict crop hygiene is important, which means removing all crop residues in case these are infected. In a greenhouse or other confined area, **soil sterilisation** may be carried out. Both these measures are particularly important in preventing the spread of viral diseases.

Certified disease-free stock can be obtained. For example, plants grown from meristem-tip cultures will be virus-free. Seed potatoes from Scotland are grown in areas where aphids only occur late in the season, so they can be harvested before the maximum aphid swarms appear, and are less likely to harbour pathogens.

Sometimes a mild strain of a virus is deliberately introduced to plants, to give **cross protection** against more pathogenic varieties. The M1116 strain of TMV is virtually symptomless in some cultivars of tomatoes, and protects the crop from more harmful strains. Genetic engineers can also engineer mild strains of a virus for this purpose.

13.7 Legislation

Some of the more serious plant diseases are **notifiable,** which means that anyone finding this disease on their plants has to notify the local authorities, so that appropriate action may be taken to prevent the disease spreading. An example of a notifiable plant disease is fireblight of pear, *Erwinia amylovora.*

Legislation also exists for certain crop associations to maintain virus-free stock of certain important crop plants. This is to ensure that disease-free stock is always available, even if a serious outbreak of disease occurs.

There is also strict legislation concerning pesticides which may be used, to prevent any unnecessary harm to humans or the environment which might be caused by applying certain formulations.

Quarantine laws apply to check that diseases are not introduced into the country from abroad. However, this does not always offer enough protection. In the late 1970s, a serious virus called plum pox entered the country from infected imported plant material.

13.8 Obtaining virus-free plants

Since there are no antiviral pesticides, control of viruses is largely by good horticultural practice, as outlined above.

Another technique is to avoid viruses, by growing the crop where the virus is either absent or rare. An example of this is the growing of seed potatoes in Scotland, mentioned previously. Many potato diseases are spread by aphids, and these are rare when the ambient temperature is below 20 °C.

If planting material, such as tubers or seeds, is thought to be infected by viruses, **heat treatment** may be used. For example, tomato seed can be heated to 70 °C for 1–2 days to rid them of tobacco mosaic virus. This heat treatment kills the virus but leaves the seed viable. Growing plants may also be treated at 37–9 °C for 3–4 weeks, for example to rid potato plants of potato leaf roll virus.

Both these methods, however, have largely been replaced by **meristem tip culture** (see section 4.2.1). Actively dividing meristem cells are rarely infected with viruses, since viruses move from cell to cell quite slowly. By generating plants from meristem cultures, these are usually virus-free. Should the virus be present in the meristem, it can be treated by including a heat treatment stage, for example, heating to 30–40 °C for 3–6 weeks in the meristem culturing method. It is also possible to use an antiviral treatment in the meristem culture. These tend to be nucleotide analogues, such as zidovudine which is used in AIDS treatment (section 10.3). Although these drugs are very expensive, their use can be justified in a meristem culture, since only tiny amounts of the drug are required.

Question

1 Two derivatives (X and Y) of a newly synthesised chemical were found to display considerable fungicidal activity *in vitro*. In an experiment to compare the effects of these two potential fungicides on the control of chocolate spot disease (*Botrytis fabae*) on broad bean, the seeds were dressed at the rate of 20 g per 50 kg of seeds immediately prior to sowing. The results obtained are shown in fig 13.4.

Fig 13.4

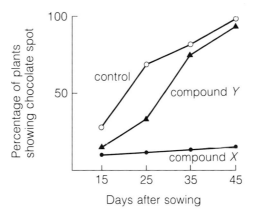

(*a*) (i) How do you explain the fact that a fungicide applied to the exterior of a seed may affect the resistance of the growing plant to fungal activity for some time after initial treatment?

(ii) Give **one** reason to account for the difference in results between compound X and compound Y.

(iii) When *Botrytis fabae* was grown on malt agar containing either compound X or an equal amount of compound Y, the same degree of inhibition of growth was observed on both media. How can this observation be reconciled with the information given in the graph and how could your hypotheses be tested experimentally? (11)

(b) Illustrate your answers to the following questions with **named** examples of plant pathogens.

(i) Outline **three** methods that can be used to control the spread of fungal or viral diseases of plants other than by use of fungicides or insecticides. (3)

(ii) Describe **three** examples to show different ways in which plant pathogens survive the winter. (6)

Total = 20 marks

JMB Option C June 1988

Appendix A guide to the sizes of microorganisms

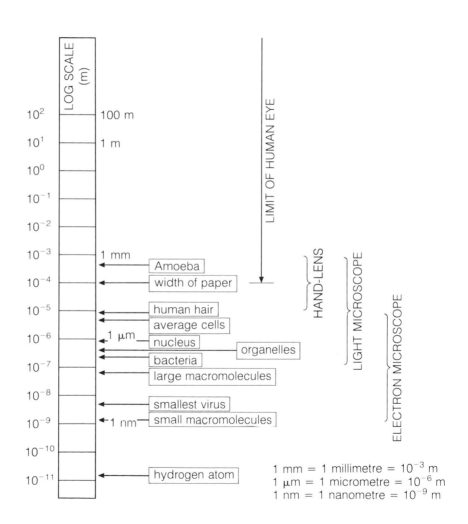

$$1 \text{ mm} = 1 \text{ millimetre} = 10^{-3} \text{ m}$$
$$1 \text{ } \mu\text{m} = 1 \text{ micrometre} = 10^{-6} \text{ m}$$
$$1 \text{ nm} = 1 \text{ nanometre} = 10^{-9} \text{ m}$$

Glossary

abzyme Antibodies made by monoclonal antibody techniques which can act as enzymes and catalyse biological reactions.

adsorption A process whereby a molecule of a liquid or gas is attracted to the surface of another substance, usually a solid, a physical process.

aerobe An organism which needs molecular oxygen for its metabolism.

agar A gelatinous substance derived from seaweed (red algae) used to solidify nutrient media for growing microorganisms.

akaryotic This means 'without a cellular structure' and is used to describe organisms such as viruses.

akinete A vegetative cell which is transformed into a thick-walled, resistant spore in Cyanobacteria.

anaerobe An organism which cannot grow if molecular oxygen is present; such strict anaerobes are killed by oxygen. Facultative anaerobes will grow if oxygen is present, but can also grow in its absence.

anion A negatively-charged ion, such as chloride (Cl^-).

antibiotic A chemical produced by microorganisms, such as bacteria and moulds, that, in dilute solution, can kill or inhibit the growth of other microorganisms. They are used as chemotherapeutic agents to treat bacterial, or sometimes fungal, diseases.

antibody A protein produced by the B-lymphocytes of the immune system. Antibodies help to defend the body against pathogens and foreign molecules by binding to them and initiating their destruction.

antigen A molecule that is recognised and bound by a specific antibody.

appressorium In pathogenic fungi, an appressorium is an infective pad of hyphae which secretes enzymes and pushes its way into the epidermal cells of the host.

ascospore Found only in the ascomycete fungi, these spores are haploid and produced inside a diploid cell called an ascus. There are usually eight ascospores in an ascus since meiosis is followed by mitosis.

aseptic technique A procedure used in microbiology used to prevent contamination of cultures by microorganisms from the environment and contamination of the environment by the microorganisms being handled.

ATP   *Adenosine TriPhosphate.* This is an energy-rich compound which, on hydrolysis, breaks down to adenosine diphosphate (ADP) and inorganic phosphate (P_i). This makes energy available for metabolic activities.

autoclave   A large pressure cooker used to steam-sterilise laboratory media, glassware and metal instruments under conditions of high temperature and pressure, usually 121 °C at 103 kPa for 15 min.

autolysis   Self-digestion of a cell or organism brought about by lysosomes, cell organelles which release the enzyme lysozyme.

autotroph   An organism that is able to synthesise the organic materials it requires from inorganic substances in its environment.

base-pairing   In the DNA double helix, the two strands are held together by weak hydrogen bonds between bases, which are paired so that adenine pairs with thymine and guanine with cytosine. Thus, the sequence of one DNA strand specifies the sequence of the second.

basidiospore   Found only in basidiomycete fungi, basidiospores are produced externally by meiosis of a diploid cell, the basidium.

batch culture   A culture in which all the ingredients are added at the beginning: it is then left for the reaction to take place, after which the products are harvested.

binary fission   The process whereby a single-celled organism divides into two daughter cells.

bioaccumulation   A process whereby certain microorganisms are able to accumulate substances from the environment, either inside their cells or externally.

bioassay   A means of measuring the concentration of a substance, such as vitamins or antibiotics, by studying their effects on the growth of a microorganism.

biodegradation   The use of microorganisms to break down substances. The process is used in waste treatment and recycling.

biodeterioration   Unwanted damage caused to materials by microorganisms, for example food spoilage.

biomass   The total mass of all organisms in a particular habitat or area. Usually, the **dry** mass is referred to.

biomining   The use of microorganisms to recover valuable metals such as uranium from low-grade ores.

biosensor   An artificial biological sensory system. Recognition systems of biological chemicals (enzymes or antibodies) may be coupled with microelectronics to enable rapid, accurate detection of substances (such as sugars) in body fluids, or pollutants in water and the like.

biotechnology	The application of living organisms, or substances made by them, to make products of value to humans.
biotroph	Obligate parasites which obtain their nutrients from living cells.
B-lymphocytes	Cell responsible for the humoral immune response. When sensitised by an antigen, it differentiates into clones of antibody-producing plasma cells and memory cells.
callus	Undifferentiated plant tissue which usually develops as a result of wounding.
capneic	A term which describes an organism that grows best when carbon dioxide levels are high.
capsid	The protein coat of a virus.
catalyst	A substance which accelerates the rate of a chemical reaction, but is not used up in the process.
cation	A positively charged ion, such as calcium (Ca^{2+}).
cell culture	Growing cells or tissues in a laboratory, in or on an appropriate nutrient medium.
chemoautotrophic	An organism which uses carbon dioxide as its sole source of carbon and inorganic chemicals as its source of energy.
chitin	A tough, resistant polysaccharide which is a component of fungal cell walls.
chlorosis	Yellowing of leaves due to loss of, or reduced development of, chlorophyll.
cilium	(plural = cilia) A short, hair-like structure present on the surface of some specialised eukaryotic cells, usually numerous and arranged in rows. They beat with **metachronal rhythm** in locomotion, or to cause liquids to flow in a certain direction. In cross-section, cilia show a 9+2 arrangement of microtubules.
clamp connections	Swellings which develop between adjacent cells in the hyphae of basidiomycetes.
clone	A group of genetically identical organisms or cells which are all descended asexually from the same individual.
coccus	(plural = cocci) A spherical bacterium.
coenocytic	An organism, or part of an organism, which is multinucleate. The nuclei are not separated by cross-walls.
coenzyme	Organic non-protein substances which are essential for the efficient function of an enzyme. Several are vitamin derivatives, such as

nicotinamide adenine dinucleotide (NAD) and NADP (P = phosphate) which contain a derivative of vitamin B.

complement	A group of 11 proteins found in blood serum which help to destroy pathogens.
conidium	A spore produced by mitosis at the tip of a specialised hypha called a conidiophore.
conjugation	In bacteria, the transfer of genetic material from one cell to another by cell to cell contact; pili may be involved. In ciliated protozoa, such as *Paramecium*, the process of exchange of nuclei prior to replication.
contractile vacuole	An organelle found in freshwater protozoa used to regulate the water content of the cytoplasm.
cryophile	See **psychrophile**.
cultivar	A variety of plant found only under cultivation.
cuticle	Waxy or fatty layer on the outer wall of epidermal cells of higher plants.
cytostome	An organelle found at the end of the gullet region of a ciliate such as *Paramecium*. The organelle is in the endoplasm and here food vacuoles are formed.
density arrest	In animal tissue culture, cells stop growing once they touch each other; this is called density arrest.
diapedesis	The process by which white blood cells migrate through the walls of blood vessels into tissues; the movement resembles amoeboid movement.
dikaryon	In fungi, a mycelium with paired nuclei, each usually from a different parent.
DNA polymerase	Enzymes which synthesise DNA by copying a template strand.
DNA probe	A specific segment of DNA, which is often radioactively labelled and of known sequence. It is used to locate complementary sequences of DNA.
electrophoresis	A technique by which molecules may be analysed and separated using the movement of charged particles in an electric field.
eukaryote	An organism which has cells containing a true nucleus, bound by a nuclear membrane, and membrane-bound organelles.
explant	A piece of plant tissue which is used to initiate a plant cell or tissue culture.
exponential growth	Growth where cell numbers increase logarithmically with time.

feedstock chemicals — Chemicals used in large quantities as the starting point for the manufacture of other chemicals.

fermentation —
(a) The extraction of energy from organic compounds without the involvement of oxygen.
(b) The use of microorganisms, or enzymes extracted from organisms, to carry out a wide variety of chemical reactions.

fermenter — The tank or other apparatus in which fermentation is carried out. Usually the fermenter is equipped with devices to monitor and adjust the environmental and other conditions within the fermenter.

filament — The threadlike bodies of certain algae or fungi.

flagellum — (plural = flagella) A fine, long, whip-like organelle composed of protoplasm. It is a thread which protrudes from the cell surface, longer than a cilium but with the same $9 + 2$ arrangement of microtubules. Used in locomotion and feeding, they are common in algae, protozoa and motile gametes.

floc — A clumping together of organic particles in a polysaccharide matrix. This is important in sewage treatment since it helps to settle out organic material.

food vacuole — A temporary vesicle containing food particles, found in the cytoplasm of protozoa and other simple organisms. They are formed by phagocytosis, then digestive enzymes are poured into the vacuole to digest food.

gene cloning — Large quantities of identical individual genes can be produced and isolated using recombinant DNA technology.

genetic engineering — The application of recombinant DNA methods to confer new traits on an organism by introducing new genes into its cells.

glycolysis — This means 'splitting sugar'. A series of enzyme-controlled reactions in the cytosol which breaks down glucose to lactic acid.

halophile — An organism which is adapted to grow at very low solute potentials, such as in salt water.

haustorium — (plural = haustoria) A projection of a fungal hypha which acts as a penetrating and absorbing organ.

helper T-cell — T-lymphocyte which induces the formation of plasma cells to secrete antibodies, and secretes interleukin-2 which causes proliferation of killer T-cells.

heterocyst — A large, transparent, thick-walled cell found in the filaments of certain cyanobacteria such as *Anabaena*. They are concerned with nitrogen fixation.

heterotroph — An organism which requires organic compounds as its energy and carbon source.

HIV — Human immunodeficiency virus, shown to be responsible for the disease AIDS (acquired immunodeficiency syndrome).

hologamy — In some species of *Amoeba*, cells fuse together prior to dividing by multiple fission.

hybridoma — A hybrid cell made by fusing an antibody-producing B-lymphocyte with a myeloma cell. Hybridomas are the source of monoclonal antibodies.

hypha — (plural = hyphae) This is a single tubular filament of a fungus. Hyphae bundled together form the mycelium.

immunisation — A process rendering a host immune.

inflammation — A non-specific reaction by a host to injury or infection, characterised by pain, swelling, redness and heat.

interferons — A group of proteins which are active in the immune system. They fight viral infections and stimulate the cell-killing abilities of some immune cells. Interferons are currently being tested in cancer therapy and in the treatment of acquired immunodeficiency syndrome (AIDS).

interleukins — A group of proteins which are required for a normal immune response by initiating growth and development of immune cells. Interleukin-2 is currently undergoing clinical trials for treating some forms of cancer and AIDS.

killer T-cell — T-cell which attaches to cells and destroys them by membrane disruption and lysis.

kinin — A plant growth substance which promotes cell division (sometimes also called cytokinin).

lamellae — Layer of cellular membranes, particularly photosynthetic membranes containing chlorophyll.

ligase — An enzyme which joins together two molecules, for example DNA ligase which joins two DNA molecules together and is used in the genetic engineering process to unite DNA from different sources.

lignin — After cellulose, the most abundant plant polymer. It is a component of woody, secondary cell walls.

log, logarithm — The logarithm of a number is the exponent of that number. $100 = 10^2$. Therefore, its $\log_{10} = 2$.

lymphocyte — A type of agranulocyte, for example B and T cells.

lymphokines	Soluble substances produced by T-cells when stimulated by antigens; these assist destruction of the pathogen by indirect means, such as attracting macrophages.
lymphotoxin	Soluble substance released by T-cells sensitised by an antigen, which brings about cell damage or lysis.
lysis	A process of cell destruction, often brought about by the enzyme lysozyme.
lysogenic bacteria	Bacteria which carry phage viruses which eventually become active and produce lysis in their bacterial hosts.
lytic cycle	Virus infection that results in cell lysis.
macronucleus	A large nucleus found in ciliates such as *Paramecium*. It forms a reservoir of nuclear material, and can be seen to constrict and break down at the onset of conjugation.
macrophage	Phagocytic white blood cell.
mediator	Substances such as resazurin and methylene blue, which change colour when they are reduced. They are used as indicators in redox reactions.
memory cell	Antigen-sensitive B or T lymphocyte, remaining in the host for a long period after the immune response to the particular antigen has died down. Further exposure to the antigen will cause the memory cell to differentiate into active T-cells or plasma cells.
meristem culture	Plant cells cultured from the undifferentiated meristematic tissue from which new cells arise.
mesophile	An organism which has optimum growth between 20 °C and 40 °C, including most human pathogens.
metachronal rhythm	The coordinated way in which cilia beat together. Each cilium has an effective power stroke and a passive recovery stroke, and beats a fraction of a second before the next in line.
micronucleus	A small nucleus found in ciliates such as *Paramecium*. It divides by meiosis during conjugation.
micronutrients	Inorganic chemical elements required in only very small (trace) amounts for plant growth, such as iron, chlorine, copper, manganese, zinc, molybdenum and boron.
micropropagation	The propagation of plants by tissue culture techniques.
microtubules	Narrow (25 nm diameter) elongated tubules which are found in the cytoplasm of many eukaryotic cells and in flagella.
monoclonal antibody	An antibody produced by a clone of hybridoma cells. Monoclonal

antibody technology allows large quantities of pure antibody to be produced.

monoculture The agricultural practice of growing one crop species over a large area.

mucopeptide A component of prokaryotic cell walls (see **murein** and **peptidoglycan**).

multiple fission A means of asexual reproduction, whereby a nucleus divides several times to form numerous identical cells.

murein A peptidoglycan which is a cell wall component of prokaryotes.

mycelium Composed of a mass of hyphae tangled together.

mycorrhiza A mutualistic relationship between soil-inhabiting fungi and the roots of trees or other plants.

myeloma A tumour of the B-lymphocytes which normally produce antibodies. Myeloma cells are fused with selected cells to make hybridomas for the production of monoclonal antibodies.

natural killer cell Also called NK cells, these protect the body by causing lysis of virus-infected and tumour cells.

necrosis The death of cells or tissues.

necrotroph A parasite which obtains its food from the host cells which it has killed.

negative feedback A form of inhibition important in the coordination of the metabolism of cells. Any deviation from the norm sets into action the appropriate corrective mechanism which restores the norm.

neutrophil Highly phagocytic granulocyte.

nucleotide These are the building-blocks of the nucleic acids. Each consists of a sugar (ribose or deoxyribose) to which is attached a phosphate group and an organic base.

oncogene A gene that causes cells to undergo cancerous transformation.

opsonin A type of complement protein or antibody which reacts with an antigen and enhances phagocytosis.

paramylum Food granules found in the cytoplasm of euglenoids; a starch-like polysaccharide.

passive defences This is a collective term referring to mechanical or chemical means of protecting the body against infection, non-specifically.

pathogen A microorganism or virus that causes disease.

pellicle A semi-rigid outer layer found in some ciliates such as *Paramecium*.

peptidoglycan	A macromolecule composed of amino acid and sugar units. It forms the basis of prokaryotic cell walls and is sometimes called murein or mucopeptide.
phagocytosis	The process by which certain types of cell engulf solid material and destroy it using digesting enzymes.
phagosome	Food vacuole formed when solid matter is taken into a cell by phagocytosis.
photoautotroph	Organism which uses carbon dioxide as a carbon source and sunlight as an energy source.
photoreceptor	A light-sensitive organ or organelle.
phycobilisome	Organelle found in cyanobacteria. It contains phycobilins, a group of water-soluble accessory pigments including phycocyanins and phycoerythrins for photosynthesis.
phytoalexins	Non-specific chemicals produced by a plant which inhibit the growth of potential pathogens.
pinocytosis	The uptake of dissolved material into the cell by invagination of the cell membrane.
plasma cell	An antibody-producing cell derived from a B-lymphocyte which has been activated by an antigen.
plasmid	A small, usually circular, molecule of DNA that occurs in bacteria but is not part of the bacterial chromosome. Plasmids have been used as vectors to transfer genes between species, since they carry a small number of genes.
pleomorphic	Exhibiting several different shapes.
primary cell	A cell used to initiate a cell culture, for example a skin fibroblast cell.
primary metabolism	The initial chemical processes occurring within a living cell for growth and maintenance, for example the release of energy from food.
prokaryote	An organism which consists of simple cells without a true nucleus or membrane-bound organelles.
prophylactic	The prophylactic use of a drug or chemical is to prevent an organism becoming infected with a disease.
prosthetic group	An organic group attached to a protein to form a conjugated protein. If the protein is an enzyme, the prosthetic group is an essential co-factor and the enzyme cannot function without it.
protoplasts	Plant cells that have had their rigid cellulose cell walls removed. They are fused to produce cell hybrids and used as targets for gene transfer in plant genetic engineering.

provirus	Some viruses can become lysogenic and upon invading a cell their nucleic acid becomes incorporated into the nucleic acid of the host. It is replicated with the cell nucleic acid and is known as provirus.
psychrophile	(Also referred to as a cryophile.) An organism which has optimum growth at low temperatures (below 20 °C). They can cause spoilage of frozen food.
pyrenoid	A body found in the chloroplasts of some algae, such as *Spirogyra* or the euglenoids. It is associated with the deposition of starch.
recombinant DNA	A DNA molecule that has been formed by joining together DNA segments from two or more sources.
recombinant protein	A protein made by genetic engineering, usually in bacteria, yeast or cultured cells, as the product of a gene that has been inserted into a recombinant DNA molecule.
restriction enzyme	A bacterial enzyme that cuts DNA at a specific sequence of nucleotides. These enzymes are used for making recombinant DNA.
reverse osmosis	A process used to remove excess water during an industrial process. An artificial diffusion gradient is set up across a selectively permeable membrane, which draws water across.
reverse transcriptase	Enzymes which synthesise DNA from an RNA template. In genetic engineering they are used to synthesise complementary DNA (cDNA) from messenger RNA (mRNA).
R-plasmid	A circle of DNA found in bacteria which confers resistance to antibiotics or antibodies.
secondary metabolism	This usually occurs at some specific point in an organism's life cycle, when a change is taking place, such as aging or spore formation. Antibiotics are examples of secondary metabolites.
sequencing	The determination of the order of nucleotides in a nucleic acid molecule, or the sequence of amino acids in a polypeptide chain.
serotype	A strain of bacteria which gives a specific immunological reaction.
single-cell protein	Proteins made from single-celled organisms, such as bacteria, fungi or algae, for use in human or animal foods.
Southern blotting	A technique developed by Ed Southern, which involves the separation of DNA fragments in an agarose gel by electrophoresis. The fragments are then transferred to another matrix such as nylon or nitrocellulose sheet by a 'blotting' process. The fragments fixed in the matrix are then hybridised with complementary labelled DNA or RNA probes, and the hybrids detected by autoradiography.
sporangiophore	A stalk-like structure in fungi, with sporangia at the tip.

sporangium A specialised structure in which spores are produced.

sporozoite An infective stage in the life cycle of protozoan parasite *Plasmodium*.

stem cell An immature form of bone marrow cell which divides and develops to form the many types of blood cell.

sticky ends Unpaired nucleotides at the end of a DNA double helix; they may be produced by using restriction enzymes to cut DNA at certain base sequences during genetic engineering. They will fuse with complementary sequences from another source.

stigma Light sensitive eyespot of some unicellular algae and euglenoids.

substrate A compound acted on by an enzyme and converted to a product.

therapeutic A drug or chemical is said to be used therapeutically when it is used to treat a disease which has already developed in an organism.

thermophile An organism with an optimum temperature for growth above 40 °C. Thermophiles are adapted for growth in hot temperatures such as volcanic springs.

T-lymphocyte Lymphocyte that has been programmed by the thymus for participation in cell-mediated immunity.

transcription The copying of the base sequence of DNA into a complementary sequence of messenger RNA.

transduction Process by which viruses may transfer genetic information between cells. The genetic material may be incorporated into the genome of the cell.

transformation The uptake of DNA from the medium by bacteria; this is usually a unidirectional process.

transformation foci In animal tissue culture, these are areas of overgrown cells on a monolayer of a primary cell culture, where a transforming (cancer-causing) virus or substance may be present.

trichocyst Specialised organelle, consisting of a threadlike shaft with a barb at the end, found in the ectoplasm of ciliates such as *Paramecium*. It is used as a weapon of defence or as a means of attachment during feeding.

vector In biotechnology, a vector is a DNA molecule which is used to transfer genes into cells; usually this is plasmid or viral DNA.

virion A virus particle

viroid A short fragment of naked nucleic acid (without a protein coat) which invades plant cells.

virus A particle consisting of a nucleic acid core, either DNA or RNA, surrounded by a protein coat. Viruses are obligate parasites that reproduce by entering cells and taking over the cell's own synthetic machinery.

volutin granule Granule of phosphate and related substances found as storage substances in yeast and certain bacteria.

zoonosis A disease which affects animals.

Chemical nomenclature

Throughout the text, modern names have been used for chemicals where these are well known, and sometimes the modern name has been used alongside the traditional name. However, in biology, the traditional names are still widely used; for example, citric acid. Therefore, the authors have retained the traditional names where this seemed appropriate. A table of traditional and modern names is supplied below.

Traditional name	*Modern name*
acetaldehyde	ethanal
acetic acid	ethanoic acid
acetone	propanone
aniline	phenylamine
butyric acid	butanoic acid
caproic acid	hexanoic acid
citric acid	2-hydroxypropane-1,2,3-tricarboxylic acid
diacetyl	butanedione
ethyl alcohol	ethanol
fatty acids	alkanoic acids
formaldehyde	methanal
formic acid	methanoic acid
glycerine/glycerol	propane-1,2,3-triol
lactic acid	2-hydroxypropanoic acid
mercaptans	thiols
nitroglycerine	propane-1,2,3-triyl trinitrate
polythene	polyethene
resorcinol	benzene-1,3-diol

References

Alexopoulos C.J. *Introductory mycology*, John Wiley and Sons 1980

Campbell R. *Plant microbiology*, Edward Arnold 1985 *

Clegg A.G. & Clegg P.C. *Man against disease*, Heinemann 1973 *

Clegg C.J. *Lower plants*, John Murray 1984 *

Dickinson C.H. & Lucas J.A. *Plant pathology and plant pathogens*, Blackwell Scientific 1982 *

Fay P. *The blue-greens*, Studies in Biology no.160, Edward Arnold 1983 *

Green N., Stout G. & Taylor D. *Biological science*, Cambridge University Press 1987

Hammond S.M. & Lambert P.A. *Antibiotics and antimicrobial action*, Studies in biology no.90, Edward Arnold 1978

Horne R.W. *Structure and function of viruses*, Studies in Biology no.95, Edward Arnold 1978 *

Humphries J. *Bacteriology*, John Murray 1974

Ingle M.R. *Microbes and biotechnology*, Basil Blackwell 1986 *

Ingold C.T. *The biology of fungi*, Hutchinson 1984

Jeeves T.M. & Margham J.P. *Cells, their products and interactions*, Liverpool Polytechnic 1988 *

Jones K. & Lea P.J. (eds.) *Applied and environmental microbiology*, University of Lancaster 1986

Katz J. & Sattelle D.B. *Biotechnology in focus*, Hobsons Publishing 1988 *

Land J.B. & Land R.B. *Food chains to biotechnology*, Nelson 1983

Lapage G. *Animals parasitic in man*, Dover, New York 1963

Lucas *et al Plant pathology*

Marx J. (ed.) *A revolution in biotechnology*, Cambridge University Press 1989

McKane L. & Kandel J. *Microbiology: essentials and applications*, McGraw-Hill 1985

McKean D.G. *Human and social biology*

Noble W.C. & Naido J. *Microorganisms and man*, Studies in Biology no.111, Edward Arnold 1979 *

Phillips R.S. *Malaria*, Studies in Biology no.152, Edward Arnold 1983

Postgate J. *Microbes and man*, Penguin 1986 *

Raven P., Evert R. & Curtis M. *Biology of plants*, Worth 1982

Roberts M. *Biology – A functional approach*, Nelson 1987

Sattelle D.B. *Biotechnology in perspective*, Hobsons Publishing 1988 *

Scientific American, Industrial microbiology and the advent of genetic engineering, W.H. Freeman & Co. San Francisco 1984 *

Sharp J.A. *An introduction to animal tissue culture*, Studies in biology no.82, Edward Arnold 1977

Simpkins J. & Williams J.J. *Advanced biology*, Unwin Hyman 1989

Smith J.E. *Biotechnology*, Studies in Biology no.136, Edward Arnold 1988 *

SSCR *Staffordshire biotech*, Staffordshire County Council Education Department 1985

Stanier C., Adelberg E. & Ingram J. *General microbiology (4th edition)*, Macmillan 1985

Staples D.G. *Introduction to microbiology*, Macmillan 1964

Stryer L. *Biochemistry*, Freeman 1988

Tortura G.J. & Anagnostakos N.P. *Principles of anatomy and physiology (5th edition)*, Harper and Row 1987

Webster J. *Introduction to fungi*, Cambridge University Press 1980

Williams J. & Shaw M. *Microorganisms*, Bell and Hyman 1982 *

Newsletters, National Centre for School Biotechnology, University of Reading

New Scientist special issue, 26 March 1987 *The science of AIDS*

Scientific American single topic issue *What science knows about AIDS*, 1987

Biological Sciences Review, University of Manchester School of Biological Sciences Philip Allan Publishers Ltd.

Selected references for further reading are marked with an asterisk *

Index